The COOK'S Magazine Cookbook

COOKBOOK

Edited by Michael and Judith Hill

Simon and Schuster · NEW YORK

Library of Congress Cataloging-in-Publication Data
Main entry under title:

The Cook's Magazine cookbook.

  Includes index.
  1. Cookery. I. Hill, Michael, DATE–
II. Hill, Judith. III. Cook's Magazine.
TX715.C7855 1985   641.5   85-14482
ISBN: 0-671-55481-6

CONTENTS

Introduction   *9*

1   Cocktail Foods   *11*

2   Quick First Courses   *24*

3   Soup, Chowder, Gumbo, and Chili   *34*

4   Meat and Sausages   *56*

5   Poultry and Feathered Game   *84*

6   Fish and Shellfish   *101*

7   Barbecuing, Grilling, and Smoking   *117*

8   Salads: Cold, Warm, and Main Course   *132*

9   Pasta   *145*

10 Vegetables and Herbs   *163*

11 Yeast Breads, Quick Breads, Spoon Breads, and Doughnuts   *175*

12 Pies, Cakes, and Shortcakes   *199*

13 One-Dish Desserts   *218*

14 Cookies and Candies   *233*

15 Ice Cream, Sherbets, and Ices   *248*

16 Condiments and Vinegars   *265*

Recipe Credits   *278*

Index   *280*

Photo Credits   *288*

INTRODUCTION

In this first *COOK'S Magazine* cookbook, we present the spirit of the magazine between hard covers. The magazine, like *COOK'S* readers, is up to date yet down to earth. We tell you here, as we do in the magazine, what's happening with food in America right now, along with a bit of background to put the current fashion into perspective, and we spend the bulk of our space giving down-to-work information to help you perform better in the kitchen and exemplary recipes to get you started.

This book, above all, is about cooking in America. We run the whole range from cocktail foods and first courses through pies and cakes and even condiments and vinegars. The book has been planned to strike an unusual balance between information and recipes, to be useful as a reference source as well as a cookbook. The introduction to each chapter is based on good, solid cooking principles. We recognize, of course, the especially popular American techniques—grilling, for one—and also the uniquely American categories of foods like chili and gumbo, biscuits and cookies.

Fresh, usable recipes emphasize the generally quicker and lighter dishes now in demand and reflect the interest in ingredients that were simply not available to American cooks ten years ago. The new American cooking is essentially two-pronged: Each chapter here contains both the old, classic American dishes that are not only in style once again but are a source of pride, as well as the strictly new, developing cuisine that is characterized by a multitude of ethnic influences and inventive and exciting combinations of ingredients. Very often the two types overlap, resulting in such dishes as our Wild Mushrooms on Fried Grits, Herbed Rice Muffins, Gingered Shortcake with Honey-Poached Peaches, or Papaya Cobbler.

The COOK'S Magazine Cookbook was a joint effort, a reflection of what the *COOK'S* staff believes their magazine, and therefore their book, should be. Everyone through the ranks at *COOK'S* helped, and many, many of our writers and contributors provided expertise and recipes. Our grateful acknowledgments go especially to Michael Hill, the co-editor; Mary Caldwell, who headed up recipe editing, and Malvina Kinard, Shirley Lantz, Donna Schaefer, and Emily Hughes, who helped her; to Pamela Parseghian, who led recipe development, and her staff, including Melanie Barnard and Brooke Dojny; to Tina Ujlaki and Sheila Lowenstein, both instrumental in the organization and shaping of the book; and to Sara Barbaris, who directed the photography of the dishes, and Beverly Cox, who styled them. Our thanks also to Julie Karp, the illustrator of the book.

This is a book from *COOK'S* to cooks. We hope you enjoy it.

Christopher Kimball, Publisher, and Judith Hill, Editor in Chief

The COOK'S Magazine
Bridgeport, CT 06604

Chapter

1

Cocktail Foods

As far as social historians can determine, the cocktail party, like the cocktail itself, seems to be a purely American invention. Cocktails—that is, beverages combining distilled spirits, not wine, with juice, soda, or other mixers—date from colonial days, and the word *cocktail*, of uncertain derivation, was used in print in the United States at least as early as 1806.

The cocktail party itself came into its own only with Prohibition. When alcohol could not legally be served in restaurants, the large Gatsby-like party became popular. Socialites gathered in the late afternoon or early evening before dining out at restaurants that, officially at least, did not serve liquor. And such affairs required small savory treats that could be nibbled with ease in the bustle of stand-up drinking.

With legalized drinking, the restaurant itself became the setting for cocktail foods. These might be served at the bar or at the table with before-dinner drinks. Much of bar food—the ubiquitous shelled peanuts, for instance—is salty and almost irresistible; its main function is to encourage drinking and thereby increase the restaurant's profit margin. At the table, the purpose is less blatantly commercial. Providing an extra unordered tid-

11

bit such as a tiny puff-pastry creation aims to put the patron in a happy mood while he or she determines the evening's repast. It also can inspire a sense of confidence in the culinary ability of the staff.

The private dinner party provides yet another setting for cocktail food, where it serves to take the edge off hunger and helps establish conversational ease. Also, as at a restaurant, a little bit of something nice to eat makes everyone happy and sets minds at ease about what's to come.

The last setting in which cocktail food makes its appearance is the simplest, and the provisions might more appropriately be called snacks. This occurs when you have a few friends over for drinks and to talk, watch something special on television, or plan an upcoming event. Here the food offered is generally neither meant to impress nor to relax, but to offer hospitality or sate light appetites. As hosts, we sometimes take a tip from bar food and have salty or spicy things to keep the drinks flowing and all in convivial spirits—though we say the food is to absorb the alcohol.

As the setting and purpose change for cocktail food, so do the sorts of things served. If in some culinary version of Plato's cave, there is an ideal type of appetizer, as far as we're concerned it would be a glorious combination of crisp and creamy, a crust fried to golden perfection, filled with a rich, slightly spicy, creamed stuffing. But in gastronomy, of course, the real is more important than the ideal, and with cocktail foods the reality is that variety counts.

The variety of cocktail foods begins with the simplest, the raw and the plain. Salted in the shell peanuts, potato chips, toasted pecans, macadamia nuts, unsalted cashews with raisins are among the easiest and often the best of snacks. The restaurant lazy Susan was a midwestern roadhouse tradition in the 1940s and '50s—a large, spinnable platter on a stand set in the center of the table. It was filled with carrot sticks, scallions, green and black olives, radishes, peppers, dips, corn relish, maybe some creamed herring—a sort of scaled-down and vastly Americanized version of the antipasto. Raw vegetables and one or two simply prepared dishes are still well received. For a contemporary version, you might drizzle baby vegetables with olive or walnut oil and scatter cracked peppercorns over them or dust with chopped herbs; something like our Mussels in Red Pepper Mayonnaise could be included.

While such simple delights seem suited to the informal or impromptu party, they are equally suitable in more formal situations as well. Witness the opulent Parisian restaurant Lasserre, where serious, stylish diners are served olives and potato chips (made on the premises, of course) with aperitifs.

From the raw and the plain, the next step opens up an almost infinite number of possibilities. The term *hors d'oeuvre* might be applied to anything served outside the courses of a regular menu or even to the first course, but in America, it seems most often used to refer to cooked foods in miniature. They can be created especially as a cocktail food, such as the Spicy Ham and Phyllo Triangles in this chapter, or merely be something small and otherwise served in quantity as a regular course, such as fried shrimp. Then there may be tiny versions of normally large items, such as silver-dollar-size cheese tarts. The one clear division within cocktail foods is the canapé—a small, thin piece of toast or bread topped with a tidbit or spread. *Canapé* first appeared in print in England in the 1890s referring to toast topped with anchovy, and its singular role continues to be as an accompaniment to drinks before meals.

Given the variety of cocktail foods and the different settings in which they're eaten, there are no rules for making or serving them, but here are some common-sense guidelines:

SIMPLE PREPARATIONS

One of the most frequent traps party givers fall into is the urge to complicate. Consequently, too many elaborate cocktail foods result in overfed guests and exhausted hosts. Unless you're having your party catered, think only of making one or two complicated appetizers and keep the others simple. Don't hesitate to include cut-up vegetables or other snacks requiring little preparation, such as salted nuts, as part of the spread. Use the same main ingredient, oysters, say, or duck, in two or three different preparations to minimize cooking time and maximize variety; or make several fillings for the same container as in our Stuffed Snow Peas with three fillings. For dinner parties, keep the main emphasis on the evening's menu.

EASY EATING

Cocktail parties, especially, demand finger foods. If your space is going to be at all crowded, try to avoid serving anything that needs even a fork to handle it. People are talking and want one-bite, no-squish food. Don't forget that your guests will be eating while moving around, and consider the danger to rugs and furniture. We know one person with white rugs who refuses to serve red wine, though that does seem a bit hard.

VARIETY

At a dinner party, it's best to serve just one or two different cocktail foods. But at a party, the rule should be variety. This does not mean that you need have ten or fifteen different hors d'oeuvre but that the food you have should not all be the same type. Have at least one crisp or crunchy tidbit, several raw or fresh things, and three or four kinds of cooked hors d'oeuvre or canapés as the centerpoints of the party. If one of your choices is quite spicy, make sure to balance with one or two that are mildly seasoned as well. It's nice to have one or two traditional hors d'oeuvre, for the less adventuresome. But also plan a novel or imaginative creation just for the fun of it. Because weight watching is as pervasive as it is these days, out of kindness there should probably be something low in calories to gnaw on.

SENSE OF PROPORTION

The basic idea is to serve your guests enough, but for dinner parties especially, that also means not too much. Plan just three or four hors d'oeuvre per person during the thirty to sixty minutes before sitting down to table.

It's impossible to say how much to prepare for cocktail parties since that depends on the time of day, the occasion, and the crowd. The best tactic is to overestimate the amount of simple things you'll serve, whether they be shrimp, vegetables, or peanuts, and keep a sufficient supply on hand so that you can replenish serving dishes all through the party. Have something out at the very beginning of the party so that early arrivals don't feel they've gotten there before you're ready. This also prevents guests from drinking too much alcohol without some food to balance its effects. If possible, put your canapés and cooked hors d'oeuvre out in waves, perhaps at two or three stages during a two-hour party, so that there is a constant sense that one has arrived at the height of things. Unless you're really anxious for everyone to leave at a specific time, keep one batch of hors d'oeuvre in reserve as a treat for those who linger late.

FRIED PUMPKIN OR SWEET POTATO CHIPS
WITH CAYENNE AND CORIANDER

Most of us probably aren't even aware that potato chips can be made at home, as they seem to be the quintessential manufactured snack. If they are the forerunners of the packaged salty bits that line the supermarket shelves, they are also a good food with a solid American tradition. Thick potato chips were well-known in American restaurants by the 1840s. The thin potato chip seems to have been created in 1853 in Saratoga; Moon's Lake Lodge and the Montgomery Hall Hotel there both have their partisans who claim that *their* place invented them. In either instance, food historians seem united in insisting that the thin chip was an accidental result of a chef's desire to satisfy a fussy patron who wanted potatoes sliced as thin as possible. Cold leftovers from the batch were given away free the next day. The chips, served either warm or cold, soon became fashionable, and area restaurants competed for the distinction of producing the lightest and thinnest of all. Our pumpkin or sweet potato chips are a delicious variation of the original potato chip.

Vegetable oil for deep-frying
1 *2-pound pumpkin wedge, peeled and seeded, or 2 to 3 large sweet potatoes*
¾ *cup flour*
½ *teaspoon salt*
¾ *teaspoon cayenne*
1 *cup milk*
¼ *cup chopped fresh coriander leaves*

1. Heat the oil in a deep fryer or a large, heavy saucepan to 370°F.
2. Cut the pumpkin or sweet potatoes into ⅛-inch-thick slices. If using pumpkin, cut it into manageable pieces first.
3. In a bowl, combine the flour, salt, and ¼ teaspoon cayenne.
4. Pour the milk into another bowl and dip the pumpkin or sweet potato slices into it. Coat each slice with seasoned flour and shake off the excess.
5. In 2 separate batches fry the slices until they are crisp, gently stirring the chips so that all the slices cook evenly, 3 to 5 minutes. Remove with a slotted spoon and drain on paper towels. Sprinkle with the remaining cayenne.
6. Put the coriander leaves into a large strainer and lower into the oil for about 5 seconds. Drain on paper towels, sprinkle the fried leaves over the chips, and serve immediately.

Yield: 4 servings

OYSTER FRITTERS

Oysters have long been one of our most popular predinner foods. One Bobby Melancom holds the modern record for consumption—188 in one hour at the 1972 Louisiana State Fair—but great nineteenth-century gastronomes like Diamond Jim Brady used to put away several dozen and then proceed to multicourse dinners. Of course, in those days oysters were so plentiful they were cheap. In the 1850s, oyster houses in the eastern United States used to advertise all-you-can-eat oyster specials for 6 cents.

Fresh oysters were delivered to Springfield, Illinois, by wagon across the Alleghenies—Abraham Lincoln served them at parties there. In 1842, the Erie Railroad packed oysters in ice and shipped them to Buffalo and then on to Chicago. For safety's sake, the railroad arranged to have them unloaded in Cleveland and boiled before sending them on to Chicago, where they arrived, according to the *Chicago Daily American*, "as fresh as could be desired." By the 1880s, refrigerated railroad cars had created a widespread demand all across the East and Midwest, and over 15 billion bushels a year were harvested from the Chesapeake Bay during that decade. Needless to say, the oyster beds began to be depleted and costs, consequently, started to rise. Nevertheless, fresh and smoked oysters are still among the best and most popular of cocktail foods. (See also our Smoked Oyster Canapés with Cherry Tomatoes.)

Vegetable oil
1½ cups sifted flour
¼ teaspoon salt
1 tablespoon baking powder
2 eggs, beaten
⅓ cup milk
1½ pints shucked fresh oysters, drained and chopped, ⅓ cup liquor reserved

1. Heat about 2 inches of oil in a deep fryer or a large, heavy saucepan to 370°F.
2. Stir the flour, salt, and baking powder together in a mixing bowl. Stir in the eggs, milk, and reserved oyster liquor. Fold in the chopped oysters.
3. Drop the batter by heaping teaspoons, a few at a time, into the oil. Fry until browned, turning once, about 5 minutes in all. This must be done in several batches so that the pan is not too crowded. Allow the oil to regain the correct temperature between batches. Drain on paper towels and serve immediately.

Yield: about 2 dozen fritters

STUFFED SNOW PEAS

Use any one or all of the following three fillings.

Snow peas, trimmed
Mascarpone and American Caviar
Filling

6 tablespoons crème fraîche (see Note)
   or sour cream
6 tablespoons Mascarpone or cream
   cheese, softened
1½ teaspoons lemon juice
¼ cup golden caviar

Mascarpone and Gorgonzola Filling

¼ cup Mascarpone or cream cheese,
   softened
¼ cup Gorgonzola
4 to 5 tablespoons heavy cream

Salmon and Dill Filling

¼ pound smoked salmon
2 tablespoons crème fraîche (see Note)
   or sour cream
2 teaspoons lemon juice
2 tablespoons minced fresh dill

1. Blanch the peas in boiling salted water until tender, about 1 minute. Plunge into cold water and drain. Slit open on one side and set aside.
2. For the Mascarpone and American caviar filling, mix the crème fraîche, Mascarpone, and lemon juice in a bowl. Carefully fold in 2 tablespoons caviar until just combined, being careful not to break the caviar eggs. Spoon the filling into the pea pods and top each with some of the remaining caviar. Refrigerate until 1 hour before serving.
3. For the Mascarpone and Gorgonzola filling, put the Mascarpone and Gorgonzola in a bowl and combine well with a fork. Blend in the heavy cream a tablespoon at a time until the mixture is smooth and creamy. Spoon the filling into pea pods and refrigerate until 1 hour before serving.
4. For the salmon and dill filling, puree the salmon, crème fraîche, and lemon juice in a food processor. Stir in the dill. Spoon or pipe the filling into pea pods and refrigerate until 1 hour before serving.

Yield: 16 to 20 stuffed pea pods per filling

Note: To make crème fraîche, combine in a jar 1 cup heavy cream with 1 tablespoon buttermilk, sour cream, or plain yogurt. Let stand, partially covered, 36 to 48 hours at room temperature until cream thickens. Cover and refrigerate until ready to use. The mixture will continue to thicken as it chills.

MUSSELS IN RED PEPPER MAYONNAISE

Mussels are still an undervalued shellfish. They have never really been in vogue in this country and thus are generally much cheaper than oysters or clams. Despite the succulence of this bivalve, Americans have a long history of resistance to mussels. The Indians seem not to have taken strongly to them, and the Pilgrims followed suit. According to 1620s records, New England settlers, who considered mussels "the meanest of God's blessings," fed them to their hogs. Perhaps our reluctance to take to mussels has to do with fear caused by their eating habits. They thrive in areas of brackish water and often feed on various kinds of slightly toxic plankton. Most mussels today are soaked in purifying tanks before they are sold. Generally mussels live in dark blue or blue-black shells, but some uncommon species have yellow-brown or bright green shells. The most abundant is the blue mussel found along the Atlantic shore from Canada to North Carolina.

1. Melt the butter in a large saucepan. Add the shallots, garlic, thyme, fennel seeds, wine, and bay leaf. Add the mussels, cover, and steam until the mussels open, about 5 minutes. Strain the mussels through a double thickness of cheesecloth, reserving the liquid. Return the liquid to the pan and boil until it is reduced by half, about 5 to 8 minutes.
2. Remove the mussels from their shells and chill. Reserve one-half of the shells.
3. Roast the red pepper in a hot broiler or over a gas burner until charred on all sides. When cool enough to handle, peel, cut into pieces, and remove the seeds and ribs, reserving any juice. Puree the pepper with any juice in a food processor and set aside.
4. Put the egg yolk and lemon juice into a food processor and whir briefly. With the machine running, add the oils in a thin stream and then ¼ cup of the reduced mussel liquid. Stir in pureed red pepper and season with salt and white pepper.
5. Toss the chilled mussels with the red pepper mayonnaise. Put 1 mussel in each reserved shell, top with a small bit of dill and a tiny mound of caviar. Serve chilled.

Yield: about 45 mussels

Scrub mussels in cold water and then pull off the beards, scraping with a knife if necessary.

1 tablespoon unsalted butter
2 shallots, minced
2 cloves garlic, minced
1½ teaspoons fresh thyme leaves, or ½ teaspoon dried thyme
½ teaspoon fennel seeds
¾ cup white wine
1 bay leaf, crushed
3 pounds mussels, cleaned and beards removed
1 red bell pepper
1 egg yolk, room temperature
1 tablespoon lemon juice
½ cup vegetable oil
¼ cup olive oil
Salt and white pepper
4 to 6 sprigs dill
2 tablespoons salmon caviar

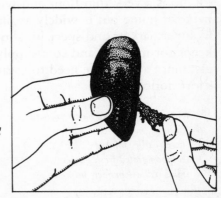

FRIED MUSHROOM PASTA

1 *tablespoon olive oil*
½ *pound mushrooms, minced*
1 *shallot, minced*
 Salt and black pepper
¼ *cup ricotta cheese*
2 *tablespoons minced prosciutto*
¼ *cup minced mozzarella cheese*
2 *tablespoons grated Parmesan cheese*
1 *small egg, lightly beaten*
1 *recipe Egg Pasta (see Chapter 9)*
 Vegetable oil

1. Heat the olive oil in a frying pan over medium-high heat, add the mushrooms, shallot, and salt and pepper to taste. Cook until the mushrooms are brown, their juices evaporate, and the mixture just begins to stick to the pan, 5 to 10 minutes. Cool slightly and combine with the ricotta, prosciutto, mozzarella, Parmesan, and egg. Adjust the seasonings.
2. Roll the pasta dough to ⅛-inch thickness. Using a round ravioli or cookie cutter, cut 2½-inch fluted rounds from the dough. Put a generous teaspoon of the filling in the center of each round. Fold each circle in half and press around the edges to seal. If the dough gets too dry to seal well, moisten the edges of each round with cold water before pressing together. Place the finished half-circles on a towel, not touching, in 1 layer.
3. In a heavy frying pan, heat 1 inch of oil to 370°F. Add the pasta packets a few at a time, being careful not to crowd in the pan. Fry until golden, turning once, 1 to 2 minutes per side. Drain on paper towels, sprinkle with salt, and serve immediately. (They could be reheated but would not be as good as when just fried.)

Yield: about 70 hors d'oeuvre

SPICY HAM AND PHYLLO TRIANGLES

Phyllo is a very thin flour and water pastry that is difficult to make at home but is widely available, either fresh or frozen, in supermarkets and specialty shops. Phyllo freezes well and keeps for months, and so a supply in the freezer is a good insurance against the need to create a special hors d'oeuvre on short notice.

10 *tablespoons unsalted butter, melted*
 6 *scallions, minced*
 4 *cloves garlic, minced*
 1 *teaspoon grated fresh ginger*
 1 *small red bell pepper, minced*

1. In a small frying pan, over low heat, combine 2 tablespoons butter, the scallions, garlic, and ginger, and cook gently until tender but not brown, 4 to 5 minutes. Raise heat to medium-high and add the red bell pepper and celery or fennel. Cook, stirring con-

stantly, until tender, for about 3 minutes. Add the ham and mix well. Remove from heat.

2. Lay 1 sheet of phyllo on a work surface and brush the entire sheet with melted butter. Cover with a second sheet and brush it with butter. Repeat with a third sheet, brushing again with butter. Top with a fourth sheet but do not butter.

3. With a sharp knife, cut the stack of layered dough into 4 squares. Cut each square into 4 equal strips. You will have 16 strips, each measuring approximately 6″ × 2″. Repeat this entire procedure with 4 more sheets of phyllo.

4. Heat the oven to 375°F. Butter a baking sheet.

5. Working with 1 stack of strips at a time (cover the remaining strips with a damp towel to prevent them from drying), put 1½ teaspoons of the filling at the lower left corner of the stack of strips. Fold the corner across to the opposite edge, as you would a flag, then fold about twice more, making a triangular package. Brush each completed triangle with butter and lay on the prepared baking sheet. Continue with the remaining strips of phyllo. The triangles can be covered and refrigerated at this point if you don't want to bake them immediately.

6. Bake the triangles in the preheated oven until golden, 12 to 15 minutes.

Yield: 32 triangles

2 *ribs celery, minced, or* ½ *cup minced fennel*
½ *cup minced Smithfield ham or other smoked ham*
½ *pound (8 sheets) phyllo dough*

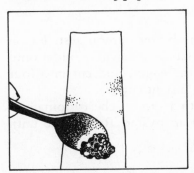

Place 1½ teaspoons of the filling at the lower corner of phyllo.

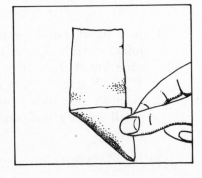

Begin folding each stack of phyllo strips as you would a flag.

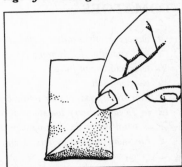

Continue folding, covering each edge of the triangle.

CANAPÉS
A little imagination can catapult the canapé from ho-hum to inspired contemporary fare. The following canapés all use traditional cocktail foods—blue cheese, oysters, smoked salmon—in fresh ways. Oysters and salmon have never gone out of favor, while blue cheese has had harder times; it is making a comeback now, however, and its sharp saltiness goes particularly well with spirits. The vogue for blue cheese dressing spawned another fashion for blue cheese dips. This dip was a staple of the party armament of the 1950s and '60s until it became so common as to be embarrassing for sophisticated hosts. Now blue cheese is returning in new combinations such as our Blue Cheese Triangles with Toasted Hazelnuts.

BLUE CHEESE TRIANGLES WITH TOASTED HAZELNUTS

½ cup hazelnuts
4 ounces unsalted butter, softened
3 ounces blue cheese, room temperature
8 very thin slices whole-wheat bread

1. Heat the oven to 375°F.
2. Toast the hazelnuts on a baking sheet in a single layer in the preheated oven until browned, 10 to 12 minutes. Rub the nuts with a kitchen towel to remove most of their skins. Chop coarsely and set aside.
3. In a bowl, cream together the butter and blue cheese. Spread each slice of bread evenly with the mixture. Trim the edges and discard the trimmings.
4. Cut each slice into 4 even triangles and garnish with the hazelnuts. Refrigerate until ready to serve.

Yield: 32 triangles

SMOKED OYSTER CANAPÉS WITH CHERRY TOMATOES

4 ounces unsalted butter, softened
1 tablespoon grated lemon zest
½ teaspoon lemon juice
¼ teaspoon salt
8 thin slices good-quality white bread
12 to 15 large cherry tomatoes, sliced
Several sprigs flat-leaf parsley
1 can small smoked oysters, drained

1. In a bowl, combine the butter, lemon zest, lemon juice, and salt. Spread 1 tablespoon lemon butter onto each bread slice, trim the edges, and cut into four 1½-inch rounds with a biscuit cutter.
2. Garnish each round with a slice of cherry tomato, a small parsley leaf, and an oyster. Refrigerate until serving.

Yield: 32 rounds

SALMON AND AMERICAN CAVIAR
CHECKERBOARD

1. In a bowl, mix the cream cheese with the dill and lemon zest. Spread 2 tablespoons of the mixture evenly onto each slice of white bread and refrigerate.
2. Spread 1 tablespoon of the mixture evenly onto each pumpernickel slice. Trim the edges and discard the trimmings. Cut each slice into 4 even squares. Put 3 strips of salmon in diagonal stripes across each. Trim the strips even with edges of bread and refrigerate the squares.
3. Remove the buttered white bread from the refrigerator. Trim the edges from the slices. Using a small metal spatula, spread about 1 teaspoon golden caviar evenly onto 4 of the slices and repeat, using sturgeon caviar, with the other 4 slices. Cut each slice into 4 even squares.
4. Decorate the golden caviar canapés with a sprig of dill and the sturgeon caviar canapés with a tiny wedge of lemon. To serve, arrange together with salmon canapés to form a checkerboard pattern.

Yield: 4 dozen squares

6 ounces cream cheese, softened
1 tablespoon chopped fresh dill, or
   ½ teaspoon dried dill
1½ teaspoons grated lemon zest
8 thin slices good-quality white bread
4 thin slices pumpernickel bread
2 to 3 ounces smoked salmon, cut into
   ¼-inch strips
1 ounce golden caviar
1 ounce American sturgeon caviar
   Several sprigs dill
3 or 4 very thin slices lemon, cut into
   tiny wedges

Lay three salmon strips diagonally on each cream-cheese-covered pumpernickel square and trim.

Chapter

2 | Quick First Courses

If we were asked to prescribe an antidote to hectic, sometimes frantic, modern life, to workaholism, and hypertension, it would be the first course. Adding an introductory dish to the simple pattern of main course and dessert signals the beginning of a relaxing meal that is to be taken at a reasonable pace, for pleasure as well as sustenance. Although many of the first courses in this chapter can also be prepared for lunch or a light supper, their primary purpose is an opening counterpoint to the more substantial main dish, a start that whets your appetite for what is to come.

A first course need by no means be elaborate. Country inns and unpretentious restaurants in France frequently serve the simplest of all first courses: just-picked vegetables, perhaps accompanied by a couple of slices of cured meat such as ham or sausage. However, things have not always been so simple, and some classes have never had to make an effort to avoid rushed eating. The French nobility, as early as the 1500s, were quite used to a score or more of dishes when dining. Meals were divided into "services," each of which often consisted of many preparations—a choice of soups, roasted meats, fish, vegetable dishes, pastries. Some of these dishes were quite spectacular, such as tiny game birds stuffed

24

within a bigger bird that was inside an even larger bird. One of Louis XIV's menus consisted of 168 garnished dishes, not including desserts.

By the eighteenth century, a wide assortment of foods was so de rigueur among the nobility that multiple courses were often considered mandatory even when the variety of foodstuffs was limited. On one occasion the duc de Richelieu was faced with planning an elaborate banquet with nothing more than "a carcasse of beef and a few roots." When the chef protested the impossibility of the task, the duke dictated a twenty-two-dish spread, almost all of which was based on beef as the main ingredient. No organ was left unturned, and the comestibles included Kidneys with Fried Onion, a Civet of Tongue, Oxtail with Chestnut Puree, and Fritters of Beef Brain.

After the French revolution, the chefs to the nobility found themselves quite suddenly unemployed, and the French restaurant was born, bringing with it the concept of multiple services or courses. At roughly the same time, Jefferson was doing his best to introduce French ideas and lavish meals to America. We had our own opulent restaurant era in the nineteenth century when, concurrent with the rise of railroad, shipping, mining, and manufacturing millionaires, luxurious continental-style places like Delmonico's were riding high. During the twentieth century, the number of the opening courses was reduced for practical reasons, resulting in the eclectic listings found under Appetizers at the top of the menu.

Since the 1950s and '60s, the most typical first course in a standard American restaurant has been a salad, included in the price of the main dish. The American love of salads at the beginning of a meal has been exported across the ocean, and fresh greens as a first course now regularly turn up on continental menus.

Until recently, when entertaining at home, we often served first courses in the form of cocktail foods—finger foods that went down nicely with a Manhattan or Old Fashioned. Much like simple home cooking the world over, the main course *was* the show, with perhaps a soup or salad as the first act. But as many American restaurants became more sophisticated and more varied, first courses also came of age at home. Pasta, the traditional

Italian first course, or a fish course was often served in small portions at the start of a meal. Warm salads became popular, and warm cheese dishes, beloved by the English but eschewed by the French until very recently, were transformed into first courses, too.

Today, first courses have no boundaries and very few guidelines; many recipes found in other chapters of this book, for instance, can be adapted for appetizers. A first course can use virtually any ingredient and should simply be light or, if its ingredients are sturdy, served in small portions. Ideally, it is a contrast in texture, flavor, and color to the other dishes planned and in general should not compete in taste with the main course. If the main dish has a rich cream sauce, keep the first course plain; if it's soft, make the beginning crisp. Don't serve three red dishes, unless it's Valentine's day. Before a meat dish, all choices are open. Before fish, it's somewhat more difficult as most meat dishes are inappropriate and the range is more or less limited to vegetables, other seafood, and pasta. In general, fish requires a lighter taste to precede it. However, rules are made to be broken, and certainly ham or pâté before sole sounds fine to us. Just be sure to think through the flavors to avoid overwhelming the taste buds with an aggressively flavored first dish before moving on to more delicate fare.

As restaurant cooking in America has embraced last-minute cooking, sautés, grilled foods, and the like, so has home cooking followed the same trend toward fresh, easily prepared foods. The recipes that follow provide both last-minute and make-ahead dishes, and preparation time for each is short enough so that it can be included smoothly in a simple, relaxing meal.

RADISH REMOULADE

1. In a bowl, toss the radishes with vinegar, mustard, caraway seeds, and salt. Cover and refrigerate for at least 2 hours.
2. Drain the radishes, return to the bowl, and add the crème fraîche or heavy cream. Mix, adding more salt, pepper, and the sugar to taste.
3. Just before serving, stir in the chives. Place the lettuce leaves on chilled plates and top with remoulade.

Yield: 4 servings

1 pound radishes, grated
½ cup white wine vinegar
2 tablespoons Dijon mustard
1 teaspoon caraway seeds
Salt and black pepper
½ cup crème fraîche (see Chapter 1, Stuffed Pea Pods, Note) or heavy cream
Pinch of sugar
1 tablespoon minced fresh chives
4 large Boston lettuce leaves

SPAGHETTI WITH PARSLEY SAUCE

1. Bring a large pot of salted water to a boil. Add the spaghetti and cook just until tender. Drain and keep warm.
2. In a large, heavy frying pan, melt the butter with the olive oil. Add the garlic and simmer for 30 seconds, stirring. Add the spaghetti, Parmesan cheese, a little salt, and a generous grinding of pepper, tossing so that the spaghetti is well coated.
3. Cover the pan for 1 minute. Turn heat off, add the parsley, and toss well. Transfer the spaghetti to a warm serving bowl or individual plates and sprinkle with extra Parmesan.

Yield: 4 servings

¾ pound spaghetti
6 tablespoons unsalted butter
1 tablespoon olive oil
1 large clove garlic, minced
3 tablespoons grated Parmesan cheese, plus extra for garnish, if desired
Salt and black pepper
3½ cups (1¾ ounces) loosely packed flat-leaf parsley with large stems removed, chopped

STEAK AND CAVIAR TARTARE WITH VODKA

1. In a small bowl, soak the horseradish in lemon juice for 3 to 4 minutes.
2. Stir in the salt, pepper, mustard, and vodka. Whisk in the oil and then combine with the sirloin. You may have to knead the meat with your hands to fully incorporate the seasonings. Mix the parsley, scallion, and capers into the mixture. Adjust the seasonings. Add the egg yolk and lightly mix it into the meat.
3. Mound the meat mixture on 4 plates, top each with a heaping teaspoonful of caviar, and serve immediately.

Yield: 4 servings

1½ to 2 tablespoons minced fresh horseradish
3 tablespoons lemon juice
1 teaspoon salt
1 teaspoon black pepper
1 tablespoon Dijon mustard
¼ cup vodka
¼ cup olive oil
1 pound lean, fresh sirloin, trimmed and coarsely ground or minced
2 tablespoons minced fresh parsley
1 small scallion, minced
2 tablespoons capers, drained
1 egg yolk
2 tablespoons black caviar

WILD MUSHROOMS ON FRIED GRITS

1¼ cups Chicken Stock (see recipe, Chapter 3)
1¼ cups milk
½ teaspoon salt
½ cup quick-cooking grits
5 tablespoons grated Romano cheese
2 drops Tabasco sauce
   Flour for dusting
5 tablespoons clarified unsalted butter
3 cups sliced or whole fresh wild mushrooms (such as chanterelles, oyster, shiitake, or morels)
1 small red onion, minced
¼ cup minced black or red radishes

1. Butter an 8″- × -8″ baking pan.
2. In a heavy saucepan, bring the chicken stock, milk, and salt to a boil. Gradually add the grits, stirring constantly, and bring back to a boil. Lower heat and cook, stirring occasionally, until thick, 5 to 8 minutes. Remove from heat and stir in 4 tablespoons Romano cheese and the Tabasco.
3. Spread the grits mixture evenly in the prepared baking pan. Chill until firm.
4. Cut the cooled grits into 3- to 4-inch rounds or squares. Dust each with flour and shake off excess.
5. In a large frying pan, heat 1 to 2 tablespoons clarified butter. Sauté the grits, a few pieces at a time, over moderately high heat, until brown on both sides, 5 to 7 minutes per side. Add more butter between batches as necessary. Remove to a warm serving platter and keep warm.
6. Sauté the mushrooms and onion in the remaining butter until soft, 5 to 8 minutes. Add the remaining cheese and radishes. Continue to cook until heated through, about 2 minutes. Adjust the seasonings. Spoon over the grits and serve immediately.

Yield: 4 servings

BAY SCALLOPS WITH LIME AND MINT

Cooking without heat but through marination is a fascinating and quite simple technique. Fish is an ideal choice for this type of preparation as there are no tough connective tissues that require more concentrated cooking. This modern recipe in which the acids in the lime juice actually cook the scallops is based on the very old dish from South and Central America called, variously, seviche, ceviche, or cebishe. Traditionally, bite-size pieces of saltwater fish are marinated in lemon juice or brine and then layered with onions, chiles, black peppercorns, and bay leaves. Oil is not included in such a marinade as it will retard the process of "cooking" the fish. In meat marinades, however, oil is often important to add fat to a dry cut.

1. In a bowl, toss the scallops with ¼ teaspoon salt, 3 tablespoons lime juice, and the lime zest. Cover and refrigerate. Marinate the scallops until they are firm and opaque, at least 6 hours, stirring occasionally.
2. Meanwhile, soak the onion in cold water for 20 minutes. Squeeze with your hands and set aside on a paper towel to dry.
3. Combine the remaining salt and lime juice with the garlic, pepper, and cayenne in a large bowl. Slowly whisk in the oil to make a dressing.
4. Drain the scallops and toss them with all but 2 tablespoons of the dressing, onion, and chopped mint. Adjust the seasonings.
5. Peel and slice the avocados, arrange on individual serving plates, and drizzle the remaining dressing over them. Mound the scallops on the plate and garnish with fresh mint leaves.

Yield: 6 servings

¾ pound bay scallops
1¼ teaspoons salt
3 tablespoons plus 2 teaspoons lime juice
¾ teaspoon grated lime zest
1 small red onion, minced
1 small clove garlic, minced
    Black pepper
⅛ teaspoon cayenne
5 tablespoons vegetable oil
3 tablespoons chopped fresh mint leaves, plus whole mint leaves for garnish
2 small ripe avocados

ROQUEFORT APPETIZER CHEESECAKE

1. Heat the oven to 350°F. Butter an 8-inch pie pan.
2. In a food processor or mixing bowl, cream the Roquefort with the butter until very smooth. Add the cream cheese and blend. Add the eggs, 1 at a time, blending after each addition until the mixture is smooth. If the mixture is lumpy, strain before continuing. Add the sour cream, chives, salt, and pepper and mix well.
3. Pour the mixture into the prepared pie pan and set the pie pan into a larger pan. Add enough hot water to come halfway up the sides of the pie pan. Bake in the preheated oven until the mixture is firm, golden, and puffy, 20 to 25 minutes.
4. Cool to room temperature (the pie will collapse) and cut into slim wedges.

Yield: 6 to 8 servings

2 ounces Roquefort cheese
2 tablespoons unsalted butter, softened
2 ounces cream cheese, softened
3 eggs
2½ tablespoons sour cream
1½ tablespoons minced fresh chives
⅛ teaspoon salt
¼ teaspoon white pepper

FRIED IPSWICH CLAMS WITH TOMATO-BASIL MAYONNAISE

Ipswich clams were named for the plethora of clam processors that sprang up around Ipswich, Massachusetts, early in this century. The clams themselves are a tender, soft-shelled species ideal for frying; they also are known as steamers for another method of cooking to which they are very well suited. Here, instead of the traditional crackermeal breading, we have substituted a flour and cornmeal mixture that makes a wonderfully crisp crust.

Tomato-Basil Mayonnaise

 2 *tablespoons olive oil*
 2 *cloves garlic, minced*
 3 *tablespoons minced fresh basil leaves*
 2 *large tomatoes, peeled (see illustrations, Chapter 16, Chili Sauce), seeded, and chopped*

1. For the sauce, heat 1 tablespoon olive oil in a frying pan over low heat. Add the garlic and cook until soft. Add the basil and stir well. Add the tomatoes and cook until just heated through, 1 to 3 minutes. Remove from heat and set aside to cool slightly.

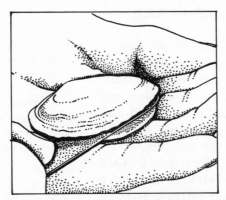

To shuck clams, push a knife between the shells and run it along one of the shells to cut the muscle that holds the clam and the shell together.

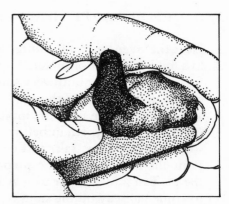

Scrape the clam free from its second shell.

2. In a small bowl, combine the egg yolk and vinegar. Whisk in the remaining tablespoon of olive oil and the vegetable oil in a slow stream. Add the tomato mixture. Season to taste with salt and pepper.
3. For the clams, heat the vegetable oil in a deep fryer or large, heavy saucepan to 350°F.
4. Meanwhile, combine the half and half, Tabasco to taste, and salt and pepper in a large bowl. Add the clams and soak for 3 to 5 minutes.
5. In another large bowl, combine the cornmeal and flour. Dredge the clams in the cornmeal mixture, coating evenly. Shake off the excess coating.
6. Fry the clams in hot oil until golden and crisp, 3 to 5 minutes. Transfer the fried clams to paper towels, season with salt and pepper, and serve immediately with the sauce.

Yield: 4 servings

1 egg yolk
½ teaspoon balsamic or *white wine vinegar*
3 tablespoons vegetable oil
  Salt and black pepper

Clams

  Vegetable oil
1½ cups half and half
  Tabasco sauce
  Salt and black pepper
4 dozen Ipswich clams, shucked
1 cup stone-ground cornmeal
2 cups flour

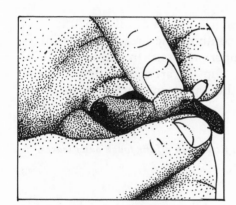

For the tenderest fried clams, remove the black skin from the neck.

FRIED BABY ARTICHOKES WITH TOMATO-ANCHOVY SAUCE

Artichokes

12 baby artichokes (see Note)
½ lemon
    Vegetable oil
½ cup dry bread crumbs
1 teaspoon minced fresh marjoram, or
    ¼ teaspoon dried marjoram
1 tablespoon minced fresh parsley
¼ teaspoon black pepper
½ teaspoon salt
1 egg

Tomato-Anchovy Sauce

2 tablespoons olive oil
1 small onion, chopped
2 tablespoons white wine
6 plum tomatoes, peeled (see
    illustrations, Chapter 16, Chili
    Sauce), seeded, and chopped
2 to 4 anchovy fillets
2 to 3 tablespoons water, if necessary
    Salt and black pepper

1. Trim the artichokes and rub the cut surfaces with lemon. Put enough salted water to cover the artichokes into a large saucepan. Bring to a boil and squeeze the juice from the lemon into the water. Add the artichokes and cook until they are just tender, about 5 minutes. Drain, pat dry with paper towels, and set aside.
2. For the sauce, heat the olive oil in a frying pan and sauté the onion over medium heat until softened but not browned, about 4 minutes. Add the wine and raise heat to medium-high. Cook, stirring, for about 1 minute. Add the tomatoes and anchovy fillets, stirring and mashing the anchovies until the sauce is slightly thickened and reduced, about 4 minutes. Add water if the sauce seems too thick. Season to taste with salt and pepper.
3. In a frying pan, heat 1½ inches of oil to 370°F.
4. In a shallow dish, combine the bread crumbs, marjoram, parsley, pepper, and salt. In another shallow dish, beat the egg. Dip the artichokes first into the egg and then into the crumb mixture to coat.

Trim the stems and cut off ½ to ¾ inch from the top. Rub all the cut edges well with lemon so that they won't discolor.

To prepare baby artichokes, first break off the tough outer leaves.

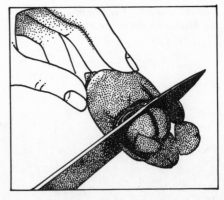

5. Fry the artichokes in the oil, a few at a time, until they are browned on all sides, about 5 minutes in all. Drain on paper towels.
6. Reheat the sauce if necessary and pour in the center of 4 warm serving plates. Arrange 3 baby artichokes (or 3 pieces of globe artichokes) around the pool of sauce and serve immediately.

Yield: 4 servings

Note: If baby artichokes are not available, use 4 small globe artichokes. Trim the stems and cut off all the outer leaves. Rub well with lemon. Cut each artichoke bottom into 3 pieces and remove and discard the fuzzy chokes.

CAJUN CABBAGE WITH SMOKED SAUSAGE

1. For the seasoning mix, combine all the ingredients in a small bowl. Set aside.
2. For the cabbage, melt the butter in a large saucepan over high heat. Add the onions and sauté for about 2 minutes, stirring occasionally. Add the cabbage, ¼ cup chicken stock, and the bay leaf. Stir in the seasoning mix and cook over medium heat, stirring occasionally, for 5 minutes.
3. Stir in the julienned apple and cook over low heat, stirring occasionally, for 15 minutes more. Add the sugar and the remaining ¼ cup stock and mix well. Cook for 2 additional minutes, stirring occasionally. Add the sausage, cook, stirring, for 5 more minutes, and serve.

Yield: 4 servings

Seasoning Mix

 1 teaspoon salt
 ¾ teaspoon sweet paprika
 ½ teaspoon white pepper
 ¼ teaspoon onion powder
 ¼ teaspoon garlic powder
 ¼ teaspoon cayenne
 ¼ teaspoon black pepper
 ¼ teaspoon dried thyme
 ⅛ teaspoon dried basil

Cabbage and Sausage

 2 tablespoons unsalted butter
 2 onions, halved then sliced thin
 ½ head cabbage, shredded
 ½ cup Chicken Stock (see recipe, Chapter 3)
 1 bay leaf
 1 apple, unpeeled, cut into ⅛-inch julienne strips
 1½ tablespoons dark-brown sugar
 ¼ pound andouille smoked sausage or any other good smoked pork sausage, such as kielbasa, cut into ½-inch slices

Soup, Chowder, Gumbo, and Chili

I n 1896 Fannie Farmer's *Boston Cooking School Cook Book* put preparation of soup into proper Victorian perspective: "It is the duty of every housekeeper to learn the art of soup making." Early in this century, canned soup was one of the first convenience foods, a great relief to overworked housewives. By mid-century, a bowl of soup more often started with a can opener than a stock-pot. The soup can is such a familiar item in our national life that Andy Warhol used it to symbolize American mass taste in early pop art works.

But making a good soup is not so hard and today is neither a duty nor a chore to be escaped. One of the regular satisfactions of any household can easily be a meal that includes bowls of homemade soup or chowder or gumbo.

The simplest way to define soup is to say that it's made in a pot or pan and served in a bowl to be eaten with a spoon. Or you can divide soups into two basic kinds—clear soup, with or without pieces of vegetables or meat, and creamy soups, often made with milk or cream or pureed vegetables. In addition, there are kin that go by other names—gumbos, chowders, and even chili—that share the techniques of soup making.

STOCK

For most soup making, the place to start is with a good stock. Stock is liquid, usually water, which has been slowly cooked with meat, poultry, or fish bones and vegetables in order to extract their flavor. The stock is then strained before being used as the base for a soup or sauce. Broth is a term sometimes used interchangeably with stock, but technically broth is the cooking liquid that results from the preparation of another dish, such as boiled beef or poached chicken. Broth can be served as a soup, of course, but unlike stock, a broth is not made primarily as a base for other dishes, and the foods from which it derives flavor are eaten, not discarded.

In professional kitchens, the process of stock making is a continual part of the routine, and a stockpot is going all the time. Despite fine resolutions, we've never been able to integrate this process into our home schedule, but since stock freezes well, several quarts can simmer away on a Sunday afternoon and be stored for future use. Canned stock is a poor substitute but can be adequate in an otherwise strongly flavored soup. Fortify it first by simmering for an hour or so with cut-up carrots and onions, herbs, and, if possible, a few meat or chicken bones.

The main types of stock prepared for soup making are beef, veal, chicken, and fish. The best and most flavorful meat soup bones are from the least expensive cuts. For chicken stock, you can use backs, necks, and wings. Freeze the scraps from whole chickens cut up for other meals until the supply is large enough to warrant getting out the stockpot. For fish stock, the remnants of fish that have been filleted can be used, and often the fish shop will let you have a batch at little or no cost. There's a wonderful satisfaction in producing something from nothing in stock making.

We find both in our own home cooking and in contemporary cooking in general that beef, veal, and fish stocks are being used less than they used to be, though this certainly needn't be true in your kitchen. Chicken stock, flavorful, yet mild and light, adapts itself readily to other flavors and has become the standard base, not only for soups but for sauces as well, much as veal stock is in classic French cooking. For modern Americans, chicken carcasses and scraps are cheaper and easier to come by than veal bones. And many of Europe's best-known chefs seem to favor its flavor, too, using it not only in meat but in contemporary fish dishes. In our "Poultry and Feathered Game" chapter, recipes for pheasant and quail call for stray parts from the birds to be simmered in chicken stock, which then becomes the game-stock basis for the sauce. In the "Meat and Sausages" chapter, chicken stock is part of veal, lamb, and beef recipes. Here it is combined with vegetables, duck, or rabbit and oysters. Altogether, a most obliging stock is chicken.

A few general rules apply to preparing a stock. Start with cold water to draw the maximum flavor from the meat and bones. Bring the ingredients and water to a boil and then reduce the heat and skim off the foam that rises to the top during the first hour. Let the stock simmer gently; don't boil it. Stock making requires some patience; you don't have to follow it constantly, but you should plan to be in the vicinity for several hours while it cooks slowly and maximum flavor is drawn from the bones and vegetables. You can't expect to produce good stock otherwise.

The exception is fish stock, which can become bitter with long cooking and is generally simmered for only 20 minutes or so with its bones. Once the bones are removed, however, the vegetables can continue to cook and the stock to simmer and reduce in order to concentrate its flavor.

After you've made your stock, let it cool slightly and then place it, uncovered, in the refrigerator until cold. Be careful, for stock will easily spoil if left too long at room temperature. Skim the surface fat off the chilled stock and then reheat it for soup making, or freeze it. If you are not using stock fairly quickly, it's best to freeze it as soon as it's cold, but it will keep in the refrigerator for several days. Bring it to a boil again before using, though, to kill any bacterial growth.

SOUP

Once you have stock according to formula, soup making itself has few rules. Of course, use good, fresh ingredients. Watch the timing when adding vegetables so that you neither undercook them and leave them half raw nor overcook them and serve them mushy. Don't boil meat in the soup pot since this can toughen it; instead cook slowly and gently. Be especially careful with cooking times and temperatures for shellfish, since it can easily be overcooked. Remember that soups keep well, normally up to a week, and that their flavor often intensifies after a couple of days' storage. So prepare soups ahead for entertaining, or make double batches for yourself, one to eat the first day and a second for later in the week.

Despite the fact that there are thousands of possible soup variations, most cooks have one or two favorites that they make over and over, often to the delight of those around them. Traditional soups such as bean soup and chicken soup, appropriate for lunchtime or simple, informal dinners, tend to be favored; but there are also contemporary soups of new and eclectic combinations, which can make sophisticated first courses. Our Curried Apple and Onion Soup and Fresh Pea Soup with Orange are examples. The Oyster and Spinach Soup in this chapter is an ideal first course for a holiday dinner, while cold soups such as the Sweet and Sour Red Cabbage Soup can revive faded summertime appetites.

CHOWDER

One member of the soup family with a long and controversial American tradition is chowder. You can still incite New Englanders with the notion of Manhattan-style clam chowder made with tomatoes instead of milk. But it is neither milk, nor cream, nor tomatoes, nor even clams, but potatoes that nearly all chowders have in common. Chowder, which shows up in English and American cookbooks as early as the eighteenth century, uses diced potatoes as a thickener, and to the surprise of many, it's almost as often made with vegetables as with seafood. For a classic example, see our Corn Chowder.

Whatever the ingredients, chowders are usually cooked by one of two methods. In one, slices of fish and vegetables are layered in a casserole, covered with liquid, and then baked or cooked over a low flame; in the other, all the ingredients are cut into chunks, put in a pot, covered with liquid, and then simmered slowly. The one key rule for either technique is not to let the soup boil or you will end up with mush.

GUMBO

As chowder is to the Northeast, so gumbo is to the Gulf states. The name *gumbo* comes from an African word for okra, *ochinnggombo*, and indeed okra, along with filé (powdered sassafras leaves), is a common thickening agent for a gumbo. As with chowders, there are regional arguments over where gumbos originated and what ingredients can be used. Southern Louisiana cooks claim to have invented the soup, but variations of gumbos are made all along the Gulf from Mississippi to east Texas. Most gumbos include seafood, but there are old recipes from the Cajun country for veal, ham, bacon, turkey, and duck gumbos. Texans often make gumbo with ham or poultry stock.

A good gumbo usually starts with a black roux, which is flour and fat cooked in a heavy pan over a low heat until it turns a dark, chocolate brown. The idea of a good roux is to get it as dark as possible without developing a burned taste. If a gumbo is thickened with okra, the gelatinous vegetable is added early in the cooking process along with other vegetables. Filé, the other traditional thickener, can be found in the spice section of most southern supermarkets. Elsewhere, it is available in specialty shops. When filé is used to thicken a gumbo, it is added after the gumbo is fully cooked. Like many soups, gumbos improve in flavor after having aged a day or so.

CHILI

If chowders and gumbos can inspire regional controversy, chili is a subject of national debate. Texans may wrongly claim to have invented many things, but they probably are right about having introduced chili to the rest of the United States. The original idea of cooking beef with native American chiles, the colored fruits of the genus Capsicum, may go back to the Aztecs. We know that Indians in the southwestern United States mixed chiles and beef or venison into a kind of meat jerky. The chile peppers preserved the meat and helped keep insects away from it, and of course gave it flavor. Ranch cooks on the Texas trail drives apparently hit upon the same use for chiles to help feed the cowboys who worked ranches and organized the cattle drives of the nineteenth century.

Like most regional specialties, there were hundreds of early variations of chili, but the first preground chili seasoning mix to allow home cooks to duplicate easily and consistently the ranch hands' dish was produced in Texas in the 1890s. Since then chili has outgrown its regional origins to the point that cooks all over the country can offer convincing arguments for the authenticity and flavor of their own concoctions.

There are no rules for making chili, but there are some basic techniques, which we tentatively tender as guidelines, not dogma. Traditionally, chili is cooked, uncovered, in a heavy cast-iron pan. Beef is the classic meat for chili, but flavorful versions can be made from venison, lamb, and pork as well. Whatever meat you choose, don't use tender, deluxe cuts. Most chili experts dice the meat by hand or run it through a meat grinder fitted with the coarsest blade. Ground beef or hamburger is often used, but it lacks the texture to make a really good chili.

The questions of tomatoes and beans will set most chili folk off on long, seldom-resolved debates. Chili can be made without either, as many purists insist it should be. But for most of us, chili means tomatoes. If used, they should be cooked well enough to dissolve them into the chili. Beans can help counterbalance the spiciness of hot chiles, and dried, not canned, beans are best. In either case, cooked beans should be added near the end of cooking the chili.

If possible, avoid the commercial chili powders, which are questionable blends put together by spice companies. Instead, find an unseasoned ground chile and season it to your taste. Add cayenne pepper to provide additional heat. Cumin is an essential seasoner, and Mexican oregano (wild marjoram) adds a special flavor. If you're not enough of an aficionado to bother to procure special ingredients, you can still stir together your own blend of chili powder that will beat the supermarket variety, just from what's on a normal spice shelf: Use paprika as the base and add cayenne, cumin, and oregano, and possibly black pepper, coriander, and a tiny touch of clove.

The final pleasure of chili making comes when the chili is in the bowl. Eat it plain or start adding the "fixins"—sour cream, chopped onions, grated cheese, diced jalapeño peppers, avocados, lime juice, salsa, coriander leaves, or just crumbled crackers.

CHICKEN STOCK

1. Put the chicken and enough cold water to cover in a large pot and bring to a boil. Skim off any foam that rises to the top. Lower heat to a gentle simmer and add the remaining ingredients. Simmer, uncovered, for about 3 hours.
2. Strain the stock, cool, and refrigerate uncovered. Remove the solidified fat from the surface before using. The stock will keep for at least 5 days, but bring it to a boil every couple of days. You can freeze it for longer storage.

Yield: about 2 quarts

4 pounds chicken carcasses, necks, backs, or wings
2 carrots, chopped
1 leek, chopped
1 onion stuck with 2 cloves
1 bay leaf
4 to 5 sprigs parsley with stems
½ teaspoon dried thyme
8 peppercorns

SOUP

SOUP Today's "new cooking" has made its reputation at least partly by putting together common ingredients in surprising ways. This has had its effect on soups, too, where both contemporary European and American chefs have taken to testing the old cooks' saw that anything goes in a soup pot. The creation of new soups takes a fine sense of taste; otherwise it becomes an exercise in shock value alone.

One source for some of our contemporary soups is regional and traditional recipes, such as pumpkin soup, common in both American Indian and early colonial cookery and here presented with a garlicky twist, and old-fashioned split pea, which we've brightened by using fresh peas and a hint of orange zest.

HEARTY DUCK AND WILD RICE SOUP

2¼ cups water
    Salt and black pepper
  1 cup wild rice
  1 4-pound duck
  2 onions, sliced
  1 clove garlic, crushed
  2 cups white wine
  2 quarts Chicken Stock (see recipe, this
    chapter)
¼ cup chopped parsley, stems reserved
½ pound fresh wild mushrooms
    (chanterelles, if available),
    chopped, trimmings reserved (about
    2½ cups)
  2 cups heavy cream

1. Bring the water to a boil with 1 teaspoon salt. Add the wild rice, stir, cover, and cook over low heat until tender, about 50 minutes.
2. Remove the breast meat from the duck with a sharp boning knife. Trim the meat of all skin and fat, and set aside. Cut the skin and fat into small pieces; set aside. Remove the leg and thigh sections and set aside. Break up the carcass and set aside.
3. In a large, heavy saucepan, cook the skin and fat over moderate heat until the fat is rendered and the skin begins to crisp, about 15 minutes. Add the carcass pieces and continue to sauté over high heat until the bones brown, about 10 minutes. Add the leg and thigh sections and brown. Add the onions and garlic and continue to sauté until the onions just begin to color, 3 to 5 minutes.
4. Remove the duck pieces from the pan and reserve the legs, thighs, and bones. Discard any remaining bits of fat but leave the skin. Pour off and reserve the melted fat.
5. Add the wine to the pan, scraping the bottom of the pan with a wooden spoon to deglaze. Boil to reduce by half. Add the stock, legs, thighs, bones, parsley stems, and mushroom trimmings. Bring to a boil and skim. Turn heat to low and continue to simmer until the liquid is reduced by half, 20 to 30 minutes. Remove the leg and thigh sections and set aside.

6. Strain the stock into a container and set aside to cool for 5 to 10 minutes. Skim off any grease that rises to the top.

7. Remove the meat from the legs and thighs and cut into ½-inch dice. Discard the bones.

8. Cut the reserved breast meat into 1"-×-¼" strips. Sauté the strips in a little of the reserved rendered duck fat until they are lightly browned, 4 to 5 minutes. Add the mushrooms, cooked wild rice, and meat from the legs and thighs. Season with salt and pepper, add chopped parsley, and toss together.

9. In another saucepan, heat the cream to a simmer and reduce gently for 4 to 5 minutes over low heat. While whisking, pour the strained stock into the cream. Bring to a boil, add the mushroom–rice–duck mixture, and simmer for an additional 4 to 5 minutes. Season with salt and pepper.

Yield: 6 to 8 servings

FRESH PEA SOUP WITH ORANGE

1. In a medium-size saucepan, bring the chicken stock to a simmer. Add the peas and sugar and cook, uncovered, until the peas are tender, about 10 minutes.

2. Strain the peas, reserving the stock. Puree the peas in a food processor or blender.

3. Push the pureed peas through a sieve and return them to the stock. Add the orange zest, cream, and salt and pepper to taste. Either heat or chill thoroughly before serving, topped with a dollop of whipped cream if you like.

Yield: 4 servings

3 cups Chicken Stock (see recipe, this chapter)
4 cups shelled fresh peas (about 4 pounds in shell)
Pinch of sugar
½ teaspoon grated orange zest
¾ cup heavy cream
Salt and black pepper
3 tablespoons heavy cream, whipped (optional)

ROASTED PUMPKIN–GARLIC SOUP

1 small (about 6 pounds), firm
   pumpkin, split in half
   Salt
6 tablespoons unsalted butter
3 to 4 heads small-cloved red garlic, or
   3 heads regular garlic, separated but
   unpeeled
4 branches fresh thyme, or 1 teaspoon
   dried thyme, plus fresh chopped
   thyme for garnish (optional)
2 cups Chicken Stock (see recipe, this
   chapter)
   Pepper Croutons (recipe follows)

1. Heat the oven to 350°F.
2. Scrape the cavities of the pumpkin halves to remove the fibers and seeds. Salt liberally and rub with 2 tablespoons butter.
3. Put the garlic cloves on a heavy baking sheet in 2 piles with 2 branches or ½ teaspoon thyme in each one. Place a pumpkin half over each pile of garlic and slide the pan into the preheated oven. Roast until the pumpkin skin begins to blister and the flesh softens, about 1¼ hours. Remove from the oven and cool until the pumpkin can be easily handled.
4. Peel the skin from both the pumpkin and garlic and discard. Press the pulp through a food mill or puree in a food processor, being careful not to overprocess.
5. Stir the garlic and pumpkin purees together with the stock in a heavy pot. Warm over low heat. Season with salt to taste.
6. To serve, stir in the remaining 4 tablespoons butter and garnish with pepper croutons and chopped thyme, if desired.

Yield: 4 servings

PEPPER CROUTONS

2 slices firm white bread, cut into ½-
   inch cubes
1½ tablespoons unsalted butter
¼ teaspoon coarsely ground black pepper
   Salt

1. Let the bread cubes dry out at room temperature for at least 15 minutes.
2. In a small frying pan, melt the butter. Add the bread cubes, sprinkle with pepper and salt to taste, and toss constantly over medium-high heat until the cubes are crisp and golden, about 3 minutes.

Yield: about ¾ cup

CURRIED APPLE AND ONION SOUP

1. In a frying pan, heat the oil and sauté the celery, chopped onion, and leek until translucent, about 10 minutes.
2. In a saucepan, make a roux by melting 4 tablespoons butter and adding the flour and curry powder. Mix thoroughly and cook, stirring over medium heat and taking care not to burn, for 8 minutes. Add ½ quart of hot chicken stock and stir until smooth. Add the sautéed vegetables and simmer over medium heat for 45 minutes.
3. Transfer the mixture to a food processor and puree.
4. In a heavy pot, sauté the sliced onions in the remaining ½ tablespoon butter until they are translucent. Add the remaining 1 quart chicken stock, bring to a boil, and cook gently until the liquid is reduced by half, 10 to 15 minutes.
5. Peel, core, and cut the apple into ¼-inch slices. Add the puree to the reduced stock and then add the apple slices and cream. Heat through, season with salt and pepper, and serve.

Yield: 4 servings

1½ teaspoons vegetable oil
2½ ribs celery, chopped
¼ onion, chopped, plus 2 small onions, sliced
½ leek, white part only, chopped
4½ tablespoons unsalted butter
¼ cup flour
1½ teaspoons curry powder
1½ quarts hot Chicken Stock (see recipe, this chapter)
1 tart apple
¼ cup heavy cream
Salt and black pepper

SWEET AND SOUR RED CABBAGE SOUP

1. In a nonreactive pot, cook the bacon until all the fat is rendered and the bacon is golden, about 10 minutes. Remove the bacon if the soup is to be served cold; leave it in the pan if the soup will be served hot. Add the leeks and cook over low heat, covered, until soft, about 15 minutes. Add the allspice, cloves, and garlic, and cook, stirring, for 2 minutes. Add the brown sugar and vinegar and stir until the sugar is dissolved, 3 to 4 minutes.
2. Add the cabbage and tomatoes with juice and cook, covered, stirring occasionally, for 30 minutes.
3. Add the chicken stock, raise heat, and bring to a boil. Reduce heat to a simmer and cook, uncovered, for 30 minutes. Add salt and pepper to taste. Serve hot or chilled with sour cream and chopped dill or chives.

Yield: 4 servings

2 ounces (about 2 slices) bacon, dried
2 leeks, minced
1 teaspoon ground allspice
¼ teaspoon ground cloves
1 clove garlic, minced
2 tablespoons brown sugar
6 tablespoons balsamic or red wine vinegar
½ head red cabbage, shredded (about 3 cups)
3 cups (about 20 ounces) minced canned Italian plum tomatoes, with juice
3¾ cups Chicken Stock (see recipe, this chapter)
Salt and black pepper
6 tablespoons sour cream
Chopped fresh dill or chives

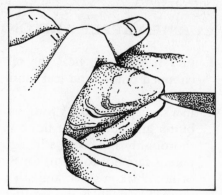

To open an oyster, first insert a knife next to the hinge.

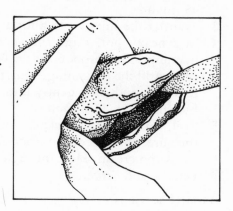

Twist the knife to open the oyster.

OYSTER AND SPINACH SOUP

¾ pound spinach
4 tablespoons unsalted butter
1 small onion, minced
½ rib celery, minced
1 leek, white part only, minced
1½ cloves garlic, minced
2 tablespoons flour
⅓ cup white wine
2 dozen fresh oysters, shucked over a
    bowl to catch liquor
2⅔ cups heavy cream
    Black pepper
    Cayenne
    Salt
    Grated nutmeg

1. Add the spinach to a pot of boiling water, bring back to a boil, and drain immediately. Press down on the spinach to remove any excess water.
2. In a large pot, melt the butter and sauté the onion, celery, leek, and garlic over a medium-low heat until soft, about 10 minutes. Add the flour and continue cooking on medium-low heat, stirring, for 3 minutes. Gradually add the wine and oyster liquor. Bring to a boil.
3. Add the spinach, stirring frequently to prevent scorching. Add the oysters and continue to cook over medium heat only until the edges of the oysters curl, 3 to 5 minutes.

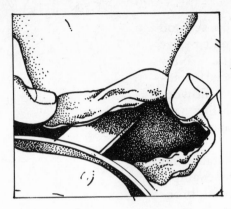

Run the knife along the top shell to sever the muscle.

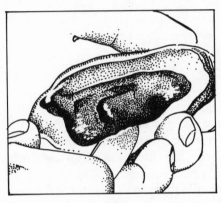

Finally, cut the oyster free from the bottom shell.

4. Transfer the mixture to a food processor and chop, being careful not to overprocess—the consistency should not be entirely smooth.
5. Transfer the mixture to a double boiler. Add 2⅓ cups cream and heat. Season to taste with pepper and cayenne. Add salt if necessary, but this soup may be salty enough.
6. Whip the remaining ⅓ cup cream lightly. Ladle the soup into bowls. Spoon dollops of whipped cream on top and dust with a grating of nutmeg.

Yield: 4 servings

CHOWDER
Clam chowder is so common on seafood restaurant menus across the country that many people don't realize there are other kinds of chowder. In fact, nineteenth-century New Englanders used a variety of seafood—oysters or mussels for instance—rather than clams in chowders. Our baked seafood chowder is based on early American recipes calling for coastal fish like haddock, whiting, or cod. You could substitute halibut, snapper, or redfish.

As chowder making spread inland with the settlers, vegetable and meat chowders appeared. Our corn chowder recipe is one example of a vegetable chowder. Other typical chowders are lima bean, broccoli, succotash, spinach, and even veal, chicken, or rabbit.

NEW ENGLAND CLAM CHOWDER

2½ cups water
24 (about 1½ pounds) soft-shell clams (see Note)
¼ pound salt pork, diced (about ½ cup)
1 onion, sliced thin
3 potatoes, peeled and cut into ½-inch dice
¾ cup milk
¾ cup heavy cream
    White pepper
    Unsalted butter
    Paprika

1. In a large pot, bring the water to a boil. Add the clams and boil for 1 minute. Remove the clams. Strain the broth through a double thickness of cheesecloth and set aside.
2. Shell the clams (see illustration, Chapter 2, Fried Ipswich Clams with Tomato-Basil Mayonnaise) and dice the meat, removing and discarding the necks and shells.
3. In a large pot, cook the salt pork over medium heat until crisp, 5 to 7 minutes. Stir in the onion and cook until softened, about 10 minutes. Add the reserved clam broth and potatoes and bring to a boil. Reduce to a simmer and cook until the potatoes are tender, about 10 minutes.
4. Stir in the milk and cream, heat gently, season to taste with white pepper, and add the clams. Serve immediately with a slice of butter and a pinch of paprika in each serving bowl.

Yield: 4 large servings

Note: Oysters or mussels can be substituted for the clams. Soft-shell or long-neck clams are common in northern New England, but you can substitute hard-shell clams with good results.

CORN CHOWDER

1. Cut the kernels from 3 ears of corn with a sharp knife. Scrape the kernels from the other 3 with the back of a knife blade. You should have about 2 cups in all.
2. In a large pot, cook the salt pork over medium-high heat until crisp, about 7 minutes. Remove the pork pieces and set aside for garnish.
3. Sauté the onion in the pork fat until softened, about 10 minutes.
4. Add the scraped and whole corn kernels. Stir in the potato and chicken stock. Bring to a boil, reduce heat, and simmer until the potatoes are tender, about 10 minutes. Add the cream, season to taste with salt and pepper and cayenne, if you desire. Stir in the parsley and serve, garnished with the reserved salt pork.

6 ears corn
2 ounces salt pork, diced (about ¼ cup)
½ onion, sliced thin
1 potato, peeled and cut into ½-inch dice
2 cups Chicken Stock (see recipe, this chapter)
1 cup light cream
  Salt and black pepper
  Pinch of cayenne (optional)
2 teaspoons chopped fresh parsley

Yield: 4 servings

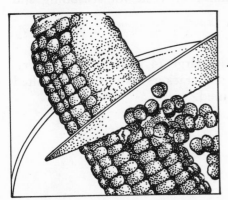

For cut kernels, cut the corn from the cob smoothly so that all the juices are retained in the kernels.

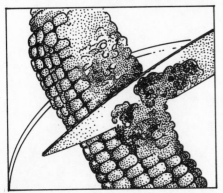

To scrape corn, use the back of a knife against the cob, pressing hard enough to get all the pulp and juice.

BAKED FISH CHOWDER

This recipe is quite authentically based on very early chowder recipes, even to the point of flavoring the milk with fish heads and bones.

2 pounds fish heads and bones
1 quart milk
3 ounces salt pork, sliced thin (about ⅓ cup)
1 onion, sliced
1 pound white fish (such as haddock, whiting, or cod), cut into about 6 pieces
1 potato, cut into ¼-inch slices
Salt and white pepper
⅛ teaspoon dried thyme
Pinch of nutmeg
1 small bay leaf
4 pilot crackers (see Note)
¼ cup white wine

1. In a pot, simmer the fish heads and bones in the milk over medium-low heat for 20 minutes. Strain and reserve the milk.
2. Heat the oven to 325°F.
3. Line the bottom of a 2-quart casserole with the salt pork. Add half the onion slices, fish, and potato slices. Season with salt and pepper and half the thyme and nutmeg. Put the bay leaf in the middle and crumble 2 crackers over all. Add the remaining ingredients, layering in the same order. Pour in wine and reserved milk.
4. Bake in the preheated oven until the potatoes are tender, 40 to 45 minutes. Taste for seasoning and serve.

Yield: 4 servings

Note: Pilot crackers are large (4 inches in diameter), sturdy, flat, unsalted dry crackers. Any firm, unsalted cracker can be substituted.

GUMBO
In spirit, Cajun and creole cooking may be the closest American approximation of the regional cuisines of France, a traditional cooking more roughly hewn and heavily spiced than haute cuisine. Such cooking is typified by the French cassoulet and bouillabaisse, and the American gumbo and jambalaya, which differ slightly in execution and style from village to village or even farmhouse to farmhouse, but which are always based on good, honest, local ingredients.

CHICKEN AND SEAFOOD GUMBO

1. Season the chicken with salt and pepper.
2. In a heavy frying pan, melt the shortening and sauté the chicken pieces until brown on all sides, about 10 minutes. Remove and set aside.
3. Add the okra, onion, and celery to the pan and sauté until the onion is soft and translucent, about 10 minutes.
4. In a large, heavy saucepan, cook the bacon until almost crisp. Remove the bacon, crumble, and set aside.
5. Combine the flour with 3 tablespoons of fat. (If there's not enough bacon fat add additional fat from the chicken pan for a total of 3 tablespoons.) Carefully cook the roux over medium heat, stirring constantly, until dark brown, 10 to 15 minutes. Be careful not to scorch the roux.
6. Add the tomato, garlic, sautéed onion mixture, bacon, thyme, bay leaf, and 2 tablespoons parsley. Stir in the chicken stock and ham. Season to taste with salt, pepper, and Tabasco. Bring to a full boil, reduce heat, and simmer, uncovered, for 1 hour. Add the chicken and simmer for 1 more hour, stirring occasionally.
7. Remove the chicken pieces and skim any surface fat from the gumbo. Remove the meat from the bones, cut into chunks, and return to the gumbo. Add the crabmeat and shrimp and simmer, stirring often, for about 5 minutes. Adjust the seasonings and stir in the filé powder. Do not boil. Serve immediately, garnished with chopped parsley.

Yield: 4 servings

Note: Filé powder must be added at the last minute, but you can prepare the gumbo ahead of time and add the shellfish and filé just before serving.

½ small chicken (about 1½ pounds), cut up
Salt and black pepper
¼ cup vegetable shortening
2 cups sliced fresh okra
1 small onion, chopped
1 rib celery, chopped
2 slices bacon
3 tablespoons flour
1 tomato, peeled (see illustrations, Chapter 16, Chili Sauce) and chopped
1 clove garlic, crushed
½ teaspoon thyme
1 bay leaf
2 tablespoons chopped fresh parsley, plus more for garnish
6 cups Chicken Stock (see recipe, this chapter)
6 ounces ham, diced (about 1 cup)
About 4 drops Tabasco sauce
1 cup cooked crabmeat
½ pound shrimp, peeled and deveined
½ to 1 teaspoon filé powder (see Note)

RABBIT AND OYSTER GUMBO

1½ *pounds rabbit, cut into pieces*
  1 *quart Chicken Stock (see recipe, this*
        chapter)
  1 *tablespoon unsalted butter*
  1 *tablespoon vegetable oil*
  2 *tablespoons flour*
  ½ *green bell pepper, chopped*
  1 *small onion, chopped*
  1 *tablespoon minced fresh parsley*
  1 *to 2 dashes of Tabasco sauce*
  ⅛ *teaspoon dried thyme*
     Salt and black pepper
  ½ *pint shucked oysters, drained*
  ¾ *teaspoon filé powder (see Note)*
  1 *cup hot cooked rice*

1. In a large pot, bring the rabbit pieces and chicken stock to a boil. Lower heat, skim off any foam, and simmer, partially covered, until the meat is very tender, about 1 hour. With a slotted spoon, lift the rabbit pieces from the pot, remove the meat from the bones, and cut into chunks.

2. In another large pot, heat the butter and oil. Stir in the flour to make a paste and cook over medium heat, stirring constantly, until the roux turns a rich, dark brown, 10 to 15 minutes. Be careful during the last 5 to 10 minutes not to burn. Add the bell pepper and onion and cook over low heat until the onion is soft and translucent, about 10 minutes.

3. Slowly strain the stock into the roux mixture, stirring constantly. Add the parsley, Tabasco, and thyme and season to taste with salt and pepper. Bring to a boil and add the reserved rabbit meat. Simmer until heated through, about 3 minutes. Add the oysters and cook just until their edges begin to curl, 3 to 5 minutes. Remove from heat.

4. Just before serving, gently stir in the filé powder. Divide the rice among 4 large soup bowls and ladle the gumbo over the rice.

Yield: 4 servings

Note: Filé powder loses its effectiveness if reheated and so must be added just before serving, even if the rest of the gumbo is prepared ahead of time. In that case, it would be a good idea to add the rabbit meat and oysters just before serving, too.

CHILI

CHILI The Southwest rightly claims pride of place in the great American chili tradition, but in the 1920s and '30s, chili parlors and chili houses became part of the urban scene all across the United States. Some of the chili enterpreneurs developed their own styles and varieties. One city, Cincinnati, became a hotbed of chili enthusiasm, driven toward its place in the history of American chili making by the experimenting of a Bulgarian immigrant named Anthanas Kiradjieff, who learned about chili at New York City hot dog stands. Later Kiradjieff moved to Cincinnati, where he opened his own hot dog place and discovered his gastronomic niche. He fiddled with his chili recipe, adding a Balkan touch with cinnamon and allspice, and eventually came up with a chili he didn't need to put on hot dogs to sell. Kiradjieff's chili parlor, the Empress, became famous for a chili hybrid—layers of chili, spaghetti, kidney beans, and, finally, onions. The whole thing was topped with grated American cheese.

Our chili recipes are for the more typical southwestern style, an innovative lamb and hominy chili, and a luscious hot pork version. But the Cincinnati chili story reminds us that when it comes to chili, most everyone's own kind is the best kind.

TEXAS CHILI

1. In a frying pan, heat the fat and sauté the onion until soft. Stir in the beef, garlic, ground chili, and cumin and cook until browned, about 10 minutes.
2. Add the salt, paprika, and water and simmer for about 2 hours, uncovered, stirring occasionally.
3. Skim any fat from the top, taste for seasoning, and serve with any combination of the garnishes, if desired.

Yield: 4 servings

1 tablespoon lard, butter, or bacon drippings
1 small onion, chopped
1½ pounds beef chuck, cut into ¼-inch dice
1 clove or more garlic, to taste
1 tablespoon or more ground hot red chili, to taste
1 to 1½ tablespoons or more ground mild red chili, to taste
1½ teaspoons ground cumin
Salt
1½ teaspoons paprika
1½ cups water
Garnishes such as tostados, avocado slices, grated cheddar cheese, diced tomatoes, sour cream, and/or chopped onions (optional)

LAMB CHILI WITH JALAPEÑO HOMINY

1½ *pounds coarsely ground lamb*
    Salt
2 *tablespoons olive oil, plus more, if necessary*
2 *small yellow onions, chopped*
2 to 3 *cloves garlic, minced*
2 *cups (14 ounces) canned Italian plum tomatoes, drained*
2 *cups water*
2½ *tablespoons ground mild red chili*
2 *tablespoons ground toasted cumin (see Note)*
2 *teaspoons black pepper*
1 *teaspoon allspice*
½ *teaspoon ground cinnamon*
½ *teaspoon dried thyme*
½ *teaspoon dry mustard*
1 to 1½ *tablespoons cornmeal (optional)*
3 *tablespoons unsalted butter*
1 to 1½ *jalapeño peppers, minced*
3½ *cups (30 ounces canned) white or yellow hominy, drained*

1. In a heavy saucepan, cook the lamb over medium heat, uncovered, and stirring often, until the meat loses its pink color but is not browned, about 15 minutes. Add salt to taste and remove any excess grease.
2. In another heavy saucepan, heat 2 tablespoons olive oil. Add the onions and garlic and cook, covered, over medium heat, stirring occasionally, until softened and translucent, about 10 minutes.
3. Add the onion-garlic mixture to the lamb. Add the tomatoes and break them up with a large spoon. Add the water and seasonings; bring to a boil. Reduce heat and simmer, uncovered, for 1 hour. Stir occasionally. Adjust the seasonings.
4. If the chili seems too thick, add up to ½ cup water more. Continue to simmer, stirring often, until the meat is tender, about 30 minutes. If the chili is too thin at the end of cooking, stir in the optional cornmeal, 1 teaspoon at a time, until the desired thickness is achieved. Simmer for 5 minutes.
5. Melt the butter in a frying pan over medium heat. When it foams, add the jalapeños and salt to taste. Cook, stirring occasionally, for 5 minutes. Add the hominy and cook until heated through, 5 to 10 minutes. To serve, spoon the hominy into bowls and ladle the lamb chili over it, or serve the chili on a platter surrounded by the hominy.

Yield: 4 servings

Note: To toast the cumin, put in a heavy frying pan and stir continuously over very low heat for 3 minutes.

GREEN CHILI WITH PORK

Besides being delicious all by itself, this chili can be served with burritos, enchiladas, or *huevos rancheros*.

1. Heat the oven to 325°F.
2. In a large, heavy ovenproof pan with a lid, heat the oil until very hot. Add the pork, reduce heat slightly, and cook, turning frequently, until well browned, about 15 minutes. Add the chicken stock, onions, and garlic. Cover and cook in the preheated oven for 2½ hours, turning the meat once at the halfway point.
3. Cool the pork to room temperature in the stock and then remove and wrap well. Pour the stock through a strainer into a bowl, pressing hard with the back of a spoon to extract all the juices from the vegetables. Refrigerate the meat and stock overnight.
4. Remove the meat from the bones and shred by pulling it apart with a fork.
5. Remove the chilled fat from the surface of the stock. Put 2 tablespoons of fat in a saucepan, and melt over low heat. Add the flour and cook, stirring constantly, for 5 minutes. Combine the stock with enough water to equal 3½ cups. Add it to the pan along with the shredded pork, green chiles, oregano, and cayenne. Bring to a boil. Reduce heat and simmer, uncovered, for 1½ hours. Stir occasionally. The chili should be very thick, the pork quite tender, and the chiles virtually dissolved into liquid. Add salt to taste.

Yield: 4 servings

2 tablespoons olive oil
1 3- to 3½-pound pork shoulder with bone
3 cups Chicken Stock (see recipe, this chapter)
2 small yellow onions, chopped
3 cloves garlic, minced
2 tablespoons flour
2¼ cups (13½ ounces) canned mild green chiles, drained, rinsed, and chopped
1½ teaspoons dried oregano (preferably Mexican)
½ teaspoon cayenne
Salt

4 Meat and Sausages

We are and always have been a nation of meat eaters. In Europe, from medieval times hunting was the preserve of the nobility and the commoner shot deer or trapped rabbits at his peril. But in colonial America, frontier equality quickly translated itself into the right of every man to provide his family with venison, to shoot squirrel or possum or rabbit for the frying pan or the stew pot.

The wide expanse of land available here almost for the claiming meant that cattle could be cheaply grazed and pigs easily kept. A sufficient amount could be slaughtered for immediate use as well as cured for sustenance through the long cold winters. As the settlers moved into the Midwest and across the Mississippi to the plains and the mountains, the whole mechanism of expansion centered around the provision of meat for those remaining behind in the East.

In time, buffalo herds disappeared to meet the demands for food of the growing cities. Cattlemen and sheepherders fought range wars in their competition to grow and sell meat to the immigrants rushing to our shores. The railroads pushed west, meeting the famous cattle trails like the Santa Fe and the Chisolm. The legend of the cowboy grew around the railhead towns—Topeka, Dodge City, Abilene, Wichita—where hundreds

of people lived literally amidst pens holding thousands of steers destined for the cattle markets and butchers in Kansas City, Omaha, and Chicago. The first great American corporations such as Armour and Swift pioneered the use of refrigerator cars to speed the slaughtered meat across the rails to markets thousands of miles from the ranches.

By the early 1900s, the steak house had become the quintessential American eatery. In 1950 the average American ate 147 pounds of meat a year; the average Frenchman got by on 94. Even as culinary sophistication took hold in the 1960s and '70s, one of the greatest economic success stories in the land was that of a Chicagoan who sold millions, then billions of cheap hamburgers to our mobile, meat-eating millions. Golden arches replaced the Coca-Cola bottle as a worldwide symbol of advancing Americanization.

So meat has been central to our cooking during most of our history. And although we're probably eating more vegetables, pasta, and fish than ever before, for millions of people in the United States and abroad American cooking starts with meat. The monochromatic emphasis on beef that highlighted the middle decades of the century has eased. This comes clear with the recipes to follow for veal, venison, and sausage. Contemporary American cooks don't ignore meat; they are, in fact, more than willing to try a traditional recipe for a forgotten stew one night and experiment with a new combination or cut of meat the next.

SELECTING MEAT

Meat is among the most versatile of cooking products. Cuts of meat can be so tender they need be cooked only minutes over a very high heat or so fibrous that they need long hours of slow stewing or braising. The knowledgeable cook can contribute greatly to the success of a meal by looking closely at the meat before buying and by knowing what cuts work best for what sorts of recipes.

Meat cooking generally aims for two qualities—flavor and tenderness. Expertly chosen and cooked meat should always offer both, though the cut as it comes from the animal may not. As it happens, the conditions

that make for tender meat also tend to lessen flavor. The texture of a piece of meat is normally determined by the amount and firmness of the connective tissue around an animal's muscles—the more there is, the less tender the meat.

In turn, the amount of connective tissue is determined by the age of an animal, its activity while alive, and the location of a particular piece of meat on the animal's body. Logically, a well-exercised muscle will produce less tender meat. To cut down on an animal's activity, ranchers neuter their male animals, which usually makes them less active. The famous Japanese Kobe beef is exceptionally tender because the animal is regularly massaged to relax the muscles, and is given little room or opportunity for strenuous exercise. In any case, the age of an animal obviously affects the texture of its meat because usually the older the animal, the more it has exercised. Most pork or lamb sold in markets today is less than six months old, while beef is normally from a mature steer over a year old.

The rule of thumb for determining which parts of an animal provide the tenderest meat is simple—the closer the meat is to a hoof or horn, the tougher it will be. While the age and activity of most animals raised for slaughter in the United States are fairly standard, it pays to ask your butcher about seasonal variations on the cuts he offers.

Flavor is a more elusive quality to define than texture. Paradoxically, the tougher the meat, the more flavorful it's likely to be. The primary indicator of flavor is the amount of fat in and around a muscle.

Fat through the flesh of an animal is called marbling. Marbling is especially important for flavor in cuts from parts of the body that get little exercise, the tender cuts from the rib and loin. Marbling also keeps these cuts, which are generally cooked with dry heat, from dehydrating and toughening. A well-marbled piece of beef or lamb should have white dots or flecks of fat distributed within the reddish flesh. Heavy or coarse marbling, however, may indicate considerable age.

The fat around a cut of beef or lamb, not within it like marbling, tells us something about how an animal was fed. A yellow outside fat layer normally means the animal was grass fed while white fat means it was raised

on a diet of corn or other grain. Grain-fed animals usually produce superior, more flavorful meat.

Many of the cooking techniques discussed in the following pages can compensate for lack of tenderness in a piece of meat, and cooking or serving meat with flavoring liquids and sauce can improve a lackluster taste. One natural process, aging, helps make meat, especially beef, both more flavorful and more tender. Beef can be aged up to six weeks in a controlled environment at a temperature of between 34° and 38° Fahrenheit. This process starts an enzymatic change that softens the connective tissue round the muscles, thereby tenderizing the meat at the same time as it intensifies its flavor.

Aging, most often done with prime-grade beef, also increases the price. Pork and lamb can also be aged, lamb for one week and pork for up to ten days. Veal should not need aging, while wild game often must be aged if it is to be tender enough to be edible.

Marinating meat, sprinkling it with commercial meat tenderizers, or scoring, grinding, or pounding it before cooking are all ways of trying to achieve the same results as aging. Effective marinades made with acidic ingredients such as lemon juice, wine, or vinegar chemically soften connective tissue. They can even be used with tender, very thinly sliced meat to render it fit for eating raw, as in our Pepper Beef. Marinades generally also contain herbs, spices, or other ingredients that impart flavor to the meat. Commercial meat tenderizers usually contain papain, a chemical derived from unripe papayas, as an active ingredient that is effective in softening the surface but rarely penetrates to the center of a piece of meat. Meat tenderizers also often include additives that can give an unappetizing flavor. Grinding, scoring, or pounding meat tenderizes it by shortening the length of the connective tissues. You can achieve much the same result by cutting it into thin slices across the grain when serving.

COOKING MEAT

Meat cookery can seem confusing. What's the difference between pan-frying and sautéing, for instance? When is one braising meat and when is one stewing it? Where does pot roasting fit in? In practice, however, cooking meat is rather simple. All the ways we cook meat fall into one of two basic categories—cooking with dry heat and cooking with moist heat. Sautéing, pan-frying, broiling, and roasting (as well as grilling, to be found in a separate chapter) are dry-heat techniques, share similar principles, and call for similar cuts of meat. Stewing, braising, pot roasting, and poaching are all ways of cooking with moist heat and therefore are also similar in concept and in the kinds of cuts chosen.

A dry-heat method is one in which meat is cooked without liquid whether on the stove, in the oven, under a broiler, or on a grill. Fat is used in some dry-heat methods, such as sautéing or pan-frying, its purpose to brown the meat while sealing its juices inside. Moist heat uses water, wine, broth, or any number of other liquids to mingle with the meat juices themselves and to impart flavor and tenderness to the dish.

In dry-heat cooking methods, the meat is essentially on its own. To be tender and flavorful, it must be a top-quality cut to begin with. Chops, steaks, rib roasts, and the like are used in dry-heat cooking. Moist heat, on the other hand, can tenderize older, tougher cuts—brisket, shank, chuck, and bottom round among them.

Roasting

Roasting is normally done in the hot dry air of the oven. For the novice, this is perhaps the trickiest of all methods of cooking meat, since it requires that large, often expensive cuts of meat be cooked to a critical degree of doneness. But unlike pan-frying or sautéing—in which the extent of doneness is equally important—it is difficult to determine by eye and hand the exact condition of the meat. Neither recommended cooking times nor meat thermometers are always precise guides. If you use a thermometer, the instant-read type is the best. Much depends on knowing how your particular oven cooks and on your own experience. On the positive side, once you have learned to gauge your oven and determined the approximate times for roasting your favorite cuts to the degree you prefer, this can be a relatively easy method of cooking an elegant main course, one that leaves you free for the preparation of other dishes while the meat is roasting.

For beef, the best pieces for roasting are prime rib, top sirloin, and top round. A prime eye of round makes a lovely roast but needs to be wrapped or coated with extra fat for sufficient moisture. For pork, choose roasts from the loin, the leg, the rump, or even the shoulder. Pork is normally roasted for a longer time at a lower temperature than beef. Lamb roasts are generally the leg, loin, rack, and shoulder. Veal roasts can be delicious—use cuts from the rump, shoulder, rack, leg, or loin.

Broiling

Like roasting, broiling in the home is usually done in the oven. The heat source, whether electric or gas, is above the meat, and cooking is regulated not by changing the temperature as in roasting, but by varying the distance between the meat and the broiling unit or the height of the flames. Thinner cuts of meat are normally broiled quickly, close to the heat, searing them quickly and leaving them juicy in the center. Larger cuts cook farther from the heat for a longer time.

As with dry-heat cooking methods, choose cuts with plenty of natural fats within the meat. Delicate or very thin pieces of meat are better sautéed or pan-fried. For beef, steaks and ground meat are commonly broiled, though our Broiled Beef and Scallop Ribbon made with prime rib is an unusual alternative that works. For lamb, choose chops, rack, loin of lamb, or butterflied, boned legs. Veal chops can be broiled, as can sausages, pork chops, and ham steaks.

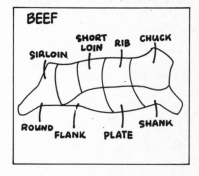

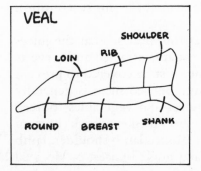

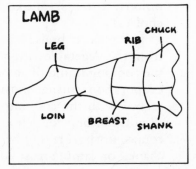

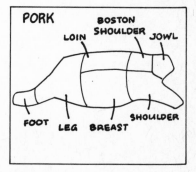

Sautéing and Pan-Frying

With sautéing and pan-frying, oil or some other fat is added to the pan. Sautéing is a quicker process than pan-frying, and less fat is normally used. Sautéing is especially suited to tender, thin cuts of meat. Good sautéing requires strict though brief concentration. Inattentiveness for even a minute can be disastrous. A well-sautéed piece of meat should have a light, crisp, golden-brown exterior. Pan-frying is much like sautéing but is generally employed for larger or thicker cuts, and more fat is used.

For sautéing, choose veal scallops or similarly thin slices of pork, lamb, or beef, such as tournedos or noisettes. Sliced pork tenderloin is a delicious choice for sautéing, as is the more traditional filet mignon. Lamb, veal, and pork chops can all be pan-fried, as can steaks that are too thin for broiling. Hamburgers and thick cuts of beef liver can also be pan-fried.

Stewing and Braising

Stewing and braising are the two most popular forms of cooking with moist heat, and although very similar in technique, there are clear differences between the two methods. Of all the forms of moist-heat cooking, true braising uses the least liquid. A piece of meat generally braises in its own juices and those of any vegetables added to the pot for flavoring. Braises can cook either on top of the stove or in the oven, but in either case the piece of meat is left whole and should fit snugly into the pot along with its accompanying vegetables (leeks, onions, carrots, and celery are the most common choices).

The meat is braised over low heat so that the juices from the vegetables and meat are extracted and serve as the cooking liquid. The pot must be covered to prevent evaporation during braising. Braised meat is generally served with the cooking juices and vegetables, pureed or not. For braising, choose beef brisket, chuck, bottom round, or short ribs of beef. Boned lamb shoulder, lamb shank, or lamb breast make good braises, as do veal shanks or veal shoulder. A pork cut such as shoulder or loin with bone left in can also be braised.

Stews are extremely popular if for no other reason than that they are very forgiving. Meat for stews is cut into pieces, usually browned, and then cooked in a pot with at least an inch of liquid—wine, beer, water, or stock. Our pork stew calls for cider. Vegetables are usually cooked with a stew and then served as part of it. The same cuts suggested for braising are appropriate. If you cook the meat slowly, it's hard not to have a successful stew.

Poaching or Simmering

Boiled beef is both a gastronomic touchstone and a misnomer. It's one of the basics in many cuisines, including American, but the meat is never really boiled since boiling for any length of time would toughen it. What we call boiled beef is actually poached or simmered in enough liquid to cover, normally broth or water, at around 200° Fahrenheit until the meat is tender, an hour or more. To poach or simmer beef, choose rump or bottom round, shoulder cuts, brisket, short ribs, or shank. Veal shank can also be poached. And although it's not done much in this country, the French have great success poaching tender cuts of meat such as the tenderloin for a short time.

BEEF

PEPPER BEEF

In principle this recipe is similar to seviche and even more closely related to the Italian beef dish Carpaccio. The meat is marinated until tenderized and then served without being cooked.

½ pound lean beef (such as sirloin), trimmed, wrapped in plastic, and frozen for 1½ hours
1 tablespoon lemon juice
1 tablespoon brine from capers, plus 2 tablespoons capers
2 tablespoons red wine
1 green bell pepper
1 red bell pepper
1 yellow bell pepper (see Note)
Vegetable oil
Pinch of cayenne
1 teaspoon dried oregano
Salt and black pepper
2 tablespoons red wine vinegar
2 tablespoons olive oil

1. Cutting diagonally across the grain, cut the well-trimmed and chilled sirloin into very thin slices. Pound them between 2 pieces of waxed paper until they are as thin as possible without tearing. Place the slices in a single layer in the bottom of nonreactive pans or a baking dish large enough to hold them without crowding.
2. Combine in a cup the lemon juice, caper brine, and red wine and sprinkle over the meat. Cover and refrigerate for at least 2 and up to 24 hours, turning slices at least once.
3. Rub the peppers with the vegetable oil and roast them under the broiler. Turn the peppers until they are charred on all sides, about 5 minutes altogether. When cool enough to handle, peel, remove the seeds and white ribs, and cut the peppers into very thin slices. Set aside in a small bowl.
4. In another bowl, combine the cayenne, oregano, salt and pepper, and vinegar. Whisk in the olive oil, stir in the capers, and pour the mixture over the sliced peppers.
5. Arrange the marinated beef on plates, spoon over the pepper mixture, and serve.

Yield: 4 servings

Note: If yellow bell peppers are unavailable, use an extra green or red bell pepper.

BROILED BEEF AND SCALLOP RIBBON

This recipe proves that meat and shellfish can be combined to good effect.

1. In a bowl, soak the scallops in the milk with the peppercorns. Cover and chill in the refrigerator for at least 45 minutes.
2. Dip the scallions into a saucepan of boiling water just long enough to soften and make them flexible, about 2 seconds. Set aside.
3. Remove the scallops from the milk; discard the milk and peppercorns. Roll the scallops in the bread crumbs and season with salt and pepper and lemon juice.
4. Heat the broiler.
5. Season the beef strips with salt and pepper. Put 1 scallion green down the middle of each side of a beef strip. Using an 8-inch skewer, pierce the end of a beef strip, making sure the skewer goes through both pieces of scallion. Add 2 scallops to the skewer, wrap the beef strip halfway around the scallops, and pierce the strip again. Continue the procedure so that the beef is skewered in a double S shape. Repeat for 3 more skewers. Drizzle each skewer of beef and scallops with about 1 tablespoon melted butter.
6. Put the skewers under the preheated broiler about 3 inches from the flame. Brown lightly on each side, about 2 minutes per side for medium-rare.
7. In a saucepan, brown the remaining 2 tablespoons butter lightly.
8. To serve, place the skewers on warm plates, then carefully remove the skewers, while holding the beef and scallops in place. Drizzle with brown butter and serve immediately.

Yield: 4 servings

¼ *pound bay scallops*
½ *cup milk*
 3 *whole peppercorns*
10 *to 12 scallions, green part only*
 1 *cup fresh white bread crumbs*
    Salt and coarsely ground black pepper
 1 *teaspoon lemon juice*
1½ *pounds prime rib of beef or strip
       steak, boned and cut into long 1
       inch wide strips, ¼ inch thick*
 6 *tablespoons unsalted butter, melted*

HERBED BRISKET

This is an elaboration on the basic braising technique. The meat is seared to give it color, and extra liquid is added both for flavor and to provide a base for the rich sauce.

2 to 2½ pounds beef brisket
⅓ cup mixed minced fresh herbs (such as thyme, marjoram, basil, chives, sage, and/or rosemary)
1 large shallot, minced
¼ teaspoon coarsely ground black pepper
2 teaspoons flour
2 teaspoons peanut oil
¼ cup dry white wine
1½ cups Chicken Stock (see recipe, Chapter 3)
1 cup water, plus more if necessary
½ cup heavy cream

1. Heat the oven to 350°F.
2. Make ¼-inch holes at 1-inch intervals in the brisket by inserting a small knife into the meat and twisting it.
3. In a small bowl, combine 1 tablespoon mixed herbs, half of the minced shallot, and the pepper. Push this mixture into the holes in the brisket. Sprinkle the meat with flour.
4. Put the oil in a heavy pan just large enough to contain the meat. Over high heat, sear the meat on all sides. Add the remaining minced shallot and most of the remaining herbs, reserving a sprinkling of the herbs for garnish.
5. Add the wine, scraping the bottom of the pan with a wooden spoon to deglaze. Add the chicken stock and water and bring to a simmer.
6. Cook in the preheated oven, adding water if necessary so that there is always at least ⅓ inch of liquid in the pan. Cook until very tender, about 2¾ hours, turning meat over every 30 minutes.
7. Remove from the oven, cool to room temperature, and then refrigerate. When cold, remove the fat from the surface of the liquid. When ready to serve, remove the brisket from the liquid.
8. You should have at least ¾ cup liquid, but not more than 1¼ cups. Add water if necessary. Bring to a simmer. Add the cream to the liquid and bring to a simmer again. Strain through a fine sieve and return to the pan. Bring the liquid back to a simmer and adjust the seasonings. If the sauce is too thin, cook up to 15 minutes more to reduce it.
9. Thinly slice the meat, cutting against the grain; heat the slices in the sauce, covered.
10. Arrange the meat on a warm serving platter, sprinkle with the reserved herbs, and serve with extra sauce on the side.

Yield: 4 servings

VEAL
In the 1930s and '40s, per capita consumption of veal in the United States was five to six times as much as in 1980. Unlike some areas of Europe where economic factors, such as limited grazing land, actually favored the production of veal over beef, the feedlot system here has generally made the raising of a mature steer more profitable both for farmer and processor. Thus veal became a specialty item, and as its price rose, consumption dropped even more. The recent emphasis on light eating may reverse the trend, and veal now appears more frequently on restaurant menus than even a few years ago.

There are three main categories of veal. *Bob veal* is from a calf less than one month old, *veal* is from a calf between one and three months in age, and *baby beef* is from a calf three to twelve months in age. Only bob veal and veal are true veal and really suitable for most veal recipes. Baby beef loses the delicate, tender quality that distinguishes veal from beef.

Milk-fed veal is considered to be the best from a gastronomical standpoint. The color of milk-fed veal is usually a pale pinkish white due to the lack of iron in the milk diet. Very little veal raised only on cow's milk ever reaches the marketplace, but there is a method of feeding veal for eleven to twelve weeks on a formula of milk solids, water, and nutrients that is used by most producers supplying milk-fed veal.

VEAL WITH SHIITAKE MUSHROOM SAUCE

3 cups *Chicken Stock (see recipe,*
    Chapter 3)
½ cup *flour*
   Salt and black pepper
1¼ pounds *veal from leg, sliced ⅛ to ¼*
   inch thick
4 tablespoons *unsalted butter, plus more*
   if needed
2 tablespoons *peanut oil, plus more if*
   needed
1 large *shallot, minced*
⅔ cup *white wine*
¼ pound *shiitake mushrooms*
1½ tablespoons *minced fresh parsley*
¼ cup *Madeira*

1. In a saucepan, reduce the stock to 1 cup by cooking for 20 to 22 minutes over a medium-high heat.
2. While the stock is reducing, combine the flour, ½ teaspoon salt, and ¼ teaspoon pepper. Dredge the veal in the flour mixture and shake off any excess.
3. In a large frying pan, heat 2 tablespoons butter and oil. Sauté the dredged veal over medium-high heat until browned, 1 to 2 minutes per side. Add more butter and oil if necessary. Remove the veal from the pan and keep warm.
4. Drain off any excess fat from the pan and add the shallot. Sauté for about 1 minute; do not brown. Add the wine and reduced stock, scraping the bottom of the pan with a wooden spoon to deglaze. Add the mushrooms and parsley and cook over medium-high heat until the liquid is reduced by half, about 2 minutes. Add the Madeira and cook, stirring, for 2 minutes more. Over low heat, swirl in 2 tablespoons butter, bit by bit, until the sauce is slightly thickened and all the butter is incorporated. Season to taste with salt and pepper.

Yield: 4 servings

VEAL CHOPS WITH CAVIAR BUTTER

1. With a boning knife, slice a pocket in each chop, making as narrow an incision as possible in its side. Insert the knife all the way into the meat but not through it and move it side to side to enlarge the pocket.
2. In a bowl, combine the softened butter, lemon zest, lemon juice, dill, chives, and shallots. Mix well and then fold in the black caviar. Add salt and pepper to taste.
3. Fill each pocket with one-quarter of the caviar butter. Secure the openings with toothpicks. Refrigerate until the butter is hard, for 45 minutes to 1 hour. Season the veal with salt and pepper.
4. In a large frying pan, heat the clarified butter or vegetable oil and sear each chop quickly over high heat for 30 seconds per side. Continue cooking over medium heat for 5 to 6 minutes per side. The chops will be slightly pink inside and browned outside. Place the chops on a warm plate and pour the pan drippings over them. Serve at once.

Yield: 4 servings

4	12- to 14-ounce veal chops, 1½ to 2 inches thick
10	tablespoons unsalted butter, softened
1½	teaspoons grated lemon zest
2½	tablespoons lemon juice
1½	tablespoons minced fresh dill, or 1½ teaspoons dried dill
2½	teaspoons minced fresh chives
2	small shallots, minced
3	tablespoons black caviar
	Salt and black pepper
	Clarified unsalted butter or vegetable oil

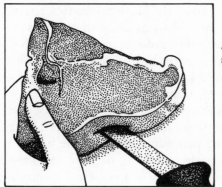

Slice a pocket in the side of each chop. Insert the knife into the meat and move it from side to side to enlarge the pocket.

LAMB
One of the small puzzles of the modern age is why spring lamb can be found in supermarkets or butcher shops in December. The answer is that although spring used to be the traditional season for the slaughter and thus sale of young lamb, new breeding and storage methods have outmoded the seasonal cycle. However, the term *spring lamb* has stayed with us as a USDA label. It indicates lamb slaughtered before it is six months old. *Genuine spring lamb* is also used as a labeling term by the USDA, and it means lamb slaughtered before four months. Baby lamb or hothouse lamb is milk fed and normally not more than six weeks of age. It is very hard to find, and although some gastronomes claim it is the most perfectly flavored of lamb, others find it a bit bland. We are decidedly with the former. All agree that yearling lamb or mutton slaughtered after at least a year of growth has a very full flavor and is little esteemed in the United States.

LAMB WITH TOMATO CHUTNEY AND MINT SAUCE

1 4-pound leg of lamb, boned and
   butterflied, bones reserved

Mint Sauce

   Reserved lamb bones from above
1 small carrot, chopped
1 small onion, chopped
⅔ cup white wine
6 cups Chicken Stock (see recipe,
   Chapter 3)
4 teaspoons white wine vinegar
1½ teaspoons sugar
   Salt and black pepper
4 teaspoons minced fresh mint leaves, or
   1¼ teaspoons dried mint
1½ tablespoons unsalted butter

1. Heat the oven to 400°F.
2. For the mint sauce, roast the lamb bones in a roasting pan in the preheated oven until they begin to brown, about 10 minutes. Add the carrot and onion and continue cooking until the bones and vegetables are all very brown, taking care not to let the ingredients burn, 45 to 60 minutes.
3. Transfer the bones and vegetables to a large pot and pour off the grease from the roasting pan. Add the wine to the roasting pan while scraping the bottom and sides with a wooden spoon to deglaze. Add the liquid from the roasting pan and the chicken stock to the pot with the bones and vegetables and bring to a boil. Reduce heat and simmer for 2 hours, skimming periodically.

4. For the stuffing, heat the white grape juice in a saucepan. Put the raisins in a bowl, pour the hot juice over, and set aside.

5. In a large frying pan, melt the butter and add the onions. Cook over medium-low heat, stirring frequently, until lightly browned and very soft, about 20 minutes. Raise heat, add the mint, ginger, and garlic, and cook for 2 minutes more. Add the honey, white wine, cherry tomatoes, and reserved raisins with white wine juice and bring to a boil. Reduce heat and simmer, uncovered, until almost all the liquid has evaporated, about 1 hour.

6. Remove from the heat and cool. Stir in the bread crumbs and add cayenne and salt and black pepper to taste.

7. Heat the oven to 450°F.

8. Season the lamb with salt and pepper on both sides and spread 1 lengthwise half with chutney. Then, starting at the side spread with chutney, roll the roast so that it will be long and thin, not short and fat. Tie well in several places with kitchen string. Put the roast into a roasting pan, fat side up, and rub all over with a little vegetable oil.

9. In the preheated oven, roast the lamb for 12 minutes and then lower the heat to 325°F and continue cooking until a meat thermometer reads 145°F for medium-rare, about 40 minutes more.

10. Meanwhile, strain the stock for the sauce and degrease. Boil until reduced to about 2½ cups, 15 to 20 minutes. Add the vinegar, sugar, and salt and pepper to taste.

11. Remove the lamb from the oven and let it rest for 10 minutes before slicing. Reheat the sauce if necessary. Thinly slice the lamb, cutting against the grain.

12. At the last minute, add the mint to the sauce. Stir in the butter; the sauce will not be thick. Serve the lamb with mint sauce on the side.

Yield: 4 servings

Tomato-Chutney Stuffing

⅔ cup white grape juice or cider or medium-sweet white wine
⅓ cup raisins
3 tablespoons unsalted butter
2 red onions, minced
1½ teaspoons minced fresh mint leaves, or ½ teaspoon dried mint
3 teaspoons grated ginger
1 small clove garlic, minced
2 teaspoons honey
¼ cup white wine
1½ pints cherry tomatoes, chopped
⅓ cup fresh bread crumbs
Pinch of cayenne
Salt and black pepper

Vegetable oil

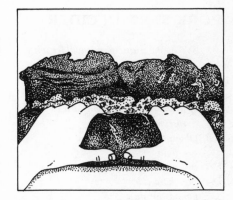

Spread chutney on half the lamb and roll it up the long way.

AMERICAN STEWS

In colonial America, stews were generally cooked in plain water or, occasionally, in stock. Using alcohol as part of the cooking liquid also was in practice—the recipe for beef stew reprinted in Hyla O'Connor's *Early American Cooking* called for "a pinte of good strong Ale." By 1900, though, mainstream American cooks mostly omitted wine and beer from stews. The 1896 edition of Fannie Farmer's *Boston Cooking School Cookbook*, for example, includes recipes for beef stew, Irish stew, and fricassee of lamb—all made with water. In the 1950s, fashionable American cooks discovered the delights of such typical European stews as boeuf bourguignon, made with red wine, and carbonnade flamande, made with beer. From there it was an easy and delicious step to contemporary American stews like our recipes featuring hard cider and California Petite Syrah.

PORK STEW IN CIDER

1 *5½-pound picnic pork shoulder with rind, boned*
   Salt and black pepper
2 *tablespoons chopped fresh rosemary leaves, or 2 teaspoons dried rosemary*
2 *tablespoons Dijon mustard*
½ *cup flour*
¼ *cup vegetable oil*
2½ *cups hard cider*
1½ *pounds turnips*
1 *pound (about 3) tart-sweet apples (such as Jonathan)*
4 *cloves garlic, chopped*

1. To prepare the pork shoulder, remove the rind and cut it into several pieces. Reserve half the pieces for another use. In a pot, cover the remaining rind with cold water, bring to a boil, and boil for 10 minutes. Drain, rinse with cold water, and reserve. Cut the meat into 2-inch cubes; there should be about 2½ pounds.

2. Season the pork cubes with salt and pepper and 1½ tablespoons fresh rosemary or 1½ teaspoons of dried. Cover and refrigerate for 24 hours.

3. Dry the meat with paper towels. In a bowl, toss the pork with the mustard. Dredge the mustard-covered pork cubes in flour and shake off the excess.

4. In a large ovenproof pot, heat half the oil. Brown the meat over a medium-high heat in 2 batches, adding the remaining oil as needed. Do not overcrowd the pan.

5. Add the cider and simmer, scraping the bottom of the pan with a wooden spoon to deglaze. Return all of the meat to the pot and add the reserved pork rind. Remove from the heat.

6. Heat the oven to 325°F (see Note).

7. Peel the turnips and cut into 1-inch cubes. You should have about 4½ cups. Peel and core the apples, cut

into eighths, and put in a bowl with the turnips. Season with salt. Add the garlic and the remaining chopped fresh or dried rosemary and mix well.

8. Put the seasoned turnips and apples on top of the meat and cover the pot tightly. Bake in the preheated oven until the apples are tender, about 30 minutes. Set aside 6 pieces of the apple for garnish. Continue cooking until the meat and turnips are tender, 1½ to 2 hours.

9. Remove and reserve the meat and half the apples and turnips. Discard the pork rind. Degrease the cooking juices. Mash the remaining turnips and apples into the juices to make a thick sauce. Return the reserved meat, turnips, and apples to the pot and reheat gently. Garnish with the 6 reserved apple pieces and serve.

Yield: 4 to 6 servings

Note: This stew may be cooked on the stove top over a very low heat.

VENISON STEW

2 pounds venison, cut into 2-inch
    chunks
1 carrot, cut into thick slices
1 small onion, quartered
½ rib celery, cut into thick slices
¾ teaspoon fresh thyme, or ¼ teaspoon
    dried thyme
  Salt and black pepper
⅛ teaspoon cayenne
2 cups dry California Petite Syrah or
    other full-bodied red wine
1 teaspoon red or white wine vinegar
2½ to 3 tablespoons vegetable oil
1 tablespoon flour
½ cup water
  Caramelized Pears (recipe follows)

1. In a mixing bowl just large enough to hold the meat and vegetables, toss the venison, carrot, onion, and celery together. Add the thyme, salt and pepper to taste, cayenne, wine, and vinegar. Cover and refrigerate for 2 to 4 days, stirring every day.
2. Drain the meat and vegetables and reserve the marinade. Sort out the vegetables from the meat and set aside. Dry the meat with paper towels.
3. In a large, ovenproof pot, heat a thin coat of oil over medium heat. Add the meat in several batches, being careful not to overcrowd, and sauté until brown, about 5 minutes a batch. Add more oil as needed.
4. Remove the last batch of meat and sauté the vegetables for about 5 minutes. Add more oil if necessary. Set the sautéed vegetables aside with the meat.
5. Heat the oven to 300°F.
6. Add more oil if necessary to the fat left in the pot to make about 2 tablespoons. Add the flour and cook over medium-low heat, stirring, until nut brown, 3 to 5 minutes.
7. Whisk in the reserved marinade. Raise heat to high, add water, and bring to a boil.
8. Return the meat and vegetables to the pot, cover tightly, and cook in the preheated oven until the meat is very tender, about 3½ hours.
9. Using a slotted spoon, transfer the meat and vegetables to a heated serving dish, cover, and keep warm.
10. To degrease and thicken the sauce, put the pot half on the burner and let only the contents over the heat come to a boil; the rest of the sauce should remain still. Lower the heat if the surface off the heat is moving. Occasionally skim and degrease the still surface. Cook in this manner until the sauce thickens and becomes shiny, about 30 minutes.
11. Meanwhile, make caramelized pears.
12. Serve the stew and pass the sauce and pears separately.

Yield: 4 servings

1. In a large frying pan, melt about 1 tablespoon butter. When foaming stops, add the pear slices in a single layer.
2. Sauté over a medium-low heat in 4 batches, using 1 tablespoon butter for each batch, until the slices are slightly softened, about 3 minutes. Return all the pear slices to the frying pan. Sprinkle with the sugar and lemon juice and raise the heat to high.
3. Continue to sauté, turning until the slices are golden and tender, about 3 minutes. Season with salt and pepper to taste.

Yield: 4 to 6 servings

CARAMELIZED PEARS

    4 tablespoons unsalted butter
1½ pounds (about 4) firm pears, peeled,
         cored, and sliced ¼ inch thick
    1 tablespoon sugar
    1 teaspoon lemon juice
       Salt and black pepper

LIVER

LIVER In American folk tradition, liver and spinach are the two foods that you eat because you should—because they're good for you, not because you like them. A quick comparison of food values from USDA tables listing amounts of nutrients per 100 grams of meat shows that in fact cooked liver has less than half the calories of porterhouse steak; a quarter the amount of fat; a third more protein; 20 percent more calcium; three times as much iron; over 1,000 times more vitamin A; and considerably more ash, potassium, sodium, phosphate, thiamin, riboflavin, niacin, and ascorbic acid. Spinach, by the way, has a tenth the calories of liver, virtually no fat, and ten times as much calcium—but in most other nutritional categories it's less impressive than liver. We love the taste of the calf's liver recipe we've selected, but have to admit it *is* good for you.

CALF'S LIVER WITH SEVEN ONIONS

This recipe calls for cooking the liver *en papillote,* a special method suited to any thin cut of meat that would normally be sautéed. Suggested accompaniments are colorful vegetables such as broiled tomatoes, sautéed snow peas, or carrots.

1. Heat the oven to 350°F.
2. In a large frying pan, melt the butter and sauté the onions and leek over medium heat until soft, 3 to 5 minutes. Add the shallots and garlic and sauté for 3 more minutes, stirring frequently. Remove from heat and stir in the scallions and chives. Season with salt and pepper.
3. Sprinkle both sides of liver slices with salt and pepper. Cut four 12-inch rounds of parchment paper or aluminum foil. Lay the paper on ungreased baking sheets and brush with oil. Position a piece of liver on a half of each sheet, leaving a 1-inch margin. Top each with one-quarter of the onion mixture. Fold the paper over to cover the liver. Fold and pleat the edges to seal securely.
4. Cook in the preheated oven for 15 minutes, a little less for rare liver. Serve immediately in the paper.

Yield: 4 servings

3½ tablespoons unsalted butter
1 small yellow onion, halved lengthwise and sliced into thin half-moons
2 small red onions, halved lengthwise and sliced into thin half-moons
1 small leek, white part only, cut into julienne strips
4 shallots, sliced thin
1½ cloves garlic, minced
6 scallions, white part only, sliced thin
3 tablespoons chopped fresh chives
Salt and black pepper
1½ pounds calf's liver, trimmed of membrane and cut into 4 thin slices
Vegetable oil

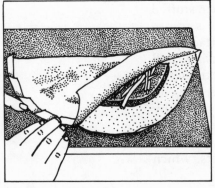

Fold the top half of paper over the liver and onions. Fold and pleat the edges, holding a finger on one fold as you make the next.

SAUSAGES
Sausage making began as an ingenious method of preserving scraps of meat. It combined the virtue of salting to retard spoilage with the economy and convenience of a strong, porous package. Depending on climate and abundance, sausages were consumed fresh, dried, or smoked.

Most often, fresh sausage is cooked and eaten within several days after it's made. Generally it is cased in intestines: fragile, slender lamb casings; stronger, larger hog casings; or fatter but tougher beef casings. Fresh sausage meat can also be wrapped in self-basting caul fat (stomach lining) or fried with no casing at all. Whatever its form, the best fresh sausages are tender, juicy, and bursting with flavor. Air-dried sausage, on the other hand, is always cased, usually in hog or beef gut, and it's prized for its firm texture and deep, complex, slightly tangy character. In wetter northern latitudes where simple air-drying is inefficient or impossible, smoked sausage became common, but it is a bit difficult to make in contemporary kitchens.

How to Make Sausages

There's been a revival of the almost lost art of home sausage making in the United States. It's an easy enough skill to master, but there are some basic guidelines to keep in mind. When you grind the sausage meat, you can use either a hand grinder or an electric one. The hand grinder gives you better control over the texture of the meat mixture, but it can be tedious work. An electric grinder set on the highest speed should give you satisfactory, uniform results.

Perhaps the most difficult part of sausage making is stuffing the meat into the casings. Casings may be made from animal intestines or synthetics; both are edible, pliable, and expand easily when stuffed with sausage meat. The most efficient way to fill casings is to use an electric stuffer. Most meat grinders include a snoutlike attachment that replaces the blades for stuffing purposes. To stuff a casing, pull a rinsed, still-wet casing over the bottom of the stuffing funnel of the meat grinder and then gather the entire casing up over the end of the funnel. Force the meat through the funnel into the casing by cranking the grinder and hold the casing as it fills with meat. When it is filled, twist or tie off links of the desired lengths. As you stuff the sausage, pack it in tightly enough to eliminate air pockets, which could cause the casing to tear and pop.

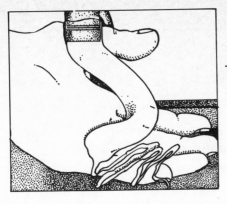

To cleanse casing of any residual salt, slip the end over the water faucet and run cool water through. The casing will swell as the water flushes through it. Keep the cleaned casings in water until ready to use.

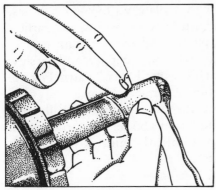

Attach the appropriate stuffing funnel to the meat grinder. Slip a wet casing over the funnel.

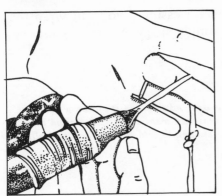

Gather the entire casing over the funnel, straightening any knots or loops.

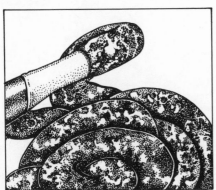

Crank the seasoned meat through the funnel and into the casing. Coil the stuffed sausage below the grinder so that there is no pull on the casing.

LAMB AND HAM SAUSAGE WITH PECANS

This is a good recipe for small sausages. The filling is complex and intensely flavorful and most appreciated as part of a mixed grill or as one of several hors d'oeuvre. Be careful to trim off all of the lamb fat; it can be unpleasantly pungent and heavy.

½ *pound lean lamb from leg or shoulder, cut into chunks*
½ *pound pork butt with about 30 percent fat content, cut into chunks*
2 *cups pecans*
5 *small cloves garlic*
2 *ounces uncooked Smithfield ham or other sweet/salty country ham, cut into small dice*
1 *teaspoon coarse salt*
½ *teaspoon bourbon*
1 *teaspoon black pepper*
1 *teaspoon chopped flat-leaf parsley*
2 *feet lamb casings, well rinsed and soaked (see Note)*

1. In a grinder fitted with a plate with ¼-inch holes, grind the lamb, pork butt, 1⅓ cups pecans, and garlic.
2. Chop the remaining pecans and add to the meat mixture with the ham, salt, bourbon, pepper, and parsley. Combine and then make a small "test" patty. Fry the patty in a skillet and taste for seasonings.
3. Stuff the mixture into the lamb casings (see illustrations, Sausages introduction above) and grill over a low flame or sauté just until the meat loses its pink color, about 8 minutes.

Yield: about 1 pound

Note: If you cannot obtain casings, you can wrap the sausages in caul fat or simply shape into patties and fry.

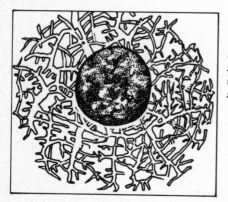

Soak lacy caul fat in warm water and then lay it out on a flat surface. Place the patties of seasoned meat on it. Cut around the meat so that the caul is large enough to fold over the meat on all sides.

COUNTRY VENISON SAUSAGES WITH SAUTÉED POTATOES AND VINEGAR

1. For the sausages, put the venison, pork, bacon, and fat into a bowl. Add the pepper, shallots, juniper berries if using, vinegar, salt, parsley, and coriander leaves. Mix well.
2. Grind the mixture in a grinder that has a plate with ¼-inch holes. In a skillet fry a small "test" patty and taste for seasonings.
3. Stuff the meat carefully into the casing (see illustrations, Sausages introduction above), holding the casing as it fills with meat. Tie off the casing to make 12 sausages.
4. Arrange the sausages on a rack, and put in the refrigerator, uncovered, so that air can circulate freely around them, for 3 days.
5. Heat the oven to 375°F.
6. For the sauce, combine the mustard, garlic, horseradish, and vermouth, and mix well.
7. For the sautéed potatoes, in the preheated oven, bake the potatoes for 30 minutes. Cool. Cut the potatoes into ½-inch slices, leaving the skins on.
8. In a large frying pan, heat the fat and sauté the sliced potatoes over a medium-high heat until well browned on both sides, 15 to 20 minutes. It may be necessary to do this in 2 batches, using half the fat for each. Drain on paper towels and sprinkle with vinegar, salt and pepper, and chopped parsley.
9. Meanwhile, in a pot of hot, barely simmering salted water, blanch the sausages for 3 to 4 minutes. Remove and pat dry.
10. In a frying pan, over medium heat, sauté the sausages until golden brown, 4 to 5 minutes per side. Drain, if necessary.
11. Serve the sausages with mustard sauce and potatoes on the side.

Yield: 4 servings

Note: You can also form sausages into patties and fry them without casings. Form the patties after the mixture has cured for 3 days in the refrigerator.

Sausages

- 1 pound venison (preferably neck), cut into chunks
- 1 pound lean pork, cut into chunks
- ⅓ pound slab bacon, cut into chunks
- ⅔ pound pork fat, cut into chunks
- 2 teaspoons black pepper
- 2 shallots, chopped
- 1 tablespoon crushed juniper berries (optional)
- 3 tablespoons red wine vinegar
- 1 tablespoon salt
- ⅓ cup chopped fresh parsley
- ⅓ cup chopped fresh coriander leaves
- 4 feet hog casings, rinsed well and soaked (see Note)

Mustard Sauce

- ½ cup grainy mustard (Pommery style)
- 1 clove garlic, crushed
- 1 tablespoon grated horseradish
- 2 tablespoons dry vermouth

Sautéed Potatoes

- 4 large baking potatoes
- ¼ cup rendered venison or pork fat
- 2 tablespoons cider vinegar
  Salt and black pepper
- 1½ tablespoons chopped fresh parsley

SUMMER SAUSAGE WITH LAVENDER

Summer sausage is dried sausage, traditionally fashioned in late fall at hog-butchering time, aged through winter and spring, and enjoyed during hot summer months. However, given a supply of fresh pork and a cool, airy cellar (steady 50° or 60° Fahrenheit), it is possible to make and serve throughout the year. For this quantity, if you divide the meat between hog and beef casings, the smaller sausages will be ready a month or two before the larger ones, and so you can enjoy each at its peak. Of course, all the meat can be stuffed into one type of casing. The finishing with lavender or other suggested aromatics is not necessary, but is very nice. Serve the sausages sliced thin with the simplest of accompaniments: good olives, radishes, a chunk of cheese, cool red wine.

1 *10-pound pork butt with about 30 percent fat content, cut into chunks*
¼ *cup salt*
   Pinch of sugar
   Pinch of saltpeter (see Notes)
   Handful of cracked peppercorns
5 *feet hog casings, rinsed well and soaked*
2½ *feet beef casings, rinsed well and soaked (see Notes)*
   Lavender buds or fennel branches or dried thyme branches

1. In a large bowl, toss the pork with salt, sugar, and saltpeter. Grind the meat mixture in a grinder with a plate that has ¼-inch holes. Incorporate the peppercorns. Shape a small "test" patty, fry in a skillet, and taste for seasonings. It should seem a bit too salty at this point.

2. Case the meat carefully (see illustrations, Sausages introduction above), stuffing each sausage tightly to eliminate air pockets and to compensate for substantial shrinkage later (30 to 50 percent). Wipe each sausage clean and tie off links with cotton string.

3. Hang in 1- to 2-foot lengths, arranging so that the sausages are not touching one another. After 1 week, they should begin to shrink and gradually develop a fine white powder on their skins. Depending on their size and the climate, they should take between 4 and 12 weeks to dry. It is often necessary to rearrange them during the first weeks to ensure even drying. At this time, wipe any sausages that are sticky and discard any with ruptured casings.

4. When they feel firm and dry, put the sausages in an open crate and strew generously with loose lavender buds, fennel branches, or dried thyme branches and store in a cool, dry place. They should be well infused

within a week and will keep a month or so at an even temperature.

Yield: about 7½ pounds

Notes: Saltpeter can be found in drugstores. It is a necessary ingredient to preserve this sausage.

If you wish, the sausage mixture for beef casings can be slightly different: Cut 6 ounces of fatback into small dice and soak in brandy or bourbon to cover for about 3 hours. Drain the fatback and discard the brandy or bourbon. Add the fatback to about half of the ground-meat mixture and use to stuff the beef casings. The fat will become nearly translucent and add a lovely perfume to the sausage.

Chapter 5
Poultry and Feathered Game

Poultry has been likened by Brillat-Savarin to an artist's canvas—the virgin surface on which the chef/artist expresses his or her creativity. The variety is great—chicken, turkey, duck, pheasant, and quail, among others—and the preparations numerous: Birds can be roasted, broiled, steamed, stewed, fried, sautéed, sauced, and served in numberless ways. In addition, poultry is good for you, most of it being low in both calories and saturated fats, and much of it is inexpensive besides.

CHICKEN

In fact, chicken is a bird that has been popular for about four thousand years; it was first domesticated in India before 2000 B.C. Every country and culture has its favorite methods of preparing it, and while the various versions have not led to any actual crusades, loyalty to local techniques can elicit strong feelings. Whether to fry chicken in lard or vegetable oil is hotly debated, as are the composition and thickness of the breading. We vote for lard and a light coating of flour (see Fried Chicken with Cornmeal Cakes and Cream Sauce).

Alexandre Dumas (*père*), French literary giant of the nineteenth century, had strong opinions on many subjects, including how to spit-roast and baste chicken: "Never, never allow a single drop of bouillon to be mixed with the butter with which you baste the chicken. Any cook, as I think I have said elsewhere, any cook, I say, who puts bouillon in the dripping pan deserves to be thrown out of the door ignominiously and without mercy."

The subject of riddle (why did the chicken cross the road) and ridicule (chicken feed, chickenhearted, featherbrained), chicken is certainly among Brillat-Savarin's most adaptable meats. For tenderness, young birds are a must. Check the breast bones: Young, tender specimens have pliable bones, old birds are more brittle. White or yellow skin makes no difference in flavor. On the East coast, yellow is more highly regarded by consumers, and so growers produce it through diet, often by adding marigold petals to the feed.

Standards of specific size and age determine which chickens are designated fryers, broilers, roasters, or stewing fowl. Fryers and broilers are the smallest and youngest, roasters are larger and a bit older, and stewing birds are the oldest still, yet are ideal for soups, stocks, and, of course, stews. Range-fed chickens, while more expensive, harder to find, and not so tender as coop-raised birds, compensate for these drawbacks with more intense flavor. They also have more protein weight and less fat than supermarket chickens.

OTHER POULTRY AND GAME BIRDS

Chicken is just one of the birds whose culinary popularity spans centuries, and now turkeys, ducks, geese, squab, and even pheasants are grown on farm, ranch, and game preserve in order to supply a poultry-craving public.

The largest of the culinary flock and a New World native, turkeys symbolize holiday festivities. There are a lot of turkeys in the United States. Over 100 million a year are produced and find their way not only to Thanksgiving and Christmas tables, but increasingly to the kitchens of diet- and budget-conscious Americans throughout the year. Turkey is high in protein and very lean, which causes it to be dry if overcooked. It is most frequently stuffed and roasted but inventive chefs are coming up with new ways of preparing it, such as our recipe for confit of turkey in which the turkey legs are cooked and preserved in fat much in the way duck and goose have long been prepared in France. To our way of thinking, the gain in flavor and moistness is worth the extra fat.

Duck is commonly raised for the supermarket. Among the several species available, the most frequently seen is Long Island duckling—raised not only in New York but in several other states. Fatty but flavorful, they can lose as much as 35 percent of their weight during cooking, as can geese. Figure on a five-pound duck for every two or three people. Other poultry (domesticated birds, commercially raised) include squab and Cornish hens. Both of these flavorful but delicate birds are tender enough for sautéing or broiling.

Geese and ducks of several species continually lure hunters to their blinds before dawn while upland game birds such as quail, partridge, and wild pheasants give purpose to a trudge through cornfields and meadows. Of the wild ducks, mallards are the biggest and most popular and are in such demand that commercial production is growing rapidly. Domesticated mallards are usually pinioned—that is, one wing tip is clipped to prevent flying, which produces a fatter, tenderer bird than in the wild—but some mallard raisers stretch netting high above pond areas to contain the birds and yet provide them with exercise opportunities. The flavor of mallards is stronger than that of Long Island duckling, and although they eat few fish, their diet of submarine plant life sometimes makes them taste as if they lived on fish alone. The fishy taste that can be all too detectable in waterfowl can be counteracted by putting a peeled raw onion in the cavity for several hours before cooking. The American canvasback duck obligingly eats only wild celery and some grasses, which give it a delicate, slightly spicy taste. Fresh duck meat should be soft to the touch, and the wing tips should be pliable. If you buy mallard whole, use the plucked heads and feet as a natural thickener for a sauce.

Because of their extensive migratory patterns, wild geese are far leaner and more muscular (in other words, tougher) than domesticated birds and are best when braised in wine or cider or well larded and roasted with a moist stuffing to prevent drying. Canada goose, blue goose, and emperor goose are among the most widely available wild species.

Pheasant, introduced to North America in the eighteenth century, is among the most common game birds and one whose flavor varies less than that of other species when raised on farms instead of in the wild. Traditionally, pheasant is hung for a week or ten days to age and tenderize, but in recent years, the custom has been to serve it within two days of the kill for a subtler, milder flavor.

Quail and other small birds, such as woodcock and snipe, should be served two or three to a person, usually sautéed and presented on toast or halved and broiled, perhaps topped with wild mushrooms or other compatible ingredients. Quail is also known as partridge in parts of the United States, although there is no true partridge native to this country. Bobwhite is another name for quail, an allusion to its lilting call. Chukar partridge, also known as Iranian or Indian rock partridge, has been successfully raised in the western states, and the population is growing on game farms. The term *partridge* can also refer to ruffed grouse, although why the word *grouse* came to mean "to complain" in the United States is incomprehensible. In Australia it means something extraordinary and wonderful, much more representative of the grouse's flavor.

FROZEN POULTRY

Since poultry spoils rapidly, freezing is often necessary. Turkey, ducks, and Cornish hens are sold frozen as frequently as fresh. The frozen flesh will always be a bit drier and stringier than fresh killed, but to ensure a minimum of difference, be sure the skin is smooth and even in color. The wrapping should be tightly sealed and contain no pink-shaded ice, which indicates that the bird has been mishandled in freezing and perhaps even thawed and refrozen.

FRIED CHICKEN WITH CORNMEAL CAKES AND CREAM SAUCE

To say fried chicken is southern is to be redundant, but there are probably as many southern variations of the dish within the South itself as there are live oaks draped with Spanish moss. This version is from Georgia's Barrier Islands and is accompanied by very southern cornmeal cakes, tiny and crisp, and topped with a traditional cream sauce made from pan drippings. For maximum flavor and crispness, the chicken should be fried in real, butcher-shop lard.

Cornmeal Cakes

3 cups water
½ teaspoon salt
1 cup cornmeal
1 egg yolk, lightly beaten

Chicken

1 2½- to 3-pound chicken, cut into 8 pieces
Salt and black pepper
⅔ cup (approximately) all-purpose flour
1½ to 2 cups lard

Cream Sauce

1 teaspoon flour
1 cup light cream or half and half
Salt and black pepper

1. For the cornmeal cakes, bring the water to a boil in a saucepan. Add salt and slowly whisk in the cornmeal. Lower heat and cook, stirring constantly, until thickened and smooth, about 2 minutes. Cool for about 3 minutes; then beat in the egg yolk. Set aside.

2. Heat the oven to 200°F.

3. Sprinkle the chicken pieces with salt and pepper. Dredge each piece with flour and shake off any excess.

4. In a large, heavy frying pan with a lid, heat the lard to about 360°F. Melted, it should be deep enough to cover the chicken pieces halfway. Put the chicken pieces into the hot fat, skin side down; cover the pan and cook over medium heat until browned, 7 to 10 minutes. Turn the chicken pieces carefully with tongs. Cover and cook for an additional 6 to 8 minutes until browned on both sides and the juices run clear. The pan should never be too crowded—you may need to fry the chicken in batches. Transfer the chicken to a baking sheet and put into the preheated oven to keep warm. Pour off all but ½ inch of the fat.

5. Drop the cornmeal batter by tablespoons into the hot fat, flatten to about 3-inch circles with the back of a spoon, and fry, turning once, until golden brown, about 5 to 8 minutes in all. Continue with all the batter to make about 12 corn cakes. Drain on paper towels and keep warm in the oven while making the sauce.

6. For the sauce, pour off most of the fat from the frying pan and stir in the flour. Add cream and stir, scraping the bottom of the pan with a wooden spoon to de-

glaze. Cook, stirring, over medium-low heat until slightly thickened, about 3 minutes. Season to taste with salt and pepper.

7. Arrange the chicken on a warm serving platter, surround it with cornmeal cakes, and pour the sauce over the chicken. Or if you prefer to keep the chicken crisp, serve the sauce separately.

Yield: 4 servings

CORNISH GAME HENS STUFFED WITH LEEKS

Braised Leek Stuffing

4 *tablespoons unsalted butter*
4 *large leeks, white and pale green part only, halved vertically and cut into thin half-moon slices*
3 *cups Chicken Stock (see recipe, Chapter 3)*
   Salt and black pepper

Cornish Game Hens

1 *tablespoon peanut oil*
4 *¾- to 1-pound Cornish game hens, wings removed and reserved*
   Salt and black pepper
4 *sprigs thyme*
¼ *cup white wine*
½ *cup Chicken Stock (see recipe, Chapter 3)*
1 *tablespoon heavy cream*
4 *tablespoons unsalted butter, cut into pieces*

1. For the braised leek stuffing, melt the butter in a large pan over medium heat. Add the leeks and sauté until soft but not brown. Add the chicken stock, cook over medium heat until almost dry, and season with salt and pepper to taste.
2. Heat the oven to 500°F. Coat the roasting pan with peanut oil.
3. Fill the birds with the stuffing and tie their legs together with kitchen string. Season the birds with salt and pepper.
4. Put the birds, breasts down, in the prepared roasting pan and cook in the preheated oven for 10 minutes. Turn breast side up and brown for 8 minutes.
5. Remove the hens and scatter their wings and thyme in the roasting pan, return the birds to the pan, breast side up, and continue cooking until just done, 25 to 30 minutes. Put the birds on a platter and return to the turned-off oven to keep warm.
6. Degrease the pan juices, bring to a boil, add the white wine, and scrape the bottom of the pan to deglaze. Add the chicken stock and reduce by half over high heat. Add the cream and simmer for 30 seconds.
7. Strain the sauce into a small saucepan, put over low heat, and add the butter bit by bit while whisking continuously. Serve the hens with the sauce passed separately.

Yield: 4 servings

CHICKEN AND ARTICHOKES WITH FRESH MARJORAM

Marjoram is a sweeter, more refined cousin of oregano. In this recipe, it adds to the equally elegant flavors of mushrooms, shallots, baby artichokes, and lightly sautéed strips of chicken breast.

8 *baby artichokes or bottoms from 8 regular artichokes*
1 *lemon, halved, plus 2 tablespoons lemon juice*
   Salt and black pepper
1 *quart cold water*
5 *tablespoons olive oil*
3 *cloves garlic, crushed with a pinch of salt*
4 *skinned and boned chicken breasts, halved and cut into 1½-inch strips*
3 *tablespoons unsalted butter*
4 *shallots, chopped*
1 *tablespoon flour*
1 *cup dry white wine or vermouth*
1 *cup Chicken Stock (see recipe, Chapter 3)*
½ *pound mushrooms, quartered*
2 *tablespoons chopped fresh marjoram leaves*

1. If using baby artichokes, break off the outer leaves down to the tender pale-green leaves. Trim the stems and cut off about ½ inch at the top. If using larger artichokes, trim the stems, cut off the tops to just above the base, and trim all around the sides of the base until no dark-green exterior is left (see illustrations, Chapter 2, Fried Baby Artichokes with Tomato-Anchovy Sauce). Rub repeatedly with lemon to prevent discoloration.

2. In a large saucepan, bring salted water to a boil with the lemon juice. Add the artichokes and simmer until just tender when pierced by a fork, about 15 minutes for the baby artichokes, 20 to 25 minutes for the artichoke bottoms. Drain the artichokes. If you have used artichoke bottoms, scoop out and discard their fuzzy chokes. Set the artichokes aside.

3. In a large frying pan, heat 4 tablespoons olive oil over medium heat. Add the garlic and cook for 1 minute. Add the artichokes and cook until lightly colored, 4 to 6 minutes. Remove the artichokes and garlic and set aside on a warm plate.

4. Sprinkle the chicken strips with salt and pepper. Heat 2 tablespoons butter and remaining tablespoon of olive oil in the pan. Add the chicken strips and cook over medium-high heat, stirring, until the chicken is just cooked, 4 to 5 minutes. Transfer to the plate with the artichokes.

5. For the sauce, reduce heat to medium, add the remaining tablespoon of butter to the pan, and stir in the shallots. Cook for 2 minutes and sprinkle with flour. Cook for 2 minutes more, stirring. Add wine and stock, scraping the bottom of the pan with a wooden spoon to deglaze. Return heat to medium-high and add mushrooms and chopped marjoram. Reduce the sauce to slightly less than 1 cup, about 15 minutes.

6. Return the chicken and artichokes to the pan to heat through, adjust seasonings, and serve.

Yield: 4 servings

PAN-ROASTED QUAIL WITH THYME AND GREEN GRAPES

1. Combine the marinade ingredients in a large non-reactive bowl. Put the quail in the marinade, cover, and refrigerate for 8 to 24 hours.

2. For the stock, heat the butter in a large, heavy pot. Add the reserved quail bones and sauté over medium-high heat until the bones are golden brown, 8 to 10 minutes. Add the onion, carrot, celery, and leek to the pot. Reduce heat to low and cook vegetables until they are soft, about 10 minutes. Add the chicken stock and bring to a boil, skimming any foam that forms on the surface. Add garlic and simmer 1 hour. Strain, discard the vegetables and bones, and let the stock cool. Remove any fat that rises to the surface.

3. Remove the bouquet garni from the marinade, squeeze out the excess oil, and put the bouquet in the stock. Reduce the stock over high heat to 1½ cups.

4. Remove the quail from the marinade and pat dry. Season the quail with thyme, and salt and pepper to taste.

5. In a large frying pan, melt 8 tablespoons butter over medium-high heat. Add the quail and cook until golden brown and the thigh meat is just springy to the touch, 2 to 4 minutes per side. Sauté in 2 batches if necessary. Remove and keep warm.

6. Pour off the fat from the pan and add the grape juice, scraping the bottom with a wooden spoon to deglaze. Reduce over high heat to ½ cup, about 15 minutes. Add the reduced stock. Reduce again by half, 15 to 20 minutes. Adjust the seasoning and toss in the grapes. Heat through but do not cook. Swirl in the remaining 2 tablespoons butter. Pour the sauce over the quail and serve at once.

Yield: 4 servings

Marinade

- 1 cup olive oil
- 1 bouquet garni (12 cracked black peppercorns; 2 bay leaves, broken; 6 sprigs each thyme and parsley tied in cheesecloth)

Quail

- 8 6-ounce quail, split in half, backbones removed and reserved for stock
- Salt and black pepper
- 2 teaspoons chopped fresh thyme, or ½ teaspoon dried thyme
- 10 tablespoons unsalted butter
- 1½ cups white grape juice
- 32 green seedless grapes, split

Quail Stock

- 4 tablespoons unsalted butter
- Reserved quail bones
- 1 onion, chopped
- 1 carrot, chopped
- 1 rib celery, chopped
- 1 leek, chopped
- 1 quart Chicken Stock (see recipe, Chapter 3)
- 10 cloves garlic, unpeeled

To divide squab in four, first remove the legs. Then cut the breasts away from the bone, leaving the wing, with its bone, attached to the breast meat. Reserve the carcass.

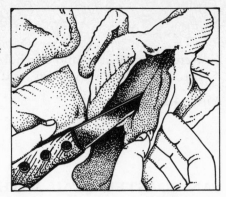

CHICKEN AND SQUAB STEW

This dish is excellent reheated, but do not poach the breasts until ready to serve to avoid toughening the meat. The stew lends itself to variations and can be made with veal or lamb instead of squab.

1 3½-pound chicken, cut into 8 pieces, breasts boned, skinned, each split in half crosswise, all bones reserved
2 squabs, cut into 4 pieces, breasts boned, carcasses reserved
¼ cup olive oil
Salt and black pepper
1 small fennel bulb, cut into ¼-inch strips
1 red bell pepper, cut into ¼-inch strips
4 carrots, diced
2 turnips, diced
2 ribs celery, diced
1 leek, diced
1 large onion, diced
¼ cup minced fresh basil, or 1 tablespoon dried basil
1 sprig fresh rosemary, or ½ teaspoon dried rosemary
3 large cloves garlic, minced
3 cups Chicken and Squab Stock (recipe follows)
½ cup Tomato Sauce (recipe follows)

1. Pat the chicken and squabs dry with paper towels. In a large frying pan, heat the olive oil and brown the chicken and squab pieces, being careful not to crowd the pan. Transfer to a plate, season with salt and pepper, and set aside.
2. Put half the fennel and half the vegetables into a large pot. Season with salt and pepper and combine with half the basil, rosemary, and garlic. Put the chicken and squab pieces, except the breasts, on top of the vegetables, along with any accumulated juice. Cover with the remaining vegetables and seasonings. Pour stock over all.
3. Cover tightly and bring slowly to a boil. Lower heat and simmer until tender, 1 to 1½ hours. Remove the meat and vegetables and set aside; strain the liquid. Degrease the liquid, return to the pan, and boil to reduce to 2½ cups.
4. Add the tomato sauce to the liquid, bring to a boil, and adjust seasonings. Add the breasts and poach until just cooked through, 5 to 6 minutes. Remove breasts and set aside. Reheat the chicken, squab, and vegetables in the sauce.

5. Transfer the vegetables to a warm bowl or tureen, add the chicken and squab pieces, and top with the breasts. Pass the sauce separately.

Yield: 4 servings

1. Heat the oven to 450°F.
2. Pour the olive oil into a large roasting pan. Add the chicken and squab carcasses, necks, trimmings, carrot, celery, and onion. Roast, stirring occasionally, until the vegetables and bones are browned but not burned, 30 to 40 minutes.
3. Add the tomato, bouquet garni, water, salt, and pepper to taste. Lower heat to 400°F and continue cooking until the liquid is reduced by half.
4. Strain the stock and, with the back of a spoon, press the bones and vegetables to extract all flavor. Degrease.

Yield: 3 cups

CHICKEN AND SQUAB STOCK

¼ cup olive oil
　 Carcasses, necks, and trimmings from chicken and squabs
1 carrot, quartered
1 rib celery, quartered
1 onion, quartered
1 tomato, quartered
1 bouquet garni (thyme, bay, and parsley leaves)
6 cups water
1 teaspoon salt
　 Black pepper

1. Heat the olive oil in a large frying pan. Add the onion and cook until soft, but not brown. Add the garlic, tomatoes, sugar, and salt and pepper to taste. Stir and cook, covered, until the tomatoes are soft, about 30 minutes. Add the basil or parsley and cook for another 5 minutes.
2. Puree in a food processor. Adjust the seasoning.

Yield: ½ cup

TOMATO SAUCE

1½ teaspoons olive oil
1 tablespoon chopped onion
1 small clove garlic, minced
2 tomatoes, chopped, or 1 8-ounce can plum tomatoes, drained
¼ teaspoon sugar
　 Salt and black pepper
1 tablespoon minced fresh basil leaves or parsley

TURKEY CONFIT

Traditionally, confit is made of duck or goose, slowly cooked and then preserved in its own fat. Since turkey is far leaner than either of these fowl, another source of fat is required. You can use rendered chicken fat (sometimes called "schmaltz"), rendered pork fat, or melted lard. This is an ideal make-ahead dish since you must allow two days for the marination and, once cooked, the confit keeps for weeks.

2   *1½-pound turkey legs*
2   *teaspoons coarse salt*
    Black pepper
2   *teaspoons dried thyme*
1½ *teaspoons dried sage*
¼   *teaspoon ground allspice*
½   *cup olive oil*
½   *cup peanut oil*
5   *cloves garlic, crushed*
5   *to 6 cups rendered chicken or pork fat*

1. With a paring knife, score the skin on each turkey leg near the end of the leg bone in order to expose the tendons. With a pair of pliers, pull the tendons out one by one, holding onto the thigh with a towel. (There are about 10 to 12 tendons per leg.) Feel up and down the leg to make sure all the tendons have been removed.
2. Rub each turkey leg with salt and pepper. Sprinkle with thyme, sage, and allspice. Put the legs in a flameproof casserole and pour the olive and peanut oils over them. Add garlic and refrigerate, covered, for at least 48 hours.
3. Heat the oven to 325°F.
4. Heat the chicken or pork fat in a large saucepan until bubbling and pour enough over the turkey legs to cover them. Bring the casserole to a simmer on top of the stove. Transfer to the preheated oven and cook for 1½ hours.
5. Allow the turkey to cool completely in the fat. The confit can be kept, covered, completely immersed in fat, and refrigerated, for several weeks.
6. To serve, reheat the legs, completely immersed in fat, for 20 minutes over low heat. Remove from the fat and sauté in 2 nonstick frying pans over medium heat until they are crisp, about 5 minutes per side.

Yield: 4 servings

DUCK BREASTS WITH CIDER SAUCE

A frequent problem in roasting duck is that by the time the legs are done, the breast is overcooked. Since this recipe uses only the breast, the cooking-time dilemma is solved. Use the legs and carcass for making a rich duck soup or stew, roast the legs, or make them into a confit (see Turkey Confit above).

1. For the sauce, combine the butter and sugar in a large, heavy saucepan. Cook, stirring, over medium heat until the sugar dissolves and caramelizes just to a golden brown, 3 to 5 minutes.
2. Remove from heat and carefully add the apple cider (stand back; the mixture splatters). Add the cloves, cinnamon, and brandy. Bring to a boil over high heat, stirring until the caramelized sugar dissolves. Lower heat and simmer, covered, for about 15 minutes.
3. Whisk the dissolved arrowroot into the cider mixture and cook over medium heat, still whisking, for 1 minute. Season with salt and pepper and set aside.
4. Sauté the duck skin pieces in a large frying pan over medium heat until fat is rendered. Strain and return the fat to the pan. Save the crisp skin for another use, such as in a salad.
5. Peel and core the apple and cut it into ½-inch slices. In another large frying pan over medium-low heat, melt the butter. Arrange the apple slices in a single layer and sauté gently, turning once, until lightly browned, 5 to 8 minutes in all. Leave the apple slices in the pan to keep warm.
6. Heat the rendered duck fat over medium-high heat. Sprinkle the duck breasts with salt and pepper. When the fat is hot, put the duck breasts in the pan and sauté for 2 to 3 minutes per side for rare meat.
7. Warm the brandy in a small saucepan. Pour over the duck breasts, stand back, and ignite. When the flames have subsided, transfer the meat to a cutting board and let it rest for 3 minutes.
8. Gently reheat the apples and sauce. Thinly slice the duck diagonally across the grain. Transfer the slices to a warm serving platter or individual plates and spoon the sauce over and around the duck. Garnish with apple slices.

Yield: 4 servings

Cider Sauce

 1 tablespoon unsalted butter
1½ tablespoons sugar
 2 cups apple cider
 2 cloves
 1 1-inch piece cinnamon stick
 2 tablespoons apple brandy
 4 teaspoons arrowroot dissolved in 1 tablespoon water
   Salt and black pepper

Duck

 4 5- to 6-ounce boneless duck breasts cut from 4½- to 5-pound ducklings, skin removed, chopped, and reserved
 1 large apple
 3 tablespoons unsalted butter
   Salt and black pepper
 2 tablespoons apple brandy

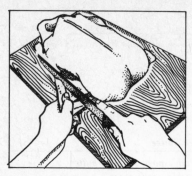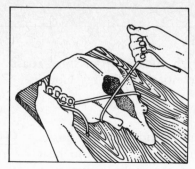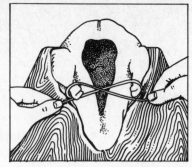

To truss poultry, first cut the wings off at the second joint and reserve for stock. Cut a piece of string about a yard long. Slide it under the end of the bird and then cross it over the legs. Slide the string under the legs.

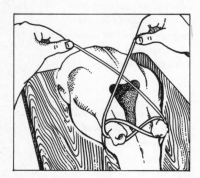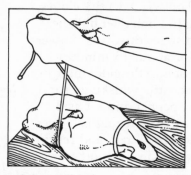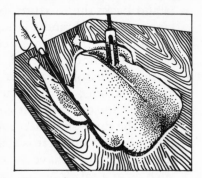

Criss-cross the string over the breast and then pull it down along the thighs. Turn the bird over and secure the wings to the body with the string. Cross the string, flip the bird back over, and knot it securely over the legs. Cut off excess string. To carve a bird, first remove both legs, pulling the drumstick and thigh away from the body and cutting down through the joint.

ROAST GOOSE STUFFED WITH WILD RICE AND CRANBERRIES

Game birds such as geese were among the most abundant of resources available to the Iroquois and Algonquin tribes; the wild rice and cranberries in the stuffing are other of nature's seasonal treats. Basting the goose with maple syrup adds yet another authentic American ingredient to this dish.

Wild Rice and Cranberry Stuffing

3 cups water
3 tablespoons vegetable oil
1 cup wild rice
8 scallions, chopped
1 teaspoon salt
1 teaspoon chopped fresh dill, or ¼ teaspoon dried dill
1 cup fresh cranberries

1. For the stuffing, bring the water to a boil in a large pot, and add 1 tablespoon oil. Add the wild rice and reduce heat to a simmer. Stir thoroughly. Cook, covered, over low heat for 40 minutes. Meanwhile, in a frying pan, heat the remaining 2 tablespoons oil and sauté the scallions for 3 minutes; set aside.

2. Uncover the rice and stir in the sautéed scallions, salt, dill, and cranberries. Simmer, uncovered, until all the liquid is absorbed, an additional 10 minutes.

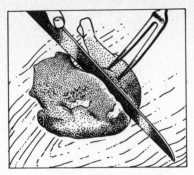 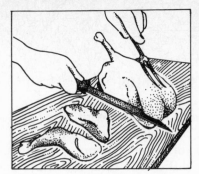 

Cut each leg in half, separating the drumstick and the thigh pieces. Cut off each wing, angling down to the joint and severing it. Carve the breast, one side at a time, into long slices.

3. Meanwhile heat the oven to 450°F.

4. If using a wild goose, rub it thoroughly with oil, inside and out.

5. Put the onions into the cavity of the goose, spoon in the wild rice and cranberry stuffing, and truss. Sprinkle the goose with allspice. If using a wild goose, cover the breast with an oil-soaked cheesecloth.

6. Put the goose on a rack in a roasting pan and surround it with celery. Pour a scant 1 inch of water into the bottom of the pan. Put the goose into the preheated oven and immediately reduce the heat to 350°F.

7. After 30 minutes, baste the goose with the pan drippings and maple syrup and lightly prick the skin all over to release the fat. Roast until the juices run clear when the thigh is pierced with a fork. Thigh temperature should reach 185°F and stuffing register 160°F, about 17 minutes per pound for wild goose, or 20 minutes per pound for domestic. If you are roasting a wild goose, remove the cheesecloth during the final 30 minutes of roasting so that the goose will brown.

8. Remove the goose from the oven, scoop the stuffing into a baking dish, and put it in the turned-off oven to keep warm.

9. Transfer the goose to a warm serving platter. (For carving instructions, see illustrations.) Degrease the pan juices and season with salt and pepper. Serve the goose and pass the stuffing and pan juices separately.

Yield: 9 to 11 servings

Goose

1	*9- to 11-pound wild Canadian or domestic goose*
¼	*cup vegetable oil*
6	*small white onions*
1	*teaspoon ground allspice*
4	*ribs celery*
⅓	*cup maple syrup*
	Salt and black pepper

YOUNG PHEASANTS MANDAMIN

Mandamin is the Chippewa Indian word for corn, and blanched kernels and cubes of corn bread add color and texture as well as flavor to this dish. Since young pheasants, about 1 pound each, might be difficult to find, substitute one 4-pound pheasant or four squabs or Cornish hens.

Pheasants

½ cup vegetable oil
4 1-pound pheasants, legs, thighs, and breasts separated from carcass, breasts boned, all bones reserved
½ cup dry white vermouth
1 quart Chicken Stock (see recipe, Chapter 3)
Salt and black pepper
2 ounces pheasant livers, soaked overnight in milk to cover
2 tablespoons unsalted butter, softened

Corn Dressing

4 tablespoons unsalted butter
4 ounces wild mushrooms, cut into ¼-inch dice
1 tablespoon minced onion
Kernels cut from 2 ears of corn
1 tablespoon chopped fresh herbs (such as basil and parsley)
Salt and black pepper
1 4"-x-4" square corn bread (see Corn Bread Loaf, Chapter 11), cut into ¼-inch cubes

1. Heat the oven to 400°F.
2. Put ¼ cup oil in a shallow roasting pan and heat in the preheated oven for about 5 minutes. Break each carcass. Put all the pheasant bones in the roasting pan and cook, stirring occasionally, until browned, 20 to 25 minutes. Reduce oven heat to 200°F. Pour off grease and add wine, scraping the bottom and sides of the pan with a wooden spoon to deglaze.
3. Add the stock to the bones. Reduce, uncovered, over moderately high heat to about 1½ cups and strain.
4. For the corn dressing, melt 2 tablespoons butter in a frying pan until it foams. Add mushrooms and onion and sauté until onion turns translucent, about 5 minutes. Blanch the corn kernels in a pan of boiling water for 1 minute. Drain. Add herbs and all but 1 tablespoon of the corn to the mushroom mixture; toss for 1 minute, and season with salt and pepper. Lower the heat and stir in 2 additional tablespoons butter until melted. Gently fold corn bread pieces into mixture. Make sure all ingredients are well distributed but do not mash. Keep warm in a low oven.
5. In a heavy frying pan, heat the remaining ¼ cup oil. Season the pheasant sections with salt and pepper and sauté until golden brown on both sides and just done, 10 to 12 minutes in all, or longer for a larger bird.
6. Transfer the pheasant sections to a platter and keep warm in low oven. Remove the livers from the milk. Discard the milk. Add the livers to the frying pan and sauté for 1 minute. Put the livers into a small bowl and cool slightly. With a fork, mash the livers and combine with 2 tablespoons butter.
7. Reheat the stock in a saucepan. Whisk in the liver butter until well blended, adjust the seasoning, and strain.

Spicy Ham and Phyllo Triangles, p. 20

Fried Mushroom Pasta, p. 20
Radish Remoulade, p. 27

Bay Scallops with Lime and Mint, p. 28

Oyster and Spinach Soup, p. 46
Pepper Beef, p. 64

Lamb with Tomato Chutney and Mint Sauce, p. 70

Veal with Shiitake Mushroom Sauce, p. 68
Fried Catfish with Mustard Sauce, p. 109

Swordfish Tonnato with Lemon-Thyme Mayonnaise, p. 114

Crabs Grilled on a Bed of Seaweed with Fresh Ginger Sauce, p. 122

8. Arrange 4 plates with some corn bread mixture in the center, surrounded by the pheasant sections. Coat the meat with the sauce, sprinkle with the reserved tablespoon of corn kernels, and serve.

Yield: 4 servings

GUINEA HEN SAUTÉ WITH NEW ENGLAND FALL VEGETABLES

Butternut squash, chestnuts, apples, and cider lend a distinctly autumnal aura to this recipe. Guinea hen is available at poultry shops and on game farms but is not found in the wild in the United States. Guinea fowl have such a cacophonous call that they are sometimes used as watch birds—their screeching will alert farmers to the presence of interlopers in the barnyard. Since guinea fowl are recalcitrant and independent birds that refuse to lay eggs if confined, raising them on a commercial scale has been less than a screaming success. If you can't find guinea hens, substitute pheasant.

¾ cup vegetable oil
2 2½- to 3-pound guinea hens or pheasants, cut up (see Notes)
4 tart apples
1 cup cider vinegar
2 cups apple cider
1 cup white wine
4 cups Chicken Stock (see recipe, Chapter 3)
8 sprigs thyme, or 2 teaspoons dried leaf thyme
2 cups heavy cream
20 whole chestnuts, shelled and cooked (see Notes)
1 pound butternut squash, peeled and cut into fine julienne strips
Salt and black pepper

1. In a large, heavy frying pan, heat the oil and sauté the hen pieces, skin side down, until browned, 2 to 3 minutes on each side. Sauté in batches if necessary to avoid crowding the pan. Remove from the pan and pour off the grease. Return the hen parts to the pan, chop 1 of the apples, and add to the pan. Sauté for 1 minute.

2. Add the vinegar to the pan and scrape the bottom and sides with a wooden spoon to deglaze. Cook gently until the acidic bite of the vinegar is cooked out, 3 to 4 minutes. Add the cider and white wine and simmer for 4 minutes. Add the stock and thyme. Bring to a boil, reduce heat, and simmer, covered. Cook the breasts until tender, about 15 minutes more for guinea hen or 5 to 8 minutes for pheasant; remove the breasts. Continue cooking the thighs and legs for another 10 to 15 minutes.

3. Remove the thighs and legs. Discard the back and wings and skim the grease from the surface of the sauce.

4. Over medium-high heat, reduce the sauce to about

⅔ cup, 15 to 20 minutes. Stir in the cream and simmer until slightly thickened, about 7 minutes. Strain through a fine sieve into a saucepan, add the chestnuts, and simmer for 1 minute.

5. Peel, core, and cut the remaining apples into thin julienne strips. Add the apples and julienned squash to the sauce and simmer until tender, 2 minutes. Taste for seasoning and adjust as necessary.

6. Return the hen pieces to the pan, heat through, and serve with chestnuts, apples, and squash scattered over them.

Yield: 4 servings

Notes: Cut the birds into leg, thigh, back, wing, and breast sections. Cut each breast piece in half.

If using fresh chestnuts, cut a small cross in the bottom of each shell. Put the nuts in a saucepan, cover with water, and bring to a boil over high heat. When boil is reached, remove the pan from heat. Take only a few chestnuts out of the water at a time, cool just enough to handle, and peel. (Once the chestnuts cool thoroughly, peeling is difficult.) Return all the chestnuts to their pan. Add water as necessary to cover well, and simmer until tender, about 45 minutes.

Chapter

6 Fish and Shellfish

I n the plastic-wrapped world of the modern food shopper, fish is an anachronism. Mass production and marketing have resulted in much standardization of food products, but with fish, we are still in the realm of mystery. Buy a steak in most butcher shops or supermarkets, and you can count on getting a reasonably good, predictable piece of meat, one that will roughly correspond to the price you've decided to pay. Not so when choosing fish. Some two hundred edible species swim our lakes, streams, and ocean areas, and while many of them aren't caught or marketed commercially, enough are so that the shopper in a fish market first faces the problem of wondering which fish taste how and what ones are suited for varying kinds of cooking. After that come further complications. Should you buy whole or filleted fish? How can you tell if fish are really fresh? Are frozen fish ever good? How much should you buy for a serving?

It's no surprise that many people simply give up and don't cook fish or, if they do, choose the path of least resistance and buy something familiar like flounder or turbot, no matter what preparation they have in mind. Yet despite the difficulties, or perhaps, for those who yearn for a return to more interesting culinary choices, because of them, fish cookery has again become fashionable.

Nutrition and diet-consciousness are two reasons. Fish offer splendid nutritional value; most varieties are good sources of protein, minerals, and important B-complex vitamins. And fish are usually low in calories, normally less than 100 calories per quarter pound for lean fish, such as sole or flounder, to about 200 calories for fatter fish such as salmon. They are also generally low in sodium and in fats, and the fat that is there is mostly polyunsaturated.

As with most culinary projects, the best way to know which fish to choose and how to cook them is through experience, but there are some general guides that can help the novice and that are useful even for the more experienced cook. Let's look first at some of the ways to differentiate among fish before surveying the main types of fish and shellfish available in the different regions of the United States.

CATEGORIES OF FISH

Saltwater and Freshwater Fish

Although an obvious distinction, this is one that's of only minor value for the cook. In general, neither freshwater nor saltwater fish lay claim to better flavor or texture. There's greater variety among saltwater fish, of course, but perhaps the biggest difference is that freshwater fish are now much less fished commercially than previously and are generally more threatened by such dangers as acid rain and industrial pollution than saltwater species. Freshwater fish, however, are more adaptable to aquaculture or fish farming, and some varieties, trout and catfish, for instance, are being raised extensively in commercial fish farms.

Lean and Oily Fish

This is one of the most useful general ways of categorizing fish types. Lean fish are those that have from 1 to 5 percent body fat and whose body fat is generally concentrated in the liver and therefore is removed when the fish are cleaned. In general, lean-fleshed fish are firm textured, white fleshed, and mild flavored. They are normally smaller and more delicate than oily fish and usually require shorter cooking times. Since they have little moisture in their flesh, they can dry out easily during cooking and are classically cooked by poaching, steaming, or sautéing. However, if basted during cooking, lean-fleshed fish can be baked, broiled, or grilled. Among the most common saltwater lean fish are flounder, sole, snapper, sea bass, and porgy.

Oily fish have from 5 to 50 percent fat in their flesh, and the fat is more or less equally distributed throughout the fish. The fat, or oil, makes their flesh darker and more flavorful, especially in those at the high end of the fat-content scale. Since these fish usually are moist, they can be cooked by most dry-heat methods, such as baking, broiling, and grilling. The most common oily-fleshed fish are mullet, pompano, salmon, tuna, mackerel, bluefish, catfish, trout, and whitefish.

Since the most vexing question in cooking fish is often that of finding an acceptable substitute for the fish specified in a recipe, one of the best rules of thumb to know is that lean-fleshed fish can almost always be substituted for other lean-fleshed fish. Generally this is also true for oily-fleshed fish, but be careful not to use only moderately fatty fish such as pompano in recipes designed for very fatty fish such as mackerel or bluefish.

A typical flatfish has two sets of thin and narrow fillets, one from the top and one from the bottom of the fish.

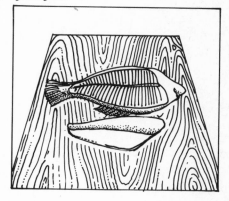

Flatfish and Roundfish

Roundfish have thicker fillets, one on either side of the backbone.

Most flatfish are also lean fish and can be substituted one for another in recipes, although flavor and texture do vary. Flatfish are generally very thin and are normally separated along a central backbone into two sets of quite thin and narrow fillets. They are sold either whole or filleted. Flatfish are mainly the members of the flounder family, such as sole, fluke, and turbot.

Most oily fish are round. They have two thick fillets that extend lengthwise on either side of the backbone. Depending upon their size, roundfish can be sold whole, filleted, or in butterfly fillets. Large roundfish, such as tuna, salmon, swordfish, or sablefish, are sold in steaks.

Fresh and Frozen Fish

Obviously the best fish are the ones eaten as soon as possible after they've been caught. Really fresh fish can be gotten from sport fishermen and, along the coasts or inland in some lake and river cities, from smaller commercial fishermen or markets that deal directly with local fishermen. Much of our commercial catch is kept on ice in fishing boats for several days before being unloaded and put into the distribution system. This fish can still be very good if handled properly and not kept in the wholesale or retail outlet too long. You need to find a fishmonger you can trust and also remember the basic tests to see how fresh the fish you're buying are: The eyes should be bulging and clear, the flesh firm, the gills bright, and the fishy odor should be detectable only by a cat. Generally, whole fish in a shop are fresher than fillets since many shops put the whole fish out when they get them and then fillet the ones that haven't sold for the next day.

Frozen fish can be suitable for cooking, but your chances of finding good frozen fish are lower than with fresh fish. First of all, frozen fish fillets are useless for anything except frying in a flavorful batter that will mask their mushy texture and lack of flavor. Whole fish flash-frozen shortly after being caught or, as with salmon or tuna steaks, frozen from a fish cut up immediately after the catch, can be used for most recipes. But remember that frozen foods are very likely to be badly handled in distribution and that freezing and refreezing are particularly bad for delicately flavored fish.

REGIONAL VARIETIES

Here's a rundown of some of the most popular fish by regions. Fish caught commercially in your region of the country are most likely to be in good condition in the shops. So rather than looking for fish from other areas or buying frozen fish to satisfy recipe demands, try to use local species.

New England

This is the land where codfish and flounder reign. Smaller cod, those between 1½ and 2½ pounds, are marketed as scrod. Haddock is a kind of cod also readily found in New England shops. Flounder is a general name for a number of flatfish species found off the New England coast; lemon sole, plaice, and the larger halibut are the most common. A very strong-flavored fish is the Atlantic mackerel at its prime in late summer or fall.

New England shellfish are famous. The Atlantic or Maine lobster is taken all along the coast. Scallops are widely available, both sea scallops and the smaller, sweeter bay scallops. Oysters are practically synonymous with New England, and they're found from Maine to Connecticut. Clams are another New England staple. Hard-shells (quahogs) and soft-shells (steamers) are the two main varieties. Hard-shells are most often eaten in chowders or raw, while soft-shells are considered best steamed or fried.

Middle Atlantic

In addition to most of the fish varieties found in New England, the Middle Atlantic region has some species primarily its own—particularly in the Hudson River and the Delaware and Chesapeake Bay watersheds. Bluefish, a strong-flavored oily fish, is in season from spring through October. Shad, though also found in New England and other areas, is a specialty in New Jersey and Pennsylvania, with a season from late winter to May. Perhaps the finest flavored fish of the whole Atlantic is the striped bass. It's now mainly taken off New York and New Jersey and in the Chesapeake Bay (where it's called rockfish). The black sea bass, from a different family altogether, is caught commercially from New York to South Carolina.

Mid-Atlantic shellfish are generally the same as those off New England. Long Island Sound is still a fertile fishery for oysters, hard-shell clams, and bay scallops. The blue crab is the king of Middle Atlantic shellfish. The hard-shell crabs are popular in Maryland and Virginia crab houses. The soft-shell crab, really a blue crab that's shed its skin during a growth stage, is a particular delicacy.

Florida and the Gulf

Red snapper, pompano, and grouper are the big three in the Florida and Gulf area. Red snapper is the one most frequently seen in markets around the country. The pompano season generally runs from October to May. Grouper is a fine white-fleshed fish, usually deep-fried or poached. In Florida and the Keys, it's particularly prized in chowders. The red drum, better known as the redfish, is primarily fished commercially in the Gulf, and is best known in the famous Cajun dish, blackened redfish.

Oysters are about as common in the Gulf as along the Atlantic coast; they're more often found fried in restaurants here than in the North. The Indian River oyster, sold only locally in Florida, is ranked among the best of all oyster types. Blue crabs are caught off Florida and in the Gulf, but the region's most prized crab is the flavorful, meaty stone crab. It's scarce, expensive, and delicious during its season, which runs from winter into early spring. Shrimp are the real backbone of the Gulf fishing industry, and locally caught fresh shrimp are among the best of American seafoods. The Florida lobster or spiny lobster is less meaty than the Atlantic lobster. One freshwater shellfish is found in the South —the crayfish, staple of Louisiana Cajun and Creole cookery.

Midwest and Plains States

What middle America lacks is a nearby ocean; what it has is good freshwater fish. Trout is one of the finest of table fish and certainly among the most popular and available, since it's easily raised in hatcheries. The most commonly sold species is the rainbow trout, but brook trout and lake trout can also be found. Catfish are caught all through the Midwest in the Mississippi and Missouri river valleys. Channel, blue, and white catfish are the most common. Catfish is traditionally deep-fried but can also be stewed, poached, or broiled.

Pike are found in the North Central and northern Midwest; northern and muskies are popular game fish caught commercially in Canada for export to the United States. The most popular commercially fished pike in the United States and the most interesting gastronomically, the walleye, is not a pike at all. It's really a member of the perch family. Walleye is a delicate-fleshed, flavorful fish and, although not a flatfish, can be substituted for sole or flounder. The yellow perch is delicious panfried and is caught in commercial quantities around the Great Lakes. Another Great Lakes fish caught commercially is the whitefish. Small smoked whitefish are usually marketed as chubs. The coho salmon caught in the Great Lakes is not generally considered the gastronomic equal of either the Atlantic or Pacific salmon.

The only freshwater crustacean is the crayfish. Over 250 species occur in North America alone, and while they are most common in Louisiana and the Gulf states, crayfish can be found in the rivers and streams of the Midwest and North Central United States as well. As yet crayfish are neither caught nor marketed commercially in those regions.

Pacific Coast

Salmon and tuna are the most commonly known Pacific coast fish. The coho, chinook, and sockeye salmon are the big three West coast species with the chinook or king salmon considered the best; the coho or silver salmon is thought next best and is generally slightly less expensive. Tuna is another oily fish often sold in steaks or fillets. Albacore is the most desirable, while yellowfin tuna is most common. Swordfish are found off the coast of southern California and are fished commercially there. This is a moderately oily fish, usually sold in steaks and much esteemed.

Of flatfish, the best Pacific varieties are the petrale and rex soles. The rex sole is smaller and more scarce than the petrale. The sand dab is another small flatfish, traditionally popular in northern California and the San Francisco Bay area. White sea bass, often sold simply as sea bass on the West coast, has become scarce and expensive. The Pacific mackerel is as common as its

Atlantic counterpart and on the West coast, as in the East, generally undervalued by cooks.

Oysters and crabs lead the shellfish parade along the West coast. The Olympia oyster is native in the Northwest and, while very small, is at least one of the best on either coast—in our mind, they're the best in the world. The Dungeness and king crabs are the principal crab species on the Pacific coast. The Dungeness is most common from California north to Washington. It's in season from October to May. The king crab is found in the cold Pacific waters from Washington to Alaska. Abalone is one shellfish found on the Pacific coast but not the Atlantic. Abalone is such a rare delicacy that California law now forbids its exportation from the state. Shrimp are caught all along the Pacific coast from lower California to Alaska. Spot shrimp or Monterey prawns are the most popular southern California species. Crayfish, once bountiful in the Sacramento River, are now raised in California, too.

BROILED LEMON SOLE

If you can't find fresh lemon sole or flounder use nearly any other white-fleshed fish from pike or trout to sea bass or pompano for this simple, yet delicious broiled-fish recipe.

1. Between sheets of waxed paper or plastic wrap, pound the fillets gently with a mallet or rolling pin to even thickness.
2. Heat the broiler.
3. In a frying pan, heat the olive oil over low heat. Add the onion and sauté until soft, about 6 minutes.
4. Put the fish in a baking pan in 1 layer. Season with salt and pepper. Slice the butter and distribute over the fish. Top with the sautéed onions and sprinkle with the herbs.
5. Broil about 3 inches from heat source until the fish tests done, about 5 minutes. Serve immediately on warmed plates.

Yield: 4 servings

1⅓ *pounds lemon sole fillets*
  2 *tablespoons olive oil*
  1 *large red onion, sliced thin*
     Salt and black pepper
  3 *tablespoons unsalted butter*
  2 *tablespoons minced fresh chives*
  2 *tablespoons minced fresh tarragon
       leaves* or *chopped fresh dill*

FRIED CATFISH WITH MUSTARD SAUCE

1. For the sauce, melt the butter in a saucepan. Add the onion and sauté over low heat, stirring frequently, until softened but not browned, 3 to 4 minutes. Add the wine and cook, uncovered, over medium heat until the liquid is absorbed, 5 minutes. Add the cream and over medium heat reduce by one quarter, about 3 minutes.
2. Remove from heat and stir in the parsley and mustard. Season to taste with salt and pepper. Set aside.
3. For the fish, heat the oil in a deep-fat fryer to 370°F.
4. In a bowl, combine flour and cornmeal. Dry the fish well with paper towels, season with salt and pepper, and then dredge in the flour-cornmeal mixture. Fry the catfish until golden brown, about 4 minutes. Drain on paper towels. Reheat the sauce gently and serve with the catfish.

Yield: 4 servings

Mustard Sauce

  2 *tablespoons unsalted butter*
  1 *onion, minced (about ¾ cup)*
 ½ *cup dry white wine* or *vermouth*
  1 *cup heavy cream*
 ½ *cup minced flat-leaf parsley*
  2 *tablespoons Dijon mustard*
     Salt and black pepper

Fish

     Vegetable oil for deep-frying
 ½ *cup flour*
 ½ *cup cornmeal*
  2 *pounds skinned catfish fillets*
     Salt and black pepper

SAUTÉED SOFT-SHELL CRABS WITH GINGER-LIME BUTTER

Virtually unknown in Europe, the soft-shell crab is an all-American delicacy. All crabs shed their shells while growing, and a soft-shell crab is simply one caught and then cooked during that shell-less period. The Atlantic and Gulf blue crab is the only crab species meaty enough to be suitable for cooking in this state, though, and so it's become synonymous with the term *soft-shell crab*. The season for soft-shells starts in the Gulf in the spring and then continues up the coast to Northern Carolina, the Chesapeake Bay, Long Island, and New England during the summer.

Ginger-Lime Butter

 1 small shallot, minced
 9 tablespoons unsalted butter, softened
 2 tablespoons minced fresh ginger
 ½ clove garlic, minced
 1 teaspoon minced lime zest
 ½ teaspoon minced lemon zest
 3 tablespoons lime juice
 1 teaspoon lemon juice
 ½ teaspoon salt
 ¼ teaspoon white pepper

Crabs

 12 soft-shell crabs
     Flour
 6 ounces unsalted butter, clarified, or 6 tablespoons butter and 6 tablespoons oil

1. For the ginger-lime butter, sauté the shallot in 1 tablespoon butter for 1 minute. Then in a food processor, puree the sautéed shallot and all remaining ingredients.
2. Put the ginger-lime butter on a piece of waxed paper or plastic wrap and roll into a 6-inch-long cylinder. Chill until firm, at least 1 hour. The butter can be refrigerated for up to 2 weeks or frozen for several months.
3. Dust the crabs lightly with flour and shake off excess. Heat enough clarified butter or a combination of butter and oil in a large, heavy frying pan to film bottom. Sauté a few crabs at a time over medium heat until crisp, 3 to 4 minutes per side. Continue sautéing in batches, adding more butter or butter and oil as necessary.
4. Top each crab with a ½-inch pat of ginger-lime butter and serve immediately.

Yield: 4 to 6 servings

SCALLOPED OYSTERS

Except for the chopped parsley garnish, this is an old traditional recipe from the South—a simple and delicious way to serve oysters fresh from the ocean.

1. Heat the oven to 375°F. Butter a small, shallow baking dish.
2. In a saucepan, melt 4 tablespoons butter. In a large bowl, combine bread crumbs, oyster crackers, and melted butter. Spread one-third of the mixture in the prepared baking dish. Put half the oysters over the top of the mixture.
3. Mix the pepper and cayenne and sprinkle half over the oysters. Repeat layering with half of the remaining crumb mixture, the rest of the oysters, and the seasonings. Top with the remaining crumb mixture, drizzle the cream over the bread crumbs, and dot with the remaining tablespoon of butter.
4. In the preheated oven, bake the casserole until brown on top, about 25 minutes. If it doesn't brown, put under the broiler for a few seconds. Scatter the chopped parsley over the casserole and serve.

5 tablespoons unsalted butter
½ cup fresh bread crumbs
1 cup coarse-crushed oyster crackers
1 pint shucked oysters, drained
  Pinch of black pepper
¼ teaspoon cayenne
⅓ cup light cream or half and half
1 tablespoon chopped fresh parsley

Yield: 4 servings

CHOCTAW SHRIMP STEW

The Choctaw, one of the major southeastern horticultural tribes, were noted farmers and fishermen.

1. In a frying pan, heat the oil and sauté the scallions, dillseed, celery, and diced peppers until the scallions are soft, about 3 minutes. Remove from heat and set aside.
2. In a large pot, bring the water to a boil. Add the Jerusalem artichokes, corn, salt, and Tabasco, and simmer, stirring, for 15 minutes. Add the sautéed ingredients, chopped dill, and minced parsley.
3. Return to a boil and drop in the shrimp. Simmer for 5 more minutes, stirring occasionally. Remove from heat and stir in filé until well blended. Taste for seasoning. Serve hot, garnished with additional parsley and dill.

3 tablespoons sunflower seed oil
3 scallions, chopped
1¼ teaspoons dillseed
½ small rib celery, diced
1 red bell pepper, diced
1 green bell pepper, diced
4 cups water
⅓ pound Jerusalem artichokes, scrubbed and sliced thin
  Kernels cut from 3 ears of corn
  Salt
  Few drops Tabasco sauce
2 teaspoons chopped fresh dill, or ¼ teaspoon dried dill
2 teaspoons minced fresh parsley
1 pound shrimp, peeled and deveined
1½ teaspoons filé powder dissolved in about ⅓ cup water (see Note)
  Parsley leaves
  Dill sprigs

Yield: 4 servings

Note: Filé, a thickening agent, will become ropey if reheated. Be sure to add at the very end.

BRAISED MONKFISH WITH CURRIED FRUIT

As the most prized fish varieties such as snapper or sole or striped bass become increasingly hard to find, experts suggest substituting less well-known kinds. Monkfish has been one of the most successful of these to the point that it is now fashionable and no longer so inexpensive as it was. Known as *lotte* in France, where it's a staple in the cooking of the Mediterranean regions, monkfish is sometimes called lobster fish or poor man's lobster because it has a texture reminiscent of lobster meat. This new recipe is surprising yet not so odd to the palate as it may sound in reading.

3 pounds monkfish, trimmed of
    membrane and cut into 2-inch
    pieces, bones reserved for stock
    Salt and black pepper
2 tablespoons vegetable oil
2 tablespoons unsalted butter
½ cup flour
½ cup dry vermouth
10 shallots, minced
2 teaspoons curry powder
½ cup chopped dates
½ cup chopped dried apricots
½ cup chopped prunes
½ cup dried currants soaked in 2
    tablespoons Grand Marnier
1 to 1½ cups Fish Stock (recipe
    follows)
    Lemon wedges

1. Pat the monkfish pieces dry with paper towels and season with salt and pepper.
2. In a large frying pan with a lid, heat the oil and butter over medium-high heat. Dredge the fish pieces in flour and shake off excess. Brown the fish quickly. Transfer the browned fish to paper towels to drain.
3. Pour off the excess oil and add the vermouth, scraping the bottom of the pan with a wooden spoon to deglaze. Add the shallots and cook slowly, covered, stirring every minute or so, until softened, about 3 minutes. Be careful not to burn the shallots.
4. Add the curry powder and cook, stirring, for 1 minute. Add the dried fruit and stir well. Gently put the drained, browned fish on top. Add enough fish stock to almost cover the fish. Cover and cook until the fish just tests done, 5 to 8 minutes.
5. Transfer the fish to a platter and keep warm. Raise heat to high and reduce the cooking liquid by one third, stirring constantly, about 5 minutes. To serve, spoon the sauce around the fish and garnish with lemon wedges.

Yield: 4 servings

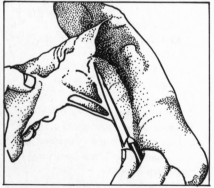

**Trim the monkfish of any membrane
prior to cooking.**

1. In a pot, melt the butter, add the onion, and cook over low heat until the onion is soft, 5 to 10 minutes.
2. Add the bones and cook, stirring well, for 2 minutes. Cover the bones with enough cold water so that they float, add the bay leaf, thyme, salt, and peppercorns, and bring to a simmer. Simmer, skimming frequently, until the mixture is reduced to about 1½ cups.
3. Strain through a fine sieve. The stock can be refrigerated for several days or frozen.

Yield: about 1½ cups

FISH STOCK

1 teaspoon unsalted butter
1 small onion, chopped
    Bones from monkfish
1 bay leaf
1 sprig fresh thyme, or ¼ teaspoon dried thyme
    Pinch of salt
3 peppercorns

SHAD ROE IN LEMON-CHIVE BUTTER

Shad, a harbinger of spring, follows the warm weather right up the coast. It's seasonal in Florida around January and may not arrive in Maine until July. The delicate roe is anticipated as eagerly as the fish.

1. In a bowl, soak the shad roe in milk for 10 minutes. Drain and pat dry. Discard milk. Dredge the roe in flour and lightly brush off any excess.
2. The roe should be sautéed in 2 frying pans or in batches. Heat about one third of the clarified butter or 4 tablespoons butter and 1 tablespoon oil per batch. Sauté the floured roe until golden brown, 6 to 7 minutes per side. Be careful when turning the shad roe, or it may burst. Remove from the pan and keep warm.
3. Add the wine to the butter in the pan and heat, scraping the bottom of the pan with a wooden spoon to deglaze. Combine the contents of 2 pans, if using, into 1. Add the chives and remaining butter and heat until the butter is golden brown. Stir in the lemon juice, season with salt and pepper, and pour over the shad roe. Serve immediately.

Yield: 4 servings

4 pairs shad roe (10 ounces each)
2 cups milk
    Flour
½ pound unsalted butter, clarified, or 7 ounces unsalted butter plus 2 tablespoons vegetable oil
2 tablespoons dry white wine
4 tablespoons chopped chives
2 tablespoons lemon juice
    Salt and black pepper

SWORDFISH TONNATO WITH LEMON-THYME MAYONNAISE

This recipe is an inventive variation on Vitello Tonnato, an Italian veal dish made with a similar sauce. Swordfish is scarce and very expensive—one reason that the mako shark, caught especially off the Atlantic coast and with a taste and texture that are somewhat the same, is occasionally sold in markets as swordfish. It often is a good substitute. The season for fresh swordfish is during the summer and fall.

Swordfish

- 1 pound swordfish steak
- 2 sprigs lemon thyme, or ¼ teaspoon dried thyme plus a few drops lemon juice
- 1 small bay leaf
- ½ to ¾ cup dry white wine or vermouth

Mayonnaise and Garnish

- 1 egg, room temperature
- 1 egg yolk, room temperature
  Salt and black pepper
- 2 tablespoons lemon juice
- 1½ teaspoons minced fresh parsley
- 1 tablespoon chopped lemon thyme, or 1 teaspoon rubbed thyme plus more lemon juice to taste
- 9 tablespoons vegetable oil
- 3½ ounces canned water-packed tuna fish, drained
- 3 tablespoons capers
- 6 anchovy fillets
- 6 tablespoons olive oil
- ¼ small red onion, sliced thin
- 4 black Niçoise olives
- 1 egg, hard-cooked and quartered

1. Heat the oven to 400°F.
2. Put the swordfish, lemon thyme sprigs, and bay leaf in a nonreactive baking dish. Add enough wine to barely cover the fish and cover baking dish with foil. Bake in the preheated oven until the swordish just tests done, 8 to 12 minutes. Remove from the oven, uncover, and let cool.
3. For the mayonnaise, combine the egg, egg yolk, ¼ teaspoon salt, ½ tablespoon lemon juice, parsley, and lemon thyme, and beat for 1 minute. Whisk in the oil, first drop by drop, and then in a thin stream as the mixture begins to thicken.
4. In a food processor, whir together the tuna fish, 1½ tablespoons capers, 2 anchovies, and the remaining 1½ tablespoons lemon juice. Gradually add olive oil to make a smooth emulsion. Fold the tuna mixture into the mayonnaise and season to taste with salt and pepper.
5. Remove the swordfish from the liquid. (The liquid can be saved for a fish stock.) Cut into ¼-inch-thick slices. Spoon some of the mayonnaise sauce onto a serving plate or individual plates. Arrange the swordfish on the sauce. Spoon additional sauce down the center of the fish. Cover and chill.
6. To serve, garnish with the remaining capers, anchovies, red onion slices, olives, hard-cooked egg, and additional sprigs of lemon thyme, if you like.

Yield: 4 servings

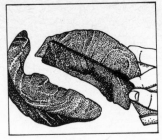

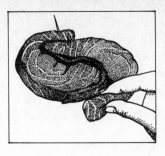

Separate boned salmon into two pieces and lay a strip of smoked salmon along the inside edge of one of the sections.

Re-form salmon steaks by wrapping the end of each side around the center section of the other side.

POACHED SALMON WITH CUCUMBER SAUCE

Canned and smoked salmon still account for most of the Pacific Northwest production of this fish. Canned salmon alone represents 7 percent of our total fish consumption in the United States, but fresh salmon, as steaks or fillets, has become increasingly common and popular in fish shops and restaurants around the country. While canned salmon is generally sockeye or pink salmon, the fresh fish is usually from the most desirable and expensive fish—the chinook and coho salmon.

1. Combine the first 8 ingredients in a deep frying pan. Bring to a boil and simmer for 10 minutes. Strain and return the liquid to frying pan.
2. Cut the salmon steaks in half and remove the bone but keep the halves of each steak together. Place a strip of smoked salmon along the inside edge of one of the sections of each steak. Re-form the salmon steaks as illustrated and secure the halves with toothpicks.
3. Bring the liquid back to a simmer, add the salmon, and cook until the fish just tests done, 6 to 7 minutes. Gently remove the fish from the liquid, cover with a little liquid, and chill.
4. For the sauce, peel the cucumbers and cut in half lengthwise. Scoop out the seeds and discard. Thinly slice the cucumbers and put the slices in a colander, toss with coarse salt, and drain for about 30 minutes. Rinse well and pat dry.
5. In a bowl, combine the cucumbers with chives, vinegar, and sour cream. Season to taste with salt and pepper.
6. Put the salmon on plates and remove the toothpicks. Top the steaks with the sauce and garnish each with caviar.

Yield: 4 servings

Salmon

4½ cups water
⅓ cup white wine
1¼ teaspoons salt
½ small bay leaf
½ teaspoon dried thyme
1 small onion, sliced
1 small bunch parsley stems
4 peppercorns, bruised
4 8-ounce salmon steaks
2 ounces smoked salmon, cut into 4 strips

Sauce

1 pound cucumbers
¾ teaspoon coarse salt
1 tablespoon minced fresh chives
2 tablespoons white wine vinegar
1 cup sour cream
Salt and black pepper
1½ to 2 tablespoons salmon caviar

GRILLED TUNA STEAKS WITH MOZZARELLA-SAGE STUFFING

4 *1-inch-thick tuna steaks*
   Salt and black pepper
2 *teaspoons minced fresh sage, or ½*
   teaspoon dried sage
2 *ounces smoked mozzarella cheese, cut*
   into thin strips
2 *tablespoons unsalted butter*
3 *tablespoons olive oil*
   Handful of woody sage twigs, soaked
   in water to cover for about 15
   minutes and then drained (optional)
5 *or 6 sage sprigs, stems tied together*
   with string

1. Heat the grill.
2. With a sharp knife, cut a deep pocket in each tuna steak by inserting the knife and then carefully moving it back and forth to enlarge the pocket. Be careful not to make the incision larger than necessary. Sprinkle salt and pepper over the surface of the fish.
3. In a bowl, toss the sage and cheese together. Stuff each pocket with the cheese mixture.
4. In a small saucepan, melt the butter with olive oil.
5. Sprinkle the drained sage twigs over the coals if desired.
6. Using the tied sage sprigs as a brush, paint each side of the fish steaks with the butter mixture. Grill until the fish is just cooked through and the cheese is melted, about 4 minutes per side, basting often with the remaining butter and oil using the sage "brush." Serve immediately.

Yield: 4 servings

Barbecuing, Grilling, and Smoking

The decade of the eighties may well be recorded in American culinary history as the renaissance of barbecuing and grilling. First popular nationwide as a suburban backyard phenomenon in the 1950s, the use of home barbecues spread, waned, and is now bigger than ever. Contemporary cooks have brought charcoal grilling to the city and revised its parameters. And ever since imaginative professional cooks got into the act, hamburgers, steaks, and the occasional shish kebab or string of sausages no longer constitute the full range of alternatives. Now on restaurant menus and at home, we're likely to see such specialties as Grilled Shrimp with Coriander Pasta or Grilled Pork Fillet with Date Chutney. At the same time that such new dishes are being invented, there is a resurgence of interest in old-fashioned barbecue.

In fact, *barbecue* is used now to describe three rather different ways of cooking, all of which involve the use of an open fire. Grilling is the culinary star of the day. No more than cooking over dry heat, grilling probably is the world's oldest cooking method, but the contemporary stage is distinguished by some startling combinations. Nearly every kind of food from duck breasts and squab to venison, fennel, and coconut now grace grills all around the country.

As we try new foods and invent new combinations for the grill, true barbecuing, on the other hand, strikes a nostalgic nerve. The open-pit barbecue has been the centerpiece of social events in the South since the eighteenth century. Barbecue aficionados insist that the only real barbecue is cooked outside in an open pit, for hours and hours. In barbecue joints in the South and in the newly fashionable barbecue restaurants in the North, long, low steel fire boxes substitute for the pit to allow for the necessary long, slow cooking. For the home cook, duplicating this practice is difficult, though heavy-duty aluminum foil used over a grill will allow gradual cooking without burning, and various other methods, such as a combination of oven and grill cooking, can approximate the tender, smoky result of barbecue.

Beef, in Texas and the Southwest, and pork, in the Southeast, are the traditional meats for barbecue. Leisurely cooking until the crucial point of tenderness where the meat all but shreds under the knife is essential to both. And the barbecue sauces—moppin' sauces to marinate or to moisten the meat while it's cooking, and soppin' sauces to eat with the meat—are regional variants. Vinegar-based sauces are still considered essential by Carolina purists. In Texas, a hot-pepper meat rub is often used. But most barbecue sauces around the country feature catsup, chili sauce, or tomato sauce with some extra regional ingredients—Coca-Cola in a recipe from Georgia, for instance; maple syrup in some parts of the Northeast; and, of course, chiles in the Southwest.

Smoking, the third of these related cooking methods, is one of the most important ways of preserving food and has a place in most cuisines, including traditional American cooking. Until recently, smoking foods was difficult to do at home, even with a grill. Now, with covered grills and with the new home smokers, it's easy to smoke foods—beef, pork, chicken, or as in our recipes, trout, game hens, or turkey.

Whether it's grilling, barbecuing, or smoking that you plan to do, there are three elements to master—the equipment, the fuel, and the fire.

THE EQUIPMENT

A typical kettle grill that can be used for grilling or smoking.

Some folks in Texas take their barbecue so seriously that they eschew commercially made grills and claim that only converted fifty-five gallon tin drums will suffice as barbecue pits. For the rest of the nation, however, there are other options. To bring the new barbecuing and grilling home, you can choose from four basic types of equipment now on the market: plain open or hooded grills, covered grills, electric or gas grills, and water smokers.

The favorite of backyards and terraces in the 1950s, the plain open or hooded grill is the cheapest model and entirely adequate for simple grilling. Included in this category are the hibachi and regulation barbecues running from the small portables to the large stand-up charcoal grills half enclosed with a metal hood.

The most popular outdoor cooker now is the covered grill, which comes in square, rectangular, or round kettle models. Versatility is the key here. Without the cover, these cookers act as plain open grills. With the cover in place, an ovenlike space is created, making roasting, smoking, or steaming possible. The kettle-shaped cooker is the best choice, since it's designed to distribute heat most evenly and effectively.

More expensive to be sure, a gas or electric grill offers quick, no-fuss outdoor cookery; both are available in all sizes, covered or not. Portable gas grills are used with a smallish tank of gas; butane-fired models also are on the market. Instead of coals, the bottoms of these units are lined with lava rocks (for gas) or ceramic tile (for electric). Some outdoor enthusiasts claim that food cooked in gas or electric grills does not attain the woodsy quality achieved over charcoal. However, if water-soaked wood chips are placed in an aluminum-foil pan directly on the heating surface, that taste can be obtained.

Cross section of a typical water smoker.

The water smoker has caught on in a big way. In these tall, cylindrical devices, a liquid, such as water or wine, sits in a pan between the heat source and the food, which cooks slowly, enveloped in a smoky haze. Juicy results are assured. Most water smokers can be used as simple open grills as well. Coal, gas, and electric versions are available.

THE FUEL

All of the excitement over the new grilling, the old barbecuing, and combinations thereof has added fuels to the fiery controversy over what to burn under the food. Mesquite, long used in the Southwest due at least partially to its cheapness and availability, is the new star and is hot in more ways than one. The heat from mesquite is quite intense (mesquite charcoal burns at 900° Fahrenheit as opposed to the 600° to 700° of regular charcoal), but it can lead to problems. Some say that while mesquite has a good flavor, it can overpower the taste of a dish if food is left on the grill too long or if the outside becomes too charred.

In California, mesquite charcoal is available in supermarkets. Farther east, it may be harder to find in retail outlets. Many home cooks get good results by using a bed of standard briquets in combination with wood chips for added smoke and flavor. Pecan, walnut, cherry, apple, or any other fruit or nut wood, as well as most hardwoods which are first soaked in water, is suitable. Avoid all softwoods such as pine, as the resin is ruinous to food.

THE FIRE

The great temptations of gas and electric grills are that they heat in ten to twenty minutes and leave your hands clean. Traditionalists will build their charcoal fire in the usual pyramid shape using enough coals to finally make a single burning layer that extends one inch beyond the food. To adjust the heat downward, spread the coals out so that there are spaces between them, removing extras to a metal container. For long cooking, it's a good idea to have additional coals warming around the edge to replenish the fire as needed.

For long, slow cooking and for smoking on a covered grill, use indirect heat. There are two ways to achieve this, each requiring an inexpensive aluminum-foil pan. The first technique is to place the drip pan in the middle of the grill floor directly under the food surrounded by smoldering coals. The other, even lower-heat, method is to put the coals on one side and the food, over the drip pan, on the other.

CHORIZO TORTAS

Grilled frankfurters are an American summer cliché, and a delicious one, but other kinds of sausage are equally adaptable to the outdoor fire. Our recipe calls for the Spanish pork sausage chorizo. If you can't find chorizo, hot Italian sausage can be substituted.

1 pound chorizo link sausages
6 tablespoons white wine
6 tablespoons olive oil
2 tablespoons unsalted butter
¾ teaspoon crushed dried hot red pepper or to taste, depending on spiciness of sausage
1 red bell pepper
1 green bell pepper or 1 large poblano chile
2 onions, cut into ¼-inch slices
4 large crusty rolls, split

1. Put the sausage links in a single layer in a large frying pan. Add the wine. Prick the sausages well on all sides. Cook over medium-high heat, turning, until the liquid is nearly evaporated, about 7 minutes. Remove the sausages and drain.
2. Heat 4 tablespoons oil with the butter and crushed pepper. Simmer for 5 to 10 minutes.
3. Heat the grill to medium hot.
4. Make a 1-inch slit in each bell pepper. Put the sausages in the center of the grill. Put the onions and peppers on the outer edge of the grill and brush lightly with the remaining 2 tablespoons olive oil. Cook until tender, 5 to 8 minutes, basting frequently with the butter-oil mixture and carefully turning once. Cook the sausages, turning, until lightly charred on edges, about 10 minutes.
5. When the sausages and vegetables are nearly done, brush the cut sides of rolls with some of the crushed pepper–butter mixture. Put on the grill, cut side down, until lightly toasted, 1 to 2 minutes.
6. To assemble the sandwiches, cut the sausages into thin diagonal slices. Remove the stems and seeds from the peppers and cut into ½-inch slices. Separate the onions into rings. Brush the bottom half of each roll with some more of the crushed pepper–butter mixture. Divide the sausages, peppers, and onions among the rolls. Drizzle with the remaining butter mixture and add the tops of the rolls.

Yield: 4 servings

DOUBLE-BARBECUED RIBS

Ribs are the quintessential barbecue food, but getting the perfect texture and flavor is a problem for the home cook. So our recipe combines slow cooking in the oven and quick grilling over the outdoor grill to give both the tender, succulent texture and the smoky, charred flavor that mean real ribs.

Barbecue Sauce

2 *cloves garlic, chopped*
1 *small dried hot red pepper*
1½ *teaspoons chopped fresh coriander (optional)*
½ *teaspoon ground cumin*
½ *teaspoon aniseed*
½ *teaspoon salt*
2 *tablespoons brown sugar*
1 *tablespoon Worcestershire sauce*
1 *cup cider vinegar*
2 *cups Catsup (see recipe, Chapter 16)*
  Tabasco sauce (optional)

4 *pounds country-style pork ribs, cut into 4 to 6 serving pieces*

1. In a blender or food processor, combine the garlic, red pepper, coriander, cumin, aniseed, salt, brown sugar, and Worcestershire sauce. Process until smooth.
2. Put the mixture into a saucepan and add the vinegar and catsup. Bring the liquid to a boil, reduce heat, and simmer, uncovered, for 30 minutes. Add Tabasco to taste, if desired.
3. Heat the oven to 300°F.
4. Arrange the ribs in a single layer in a baking pan. Pour the sauce over the ribs so that all portions are covered. Cover the baking pan with aluminum foil and bake until the meat is tender, 1 to 1½ hours.
5. Heat the grill to medium hot.
6. Using tongs, remove the ribs from the sauce and reserve the sauce. Grill the ribs, adding wood chips to the fire if desired. Cook for 5 to 10 minutes, turning so that both sides are crusty and charred. Skim any fat from the reserved sauce and serve the sauce on the side.

Yield: 4 to 6 servings

CRABS GRILLED ON A BED OF SEAWEED WITH FRESH GINGER SAUCE

The blue crab is one of the East coast's most abundant and delicious shellfish. Depending on the region, the season runs from spring through late summer, when both hard- and soft-shell crabs are usually plentiful in fish markets. The Fresh Ginger Sauce adds an Oriental touch to this all-American favorite.

1. Combine all sauce ingredients in a small bowl and set aside at room temperature for 30 minutes.
2. Heat the grill. Line a wire grill basket with a thin layer of seaweed if using.
3. Plunge the crabs into a large pot of rapidly boiling water for 2 minutes.
4. Put the crabs in the prepared basket and cook for 5 minutes longer. Serve at once with ginger sauce on the side.

Yield: 4 servings

Note: Seaweed can be purchased at fish shops and wherever crabs are sold. Or you can gather it yourself.

Fresh Ginger Sauce

4 teaspoons minced fresh ginger
4 scallions, minced
2 cloves garlic, crushed
6 tablespoons soy sauce
2 tablespoons hoisin sauce
½ to ¾ teaspoon Chinese hot pepper oil
    or Tabasco sauce
2 tablespoons dry sherry
½ teaspoon sugar

½ pound moist seaweed (optional) (see
    Note)
24 medium-sized blue crabs

MAPLE-AND-COB-SMOKED HAM

Maple twigs or chips and a corn cob give this ham its special flavor. The two are a natural pair, and some fuel packagers bag them together. Or you can collect and save your own.

1. With a sharp knife, score the top (fatty side) of the ham in a diamond pattern. Stud each diamond with a clove.
2. In a bowl, combine all the glaze ingredients. Spread the mixture over the ham. Set aside at room temperature for at least 2 hours.
3. Soak maple twigs or chips in water for at least 30 minutes. Heat the grill. Put a drip pan in the center of the grill and arrange coals around it. Add a few soaked maple twigs or chips to the drip pan.
4. The fire should be fairly low. Smoke the ham over the drip pan, covered, with the vents halfway open, for 30 minutes. Remove the cover and grid with the ham. Add more maple twigs or chips to the drip pan along with a corn cob. Put the ham back on the grill and cover. Continue to cook until the internal temperature reads 140°F, about 30 minutes more. Add about ¼ cup water to the flavoring wood whenever smoke stops coming through the vents.
5. Slice the ham and serve it garnished with apricots if you like.

Yield: 8 servings

1 4-pound, ham, fully cooked
    Whole cloves
Glaze

1 cup apricot jam
2 tablespoons Dijon mustard
1 large clove garlic, crushed
2 tablespoons soy sauce
1 tablespoon vinegar
1 tablespoon orange juice
¼ teaspoon salt

Apricots, halved and pitted (optional)

PIQUANT PRODIGAL LAMB

A covered grill as used in this recipe is a big help in cooking roasts and similar cuts, because it decreases the flaming and makes longer cooking possible. Our mint and cucumber sauces make this lamb dish a refreshing summertime treat.

Marinade

2 cups plain yogurt
4 cloves garlic, crushed
½ cup chopped fresh mint
¼ teaspoon black pepper

1 3½- to 4-pound leg of lamb, boned and butterflied
Mint leaves for garnish (optional)
Cold Cucumber Sauce and/or Spicy Mint Sauce (recipes follow)

1. Combine all the marinade ingredients in a bowl.
2. Pat the lamb dry and put in a nonreactive pan. Spoon the marinade over both sides of the lamb and cover with plastic wrap. Refrigerate for 8 to 16 hours.
3. Heat the grill. Put a drip pan in the center of the grill and arrange coals around it.
4. Drain lamb, reserving marinade. Put the lamb on the rack over the drip pan and cook, covered, with vents about three-quarters open, for 15 minutes. Baste with some of the reserved marinade. Cook for an additional 10 minutes. Turn the lamb over and baste once more. Continue to cook, covered, until the lamb is just about done, about 10 minutes for medium-rare.
5. Remove the cover and rack with the lamb. Remove the drip pan and push coals to the center of the grill. Return the rack and lamb to the fire and cook, uncovered, over direct heat until lightly browned, about 4 minutes per side. The internal temperature should read between 135° and 145°F for medium-rare.
6. Garnish with mint leaves and serve with the cold cucumber sauce and/or the spicy mint sauce.

Yield: 6 servings

For indirect heat, put the drip pan in the center of the grill with coals around it.

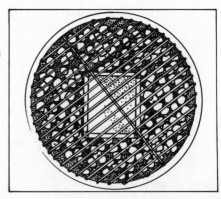

1. Put the cucumber into a colander and sprinkle with salt, vinegar, and sugar. Let stand for 30 minutes and then rinse with cold water. Drain, pressing out excess liquid with the back of a spoon.
2. In a bowl, beat the sour cream with mustard until light. Beat in the shallot, add the drained cucumber, and chill until ready to serve.

Yield: about 1½ cups

1. In a nonreactive saucepan, combine the chicken stock, vinegar, and sugar. Bring to a boil, stirring to dissolve the sugar.
2. Put ¾ cup mint in a bowl. Pour the chicken stock mixture over the mint leaves and steep for 1 to 1½ hours.
3. Strain, pushing the mint with the back of a spoon to extract the juice. Stir in the crushed peppers and the remaining 2 tablespoons mint leaves. Serve at room temperature.

Yield: about 1¾ cups

COLD CUCUMBER SAUCE

1 cucumber, peeled, seeded, and cut into small dice (about ¾ cup)
½ teaspoon salt
½ teaspoon red wine vinegar
Pinch of sugar
1 cup sour cream
1 teaspoon Dijon mustard
1 shallot, minced

SPICY MINT SAUCE

½ cup Chicken Stock (see recipe, chapter 3)
½ cup white wine vinegar
¼ cup sugar
¾ cup plus 2 tablespoons chopped fresh mint leaves
½ teaspoon crushed dried hot red pepper

GRILLED BEEF KEBABS CARIBBEAN-STYLE

The American melting pot is a sociological term, but it's a perfect image for contemporary American cooking styles as well. Kebabs are Middle Eastern in origin but experienced great popularity in our U.S. suburbs during the 1950s. We've updated this backyard classic with some flavors from one of our most recent sources of culinary inspiration—the Caribbean.

  1 coconut
 ½ teaspoon grated fresh ginger
  1 teaspoon crushed dried hot red pepper
 ¼ cup vegetable oil
 ¼ cup light rum
1¼ to 1½ pounds sirloin steak, cut into
      1½-inch cubes
  1 clove garlic
 12 scallions, trimmed to within 2 inches
      of white part
  2 seedless oranges, peeled and quartered

1. To open the coconut, pierce the "eyes" with a skewer or screwdriver. Drain off the liquid and reserve. Put the coconut in a 350°F oven for 15 to 20 minutes. Tap the coconut in several places with a hammer to loosen the shell. Split the shell with a sharp blow from the hammer. Remove the meat. Pare off the skin with a sharp knife. Grate ¼ cup coconut and break the rest into roughly 2-inch chunks.
2. In a nonreactive dish, combine the coconut liquid, grated coconut, ginger, crushed pepper, oil, and rum.
3. Add the sirloin cubes and bury the garlic clove in the center of the meat cubes. Cover with plastic wrap and refrigerate for 4 hours, stirring occasionally.
4. Heat the grill.
5. Thread the meat, scallions, orange quarters, and coconut chunks onto 4 skewers, beginning and ending each skewer with coconut. Reserve the meat marinade.
6. Grill the kebabs over medium-hot heat until the meat is done medium-rare, turning frequently and brushing with the reserved marinade, about 8 minutes in all.

Yield: 4 servings

PORTERHOUSE STEAK GRILLED OVER HERBS AND GARLIC

In a John Wayne world, all the backyard cooking would be done by men, and their dish of choice would be the porterhouse steak—perhaps with a Mexican hot sauce like our Chimichurri to make faint hearts flutter and weak eyes tear. We like the real world better than the macho fantasy, but even so, on some summer days a porterhouse steak is the right stuff—no matter who cooks it.

1. Heat the grill.
2. Score the fat around the steak. Fold the tail against the main body of the steak and attach with a small skewer or toothpick.
3. Brush the steak very lightly with oil and sprinkle with pepper. Cook on a rack over hot coals, uncovered, for 3 to 4 minutes. Turn the steak, sprinkle with salt, and cook for 3 more minutes.
4. Moisten the garlic and 4 or 5 sprigs thyme and/or oregano with water and scatter over the coals. Cover the grill and cook for 5 to 6 minutes more on each side for a medium-rare steak. Garnish with additional herb sprigs if you like and serve with chimichurri sauce.

Yield: 4 servings

Score the fat around the steak and then attach the tail to the rest of the steak with a skewer or large toothpick.

1 2-pound porterhouse steak, 1½ to 2
    inches thick
1½ teaspoons vegetable oil
    Salt and black pepper
3 or 4 cloves garlic, unpeeled
    Sprigs of fresh thyme and/or oregano
    (optional)
    Chimichurri Sauce (recipe follows)

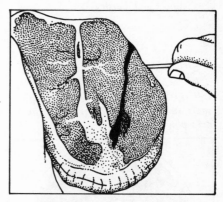

1. In a small bowl, whisk together all the ingredients.
2. Set aside for at least 30 minutes, or for a hotter sauce refrigerate for several days.

Yield: about 1⅓ cups

CHIMICHURRI SAUCE

⅔ cup lemon juice
6 tablespoons vegetable oil
2 fresh cherry peppers or jalapeño
    peppers, seeds and ribs removed,
    flesh minced
1 small onion, minced
3 tablespoons minced fresh parsley

SMOKED TROUT WITH HORSERADISH-PARSLEY BUTTER

Smoking can be done in a covered kettle grill or in a real smoker. In a smoker, racks hold the food over a pan. Either water or another liquid such as wine can be put in the pan to keep the smoky air, and hence the cooking food, moist. Add aromatics such as spices, herbs, or orange zest to the liquid if you like. The charcoal pan at the very bottom holds the source of heat, and wood chips—apple, hickory, or mesquite, for example—or grapevine cuttings will add their own distinctive flavors.

½ *cup coarse salt*
4 *quarts water*
4 *½-pound trout, cleaned, boned, and butterflied*

Horseradish-Parsley Butter

6 *tablespoons unsalted butter, softened*
1½ *to 2 tablespoons grated fresh horseradish*
Minced fresh parsley

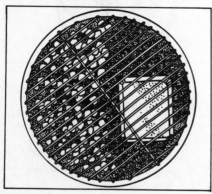

For the lowest indirect heat, arrange coals on one side of the grill and the drip pan on the other.

1. In a nonreactive pan large enough to hold the fish, dissolve the salt in the water. Add the trout and more water if necessary to cover the fish. Cover and refrigerate for 24 hours.
2. For the horseradish-parsley butter, beat the butter with the horseradish in a bowl until well combined. Cover the bowl with plastic wrap and chill for about 2 hours. Divide the mixture into 8 parts and roll each part into a ball. Roll in the parsley to cover completely. Chill the butter balls on a plate and cover until needed.
3. Soak hickory chips in cold water for 30 minutes. Heat the grill. Push all the coals to one side of the grill. The fire should be fairly low. Put a drip pan on the other side of the grill and add a handful of the soaked hickory chips to the pan.
4. Put the fish on a rack over the drip pan, skin side down. Cover the grill and smoke the fish until it is golden and just tests done, about 40 minutes. Add more soaked chips as needed to make smoke.
5. Remove the fish from the grill and put 2 balls of horseradish-parsley butter on top of each fish.

Yield: 4 servings

Notes: The fish can also be served cold with a mayonnaise sauce rather than butter. If serving cold, wrap the hot fish in foil to preserve moisture, cool, then chill until ready to serve.

Whole, dressed trout of any size up to 2 pounds can be cooked in the same manner as in this recipe. For larger fish, however, increase the cooking time to about 45 minutes, but rarely any longer or the fish will be overcooked.

SMOKED AND SIZZLED CORNISH GAME HENS

1. For the marinade, whir all the ingredients in a food processor until smooth. Pour the marinade over the hens and refrigerate, skin side down, for 8 to 12 hours.
2. Heat the grill. Put a drip pan in the center of the grill and arrange the coals around it.
3. Drain the hens, reserving the marinade. Put the hens, skin side up, on the rack over the drip pan and cook, covered, with the vents about halfway open, basting every 15 minutes with the marinade until almost done, about 1¼ hours. Add coals every 30 minutes to maintain heat.
4. For the sauce, combine all the ingredients except the sesame oil in a small saucepan. Bring to a boil, reduce heat, and simmer over medium-low heat for 4 minutes. Strain into a heatproof bowl and whisk in the sesame oil.
5. Remove the cover and rack with the hens. Remove the drip pan and push the coals to the center of the grill. Return the hens and cook, uncovered, over direct heat until almost blackened, about 5 minutes per side. Transfer to a serving platter and brush with the sauce. Serve hot or cold garnished with coriander sprigs.

Yield: 4 to 6 servings

Marinade

	Grated zest of 1 lemon
	Grated zest of 1 orange
½	cup soy sauce
½	cup oyster sauce
½	teaspoon chopped fresh ginger
2	cloves garlic
1	tablespoon chopped fresh coriander leaves
¼	teaspoon black pepper
1	small bay leaf
2	tablespoons honey

3	Cornish game hens, split, backbones removed, and hens pressed flat

Sauce

2	teaspoons vegetable oil
1	large clove garlic, minced
1	teaspoon minced fresh ginger
¼	teaspoon crushed dried hot red peppers
2	shallots, minced
1	scallion, minced
1	tablespoon soy sauce
1	teaspoon red wine vinegar
2	tablespoons brown sugar
1½	tablespoons water
2	tablespoons sesame oil

Coriander sprigs

WOOD-SMOKED TURKEY WITH TWO SAUCES

1 *12- to 16-pound turkey, trussed (see illustrations, Chapter 5, Roast Goose Stuffed with Wild Rice and Cranberries)*
¼ *cup peanut oil*
   Salt and black pepper
   Mustard Mousse Sauce (recipe follows)
   Burgundy Cherry Sauce (recipe follows)

1. Heat the smoker according to manufacturer's instructions for cooking a whole bird. Soak wood chips in water.
2. Rub the turkey all over with oil and sprinkle lightly with salt and pepper.
3. Put the turkey on the grill, breast side up, and cook, covered, for about 30 minutes. Add the moistened wood chips and continue to cook until the internal temperature reaches 185°F, about 15 minutes per pound. Add more coals and wood chips to the fire as needed. Be careful that the moisture doesn't evaporate so that an even cooking temperature and a moist, smoky environment is maintained throughout the cooking period. Avoid opening the smoker unnecessarily.
4. Cover the turkey loosely with foil and allow to stand at room temperature for about 15 minutes before carving into thin slices. The turkey can be served warm or at room temperature.
5. To serve, arrange 3 or 4 slices of turkey in the center of each plate. Put a dollop of each sauce on either side of the turkey.

Yield: 8 to 10 servings

MUSTARD MOUSSE SAUCE

3 *tablespoons dry mustard*
2 *tablespoons crushed mustard seeds*
⅓ *cup white wine vinegar*
¼ *cup dry vermouth*
2 *tablespoons honey*
1 *teaspoon salt*
1 *teaspoon minced fresh tarragon, or ¼ teaspoon dried tarragon*
2 *eggs*
½ *cup heavy cream*

1. In a small bowl, combine the dry mustard, mustard seeds, vinegar, and vermouth. Cover and let stand for 8 to 12 hours.
2. Stir in the honey, salt, and tarragon.
3. Over low heat, whisk the eggs in the top of a double boiler set over hot water until very light and foamy. Whisk in the mustard mixture and cook, stirring occasionally, until thickened, 25 to 30 minutes. Remove from heat and cool. (At this point, the mustard mousse may be kept, refrigerated, up to 1 week.)
4. Shortly before serving, whip the cream to soft peaks and fold into the mustard mousse.

Yield: about 2 cups

1. In a saucepan, combine all the ingredients except the cherries and cornstarch. Bring to a boil, stirring to dissolve the sugar. Reduce heat and add the cherries. Poach gently until the cherries are tender, 5 to 10 minutes.
2. Remove the cherries with a slotted spoon and set aside. Remove and discard the cinnamon stick.
3. Over medium heat, bring the wine mixture back to a boil and cook until reduced to about 1¼ cups, 8 to 10 minutes. Whisk in the cornstarch and cook, stirring, about 2 minutes. Strain over the cherries and stir. Serve warm or at room temperature.

Yield: about 3 cups

BURGUNDY CHERRY SAUCE

2½ cups red Burgundy wine
⅓ cup sugar
1 2-inch strip lemon zest
1 bay leaf
3 whole cloves
3 whole peppercorns
3 whole allspice berries, or *pinch of ground allspice*
1 2-inch cinnamon stick
1 pound Bing cherries, pitted
1 teaspoon cornstarch dissolved in 1 tablespoon cold water

Salads: Cold, Warm, and Main Course

ince the turn of the century, salads have been among the touchstones of American cooking. Evidently it was only after the Civil War that Americans took to serious salad eating, but once they did, they never stopped. The 1896 edition of *Fannie Farmer's Boston Cooking School Cook Book*, for instance, notes that just a few years before its publication salads were rarely seen on American tables but that by then had become "a course in almost every dinner." And even in 1896 it was pretty clear why Americans were attracted to salads. The basic features are the same today: Salads can be made in unlimited combinations, they are light and refreshing, and they are seemingly among the healthiest, if not the most nutritious, of foods.

All through this century we've continued to create new kinds of salads and salad dressings. Salads represent the invention and individuality in our culinary style. From Waldorf Salad, created at the Waldorf-Astoria in New York for the hotel's opening in 1893, to a new salad like our Asparagus and Red Pepper with Orange Zest, American cooks have pushed the limits of what defines a salad, always moving beyond the mass taste—even if the new creation then becomes a popular success and ultimately a cliché. One of the most successful commercial innovations of the last twenty years has been the salad bar, where each person becomes his or her own salad chef. And we've become more enamored with the way of living a salad seems to represent. Salads appeal to our love of the casual, the informal, the healthy, and, especially recently, to our somewhat puritanical struggle against gastronomic excess.

KINDS OF SALADS

While it's easy enough to say the salad is an essential part of contemporary American cuisine, it's a little harder to say just what defines a salad. Most salads are still meant to be served cold, but some—such as our Morel Salad on Steamed Spring Lettuce, Potato Salad with Sugar Snap Peas and Bacon Dressing, and Two Chicken Balsamico—are to be served warm. It's generally agreed that there are two kinds of salads—simple salads and composed salads, though starchy salads like bean or potato don't really fit into either category.

Simple Salads

Simple salads are usually lettuce or other greens with dressing—classically a vinaigrette, but often in the United States a creamy concoction, such as Thousand Island or blue cheese. There's a considerable lore about how to make the perfect tossed dinner salad, ranging from what sort of greens to pick and how to cut them to what kind of bowl to use and the exact proportions of a particular vinegar and oil needed for the ideal dressing. Much of this is nonsense. The best rules are the simplest ones. Choose the freshest greens available. Wash them and handle them carefully. Use good-quality vinegar and oil for the dressing and enough salt and pepper. That's all.

Simple salads can feature any of a wide variety of greens now available in supermarkets. The most popular types are iceberg (which is really suitable only shredded on top of tacos), Boston or butter lettuce, romaine, bibb lettuce, and curly green or red lettuce. But other greens besides lettuce can make a salad—cabbage, watercress, Belgian endive, spinach, arugula, and dandelion leaves can all be salad greens. And of course you can make various additions to the salad and still keep it, in theory at least, a simple salad. Shredded carrots, beets, tomatoes, sliced onions, mushrooms, croutons, cheese, bacon, boiled eggs, celery, and even beans are just the most common salad ingredients. We've seen salads that include all of the above, but in general have managed to avoid eating them.

Composed Salads

From a culinary standpoint, the simple salad can be a delight, but it's not nearly so interesting a thing to construct as what's called a composed salad, one in which several different types of ingredients are tossed or otherwise arranged together, a *salade Niçoise*, for instance. Composed salads can be served in place of a simple salad as a first course in a meal, or they can be a main course.

While tradition and classicism mark the best simple salads, composed salads are a fantasy realm. The first impact of California cuisine on the rest of the United States may have been in the early decades of this century when a series of creative composed salads tumbled out of the land of eternal sunshine and onto the plates of middle America—Cobb's Salad (invented at the Brown Derby in 1936), Crab Louis (a San Francisco original), even the very idea of a main course chef's salad.

As with much culinary art, the production of a successful composed salad is a matter of experience and style rather than rule. First think seriously about ingredient combinations. One good guideline to remember is that most ingredients that work together in a hot dish—say sausage and peppers, chicken and broccoli, corned beef and cabbage—will work together in a tepid or cold salad. A salad is an admirable vehicle for leftovers, but beware the temptation to clean out the refrigerator or the salad will look and taste just like what it is—a tawdry, leftover melange. Add carefully thought-out fresh vegetables and herbs to that bit of roast chicken or braised beef from yesterday, and you can make a new star dish. By the same token, don't let yourself be carried away with the mix-and-match syndrome. A salad should be a marriage of flavors and textures, not a baroque assemblage of every taste imaginable. Keep a central flavor focus for every salad and then play to that focus with a few complementary ingredients. Innovations like our Two Chicken Balsamico and Lamb and White Bean Salad are good models to follow.

While greens are not usually as central for a composed salad as for simple salads, they often play a role, especially for texture and color. Consider the color of the greens and of other ingredients, too, as part of the overall effect. Don't forget that much of the glamour of a good composed salad lies in the presentation. With a salad, perhaps more than any other dish, the eye does a lot of the eating.

MESCLUN SALAD

Derived from a Niçoise word for "mixture," the term *mesclun*
originally referred to a combination of young wild greens,
traditionally including frizzy escarole, wild chicory, lamb's
lettuce, and dandelion.

Vinaigrette

- 1 *clove garlic, crushed with a pinch of salt*
- 2 *shallots, cut into small dice*
- 3 *tablespoons strong red wine vinegar*
  Few drops balsamic vinegar or *squeeze of lemon juice*
- ½ *cup fruity extra-virgin olive oil, plus more if necessary*
  Salt and black pepper

Salad

- 1 *handful each of 6 very young salad greens, such as red and green lettuces, curly endive, rocket, chervil, and green chicory (about 1½ quarts)*

1. For the vinaigrette, combine the garlic-salt mixture, shallots, red wine vinegar, and balsamic vinegar or lemon juice in a bowl and let stand for a few minutes.
2. In a slow, steady stream, add the oil, whisking continuously. Season to taste with salt and pepper.
3. Put the greens into a large salad bowl and toss with just enough vinaigrette to coat lightly. Serve immediately.

Yield: 6 servings

WARM MOREL SALAD ON STEAMED SPRING LETTUCE

- 6 *ounces small fresh morels, or 2 ounces dried morels*
- ¼ *cup olive oil*
- 1 *tablespoon red wine vinegar*
- 1 *shallot, minced*
- 1 *tablespoon minced fresh parsley*
  Salt and black pepper
- 2 *tablespoons unsalted butter*
- 16 *large curly lettuce leaves*

1. Carefully wash the morels under running water until all the sand is removed. Or, if using dried morels, reconstitute them in water to cover for about 30 minutes. Drain on paper towels and set aside.
2. In a bowl, mix 2 tablespoons olive oil, vinegar, shallot, and parsley. Season to taste with salt and pepper and set aside.
3. In a frying pan over medium-high heat, warm the remaining 2 tablespoons olive oil and cook the morels, stirring constantly, until they are coated with olive oil and heated through, 3 to 5 minutes. Season to taste with salt and pepper. Transfer the morels to the dressing, toss, and set aside.
4. In a large frying pan over low heat, melt the butter,

add the lettuce, season with salt and pepper, cover, and cook until the leaves are limp but still bright green, 1 to 2 minutes.
5. Arrange 4 lettuce leaves on each salad plate and top with mushrooms. Serve immediately.

Yield: 4 servings

ASPARAGUS AND RED PEPPER WITH ORANGE ZEST

1. Cut the roasted pepper lengthwise into ⅛-inch-wide strips.
2. Bring a small saucepan of water to a boil, add the zest, and blanch for 5 minutes. Drain well, cut horizontally into fine shreds, and set aside.
3. In a pan large enough to hold all the asparagus lying flat, bring enough salted water to cover the asparagus spears to a boil. Add spears and cook, uncovered, until just done, about 4 minutes. Lift out with tongs and drain well on paper towels.
4. In a bowl, whisk together the vinegar, salt, and mustard. Still whisking, add the oil in a thin stream, and then the pepper and chives.
5. To serve, arrange the asparagus on salad plates with all tips pointing in one direction. Arrange the red pepper strips over the asparagus in 2 diagonal rows that cross in the center and point toward the tips of asparagus, forming a herringbone pattern.
6. Just before serving, spoon the vinaigrette over the salad top and sprinkle zest over all. Serve at room temperature.

Yield: 4 servings

1 small (about 4 ounces) red pepper, roasted
Zest from ½ orange, pared off in ½-inch-wide strips
1 pound asparagus, ends snapped off and stalks peeled (see illustrations, Chapter 10, Asparagus with Lemon Beurre Rouge)
1½ tablespoons red wine vinegar
¼ teaspoon salt
½ teaspoon Dijon mustard
6 tablespoons peanut oil
⅛ teaspoon black pepper
1 tablespoon chopped fresh chives

LAMB AND WHITE-BEAN SALAD

5 tablespoons red wine vinegar
2½ tablespoons chopped fresh mint, or 2
    teaspoons dried mint
2 teaspoons chopped fresh thyme leaves,
    or ½ teaspoon dried thyme
  Salt and black pepper
1 cup virgin olive oil
8 thin slices cooked lamb, trimmed of fat
1 cup dried white beans, rinsed and
    picked over
1 ham bone
1 small red onion, halved
⅓ cup chopped fresh flat-leaf parsley
¼ cup pumate (sun-dried tomatoes in
    oil), sliced into ⅛-inch × 1½-
    inch julienne strips

1. Put the vinegar, mint, thyme, and salt and pepper in a small bowl. Add the olive oil in a slow stream, whisking continuously.
2. Put the lamb slices in a shallow nonreactive dish and cover with ¾ cup of the dressing. Cover and marinate in the refrigerator for 8 to 24 hours.
3. While the lamb is marinating, put the beans in a small bowl, cover with cold water by at least 2 inches. Bring to a boil, skim off any foam, and cook for 2 minutes. Remove from heat and set aside for 1 hour.
4. Drain the beans, cover again with water by at least 2 inches. Add the ham bone and bring to a boil, skimming off any foam that rises to the top. Reduce heat, cover, and simmer until the beans are tender, about 40 minutes. Drain and remove the bone.
5. Toss the hot beans with the remaining dressing. Mince half of the onion and add to the beans. Season with salt and pepper and chopped parsley. Toss carefully, set aside, and cool to room temperature.
6. Cut the remaining half onion into thin slices. Soak the onion in cold water to crisp. Drain well.
7. To serve, spread the beans on a platter and top with the lamb slices, onion slices, and pumate.

Yield: 4 servings

CREAMY THREE-CABBAGE SLAW

Traditional American cole slaw is a bit sweet, a bit sour, and often made, as in our recipe, with old-fashioned boiled dressing.

1. For the dressing, combine the flour, mustard, cayenne, ½ teaspoon salt, and sugar in a large, heavy saucepan. Whisk in about 2 tablespoons milk to make a paste. Over medium-low heat, gradually whisk in the remaining milk and cook, stirring, until thickened and smooth, about 5 minutes.
2. In a small bowl, whisk together the vinegar, lemon juice, and egg yolk. Whisk about half of the hot milk mixture into the vinegar mixture and then return to the saucepan. Cook, stirring, over low heat until smooth and thickened, about 3 minutes. The mixture should be the consistency of thin mayonnaise. Do not boil. Stir in the celery seed and remove from heat. Season with salt and pepper to taste. Cool and then stir in the crème fraîche or sour cream.
3. For the slaw, combine all the salad ingredients in a large bowl.
4. Toss the slaw with the dressing. Cover and chill for 2 to 4 hours before serving.

Yield: 4 servings

Dressing

1½ teaspoons flour
½ teaspoon dry mustard
 Pinch of cayenne
 Salt and black pepper
1 tablespoon sugar
½ cup milk
1½ tablespoons cider vinegar
1 tablespoon lemon juice
1 egg yolk
¼ teaspoon celery seed
¼ cup crème fraîche (see Chapter 1, Stuffed Pea Pods, Note) or sour cream

Slaw

1½ cups shredded green cabbage
1½ cups shredded red cabbage
1 cup shredded savoy cabbage
1 green bell pepper, sliced thin
½ cup sliced radishes
¼ small red onion, minced
½ carrot, grated
 Salt and black pepper

Before shredding cabbage, cut the head in half vertically and remove the core.

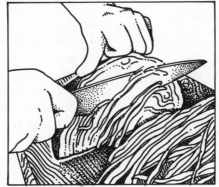

To shred cabbage, put the flat side of half the head down and cut into thin strips.

WARM POTATO SALAD WITH SUGAR SNAP PEAS AND BACON DRESSING

1 *pound small new potatoes*
2 *ounces sugar snap peas, trimmed and cut into 1-inch diagonal slices*
¼ *pound double-smoked bacon, diced*
1½ *tablespoons red wine vinegar*
1 *teaspoon Dijon mustard*
   Salt and black pepper
   Chopped fresh chives (optional)

1. In a saucepan, cook the potatoes in boiling salted water until just tender, 12 to 15 minutes. Peel, cut into ¼-inch slices, and keep warm in a covered, non-reactive dish.
2. Bring a small saucepan of salted water to a boil and blanch the snap peas until just tender, 3 to 5 minutes. Drain and keep warm along with the potatoes.
3. In a heavy frying pan, cook the bacon until crisp and golden. Remove with a slotted spoon and drain on paper towels. Discard all but ½ cup bacon fat.
4. Over low heat, stir the vinegar and mustard into the bacon fat to blend. Season with salt and pepper to taste and pour over potatoes and peas.
5. Add the reserved bacon to the salad and toss very gently; sprinkle with chives if desired. Serve immediately.

Yield: 4 servings

PINTO BEAN AND PARSLEY SALAD

½ *clove garlic, crushed with a pinch of salt*
2 *tablespoons virgin olive oil*
1⅓ *cups dried pinto beans, rinsed and picked over*
   Salt and black pepper
1 *cup chopped fresh parsley*
2½ *tablespoons minced fresh coriander leaves*
2 *small red bell peppers, chopped*
2 *ribs celery, minced*
4 *scallions, chopped, some green parts included*
2 *teaspoons minced hot chile pepper*
¼ *cup lemon juice*
4 *to 6 drops Tabasco sauce*

1. Combine the garlic-salt mixture with the olive oil in a large bowl. Set aside.
2. In a large saucepan, cover the beans with water by at least 2 inches. Bring to a boil, skim off any foam, and cook for 2 minutes. Remove from heat and set aside for 1 hour.
3. Drain the beans, cover with 2 inches water, and return to heat. Add 2 teaspoons salt, bring to a boil, skim off any foam, and reduce heat. Cook until the beans are just tender, 30 to 40 minutes. Drain.
4. Combine the beans with the garlic paste and mix well. Add the remaining ingredients and mix well. Season to taste with salt and pepper. Macerate for 2 hours before serving, tossing occasionally.

Yield: 4 to 6 servings

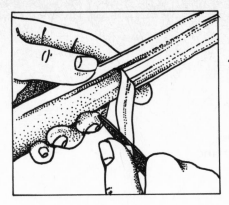

To chop celery, first peel the tough outer fibers from the celery ribs.

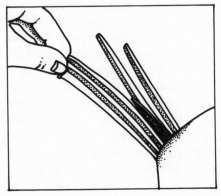

Slice the celery ribs lengthwise into strips.

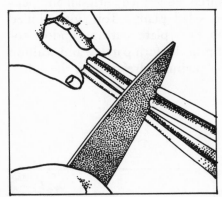

Cut the celery strips in half crosswise and stack together.

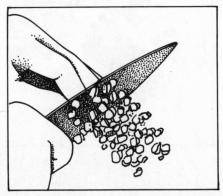

Finally, cut crosswise into dice.

SEAFOOD LOUIS

Our version of the famed salad that is synonymous with Pacific Dungeness crab and San Francisco's Fisherman's Wharf. Two restaurants in San Francisco lay claim to the invention of the dish—the now defunct Solari restaurant and the restaurant in the St. James Hotel.

Dressing

   1 *egg, room temperature*
   1 *egg yolk, room temperature*
  ¼ *teaspoon Dijon mustard*
      Salt
   1 *tablespoon lemon juice*
   5 *tablespoons olive oil*
   5 *tablespoons vegetable oil*
  ½ *cup Chili Sauce (see recipe, Chapter 16)*
   2 *to 3 drops Tabasco sauce*
  ¾ *teaspoon Worcestershire sauce*
  ½ *small green bell pepper, minced*
  ½ *rib celery, minced*
   1 *small shallot, minced*
   3 *tablespoons heavy cream, whipped to soft peaks*

Salad

   2 *cups cooked crabmeat or a combination of cooked crab, lobster, and/or shrimp*
   2 *cups shredded romaine lettuce*
   2 *cups shredded red leaf lettuce*
      Salt and black pepper
   2 *small ripe avocados, quartered and tossed with lemon juice*
   2 *small tomatoes, peeled (see illustration, Chapter 16, Chili Sauce), seeded, and quartered*
   2 *eggs, hard-cooked and quartered*
  1½ *tablespoons minced fresh parsley*
   1 *scallion, minced*

To shred leaf lettuce, separate the leaves from the head and wash and dry them. Then pile up several at once and cut through the stack into thin strips.

1. For the dressing, whir the egg, egg yolk, mustard, salt, and lemon juice in a food processor for about 10 seconds. Add the oils in a thin, steady stream through the feed tube with the machine running. Add the chili sauce, Tabasco, Worcestershire sauce, green bell pepper, celery, and shallot. Cover and chill for 2 to 8 hours. Allow the dressing to come to room temperature and, just before using, fold in the whipped cream. Taste for seasoning.
2. Cut the crab or lobster into 1-inch pieces. Leave the shrimp whole. Toss the crabmeat or seafood combination with ¾ cup dressing. Cover and chill.
3. Lightly season the shredded lettuce with salt and pepper and arrange on salad plates. Top with chilled seafood and garnish each plate with avocados, tomatoes, and eggs. Sprinkle with parsley and scallion and serve with the remaining dressing on the side.

Yield: 4 servings

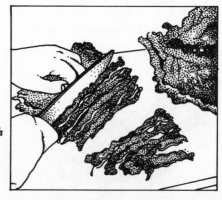

CHICKEN SALAD WITH BLUEBERRY-ORANGE VINAIGRETTE

Chicken salad has long been an all-American favorite. In the *Home Cook Book*, 1882 edition, six of the sixteen salad recipes were for chicken salad. About 100 years later, the *New York Times*' food section devoted a several-page lead article to scouting out the best chicken salads prepared in New York delicatessens and food shops. Here are two chicken salad recipes with a twist—one with a fruity vinaigrette and another that is warm and includes the livers.

1. For the vinaigrette, whisk the crème fraîche or sour cream, mustard, and blueberry-orange vinegar in a bowl. Season with salt and white pepper. Add the oil in a slow stream, whisking continuously. Adjust the seasonings and set aside.
2. In a large frying pan, arrange the chicken breasts in a single layer. Add enough cold water to cover the chicken by 1 inch and season lightly with salt. Bring to a simmer and poach until the chicken is just cooked through, 10 to 12 minutes. Do not allow the water to boil. Remove the chicken from the pan and cool slightly.
3. Pat the chicken dry and cut or tear meat into bite-size pieces.
4. In a mixing bowl, toss the chicken with half of the vinaigrette and let stand, covered, for 30 minutes.
5. Cut the orange zest strips horizontally into fine shreds. Add the orange zest shreds, scallions, celery, and walnuts to the chicken. Season with salt, pepper, and additional vinaigrette to taste. Just before serving, add blueberries and toss gently.

Yield: 4 servings

Diagonally cut vegetables are especially attractive.

Blueberry-Orange Vinaigrette

1½ teaspoons crème fraîche (see Chapter 1, *Stuffed Pea Pods*, Note) or sour cream
1½ teaspoons Dijon mustard
¼ cup Blueberry-Orange Vinegar (see recipe, Chapter 16)
Salt and white pepper
½ cup vegetable oil

Chicken Salad

3 skinned, boned chicken breasts, halved
Salt and black pepper
Zest of ½ orange, pared off in ½-inch-wide strips
2 whole scallions, sliced diagonally
2 ribs celery, sliced diagonally
½ cup broken walnuts
¾ cup blueberries

TWO-CHICKEN BALSAMICO

Herb Vinaigrette

4 teaspoons minced fresh tarragon
      leaves, or 1 teaspoon dried tarragon
2 teaspoons minced fresh savory leaves,
      or ½ teaspoon dried savory
2 teaspoons minced fresh chervil leaves,
      or ½ teaspoon dried chervil
5 tablespoons balsamic vinegar
   Salt and black pepper
¼ teaspoon ground cloves
¼ teaspoon ground coriander
2½ tablespoons virgin olive oil

Chicken

1½ teaspoons vegetable oil
1½ tablespoons virgin olive oil
3 shallots, minced
⅔ pound boned chicken breasts, cut into
      1-inch pieces
⅔ pound chicken livers, trimmed and
      halved if large
2 small heads radicchio
2 small Belgian endives
3 tablespoons toasted pine nuts (see
      Note)

1. For the dressing, combine the tarragon, savory, chervil, vinegar, 1 teaspoon salt, pepper to taste, cloves, and coriander in a bowl. Slowly whisk in the olive oil until well blended. Set aside.

2. For the chicken, pour the vegetable and olive oils into a frying pan large enough to hold all the chicken pieces without crowding. Add the shallots and sauté gently for about 3 minutes, being careful not to brown.

3. Add the chicken, raise heat to medium high, and cook, stirring, until all the pieces begin to turn golden, about 4 minutes. Add the chicken livers and sauté, tossing, until just cooked, 3 to 4 minutes. Remove the chicken and chicken livers and set aside.

4. Remove the pan from the heat and whisk the vinaigrette into the pan juices. Strain over the chicken and chicken livers and toss to combine.

5. To serve, arrange the radicchio leaves on salad plates and put the endive leaves around the edges. Put the warm chicken in the center of the radicchio and sprinkle with pine nuts.

Yield: 4 servings

Note: Toast the pine nuts in a 325°F oven until brown, 5 to 10 minutes.

Chapter

9 Pasta

We can hardly discount pasta's national heritage. However, Americans have enthusiastically adopted this Italian staple as one of their own. In fact, in recent years our fresh new approach to pasta has made it one of the primary showcases of innovative American cooking. Which is not to say that pasta is without a history here. Thomas Jefferson was probably the first American to fall under pasta's spell. He was fascinated by the tubular "maccarony" he saw for the first time in Naples. He returned to America with copious notes on pasta-producing procedures, as well as illustrated descriptions of macaroni–shaping machines. He ordered four crates of macaroni to be sent home, and he asked a friend to procure a machine so that he could produce his own. Despite Jefferson's evident enthusiasm, when his "maccarony" pie was served at the White House in 1802, it was not hailed a success by his guests.

A hundred years later, following a substantial influx of Italian immigrants, pasta began to appear more frequently. Around this time, pasta was being manufactured in New York, San Francisco, and Philadelphia. Spaghetti joints specializing in modest Italian home cooking began cropping up around the country, and acceptance gradually became more widespread. The decline in Italian imports at the outset of World War I, coupled with the introduction of Russian durum, a hard wheat high in gluten, greatly contributed to a dramatic increase in domestic pasta production. By the early 1950s, over one hundred fifty sizes and shapes were manufactured commercially in the United States.

There are two basic types of pasta dough: one is made with flour and eggs, and the other with semolina, which is milled from durum, and water. Homemade pasta and that sold commercially as "fresh" pasta are generally made from the first type of dough, while the majority of better-quality "dry" pastas are made from a paste of pure semolina and water. Semolina, milled from the wheat's yellowish endosperm, is coarser and grainier than highly refined flour, and it produces a pasta with a little more body and resilience, and more of a bite. Since semolina dough is considerably tough, elastic, and difficult to knead by hand, we do not recommend it for homemade pasta.

Fresh pasta, either homemade or store bought, is made with eggs and all-purpose flour. It is easily mixed and kneaded by hand, and the resulting dough has a rich yellow color. One of the advantages of making your own pasta is that you can color and flavor the basic dough to suit your taste or a specific recipe. Possible additions include chopped fresh herbs, resulting in flavorful green-speckled dough; pureed spinach; pureed beets, for brilliant magenta pasta that fades slightly during cooking; tomato paste, for salmon-colored dough; pureed green or red peppers; or saffron, for a vibrant yellow dish. If you decide to prepare any of these vegetable-puree variations, make sure to squeeze or drain the vegetables well to eliminate as much excess moisture as possible. In the event that your finished dough still feels sticky, knead in a little extra flour.

MAKING THE DOUGH

Pasta dough can easily be made on a marble slab, a pastry table, a large cutting board, or just on a counter top. Have your eggs at room temperature. Sifting the flour is by no means a must, but, especially in humid weather, it loosens the flour so that it will combine more readily with the eggs.

Mound the flour on your work surface and make a well in the center. Break the eggs into the well and beat them lightly with a fork or with your fingers; alternatively, you can beat the eggs in a separate bowl and then add them to the well. Any flavoring or coloring should be added to the well and combined with the beaten eggs. With one hand supporting the outer perimeter of the well, begin to incorporate the flour from around the inner wall. As the paste thickens, gradually work your way to the outer perimeter; try to keep the well intact until enough flour has been incorporated to prevent the egg mixture from seeping out. When the dough forms a cohesive ball, brush away any excess flour and begin kneading the dough with the heel of your hand. The dough should be neither sticky nor dry and crumbly. Continue kneading for 8 to 10 minutes or until the dough softens and feels pliable and elastic. Cover the dough and let it rest for a few minutes to several hours before rolling it out. The entire process can also be done in a large bowl.

Although making the dough by hand is relatively simple, it can also be accomplished in a food processor. Fit the processor with the steel blade and begin by blending the eggs and any flavorings you are using. Add the salt and 1 cup of flour and process for 10 seconds. Then, with the machine running, gradually add as much of the remaining flour as necessary until the dough forms a ball. Process for 45 seconds more, and then transfer the dough to a work surface and check its consistency, which should be silky-smooth, moist, and pliable, but not sticky. If the dough feels sticky, knead in a little extra flour by hand.

ROLLING THE DOUGH

Purists claim that hand-rolled pasta far surpasses the machine-rolled product, but rolling by hand requires strength, practice, and a fair amount of space. It is perfectly acceptable and certainly easier to turn out thin, even sheets with a hand-cranked pasta machine.

If you have prepared the basic recipe, split the dough

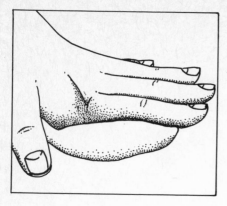

Flatten each ball of dough with your hand.

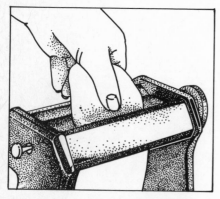

Feed the flattened dough into well-floured rollers of a pasta machine. Keep the machine's moving parts sprinkled with flour during the rolling and cutting process.

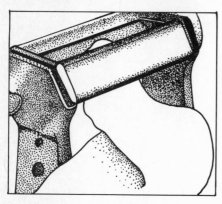

Roll the dough through the machine three or four times until it is smooth and has reached the desired thickness for the type of pasta you are making.

As the dough elongates, it will fold when it comes out of the machine.

into three even pieces and work with one at a time. Knead and flatten the dough slightly. Set the pasta machine on the widest notch (with the rollers as far apart as they will go) and feed the dough into the rollers at a 45 degree angle. Repeat this step at the same setting three or four times or until the dough becomes smooth and rectangular. Then roll the dough through each successive setting at least once until you have the desired thinness. Make sure as you feed the dough into the rollers that it remains as straight as possible, otherwise the dough will crease or wrinkle, and it may even tear. If, as the dough stretches and elongates, it becomes unwieldly, cut it in half and continue. Keep in mind that the width of the dough will always be about six inches.

Once the dough has been rolled out, you can cut or shape it as you wish. Standard rolling machines come with two dies, one for cutting thicker, fettuccine-type strands, and one for thinner, linguine-type ribbons. If you are preparing a filled pasta, like the Shrimp and Fennel Triangles or the Green Pepper Capelletti with Red Pepper Sauce that follow, it is advisable to roll out just one sheet of dough at a time to prevent it from drying out. Work as quickly as possible, cutting, filling, shaping, and sealing the dough. As long as the edges remain moist, they will adhere well, and the dough will not crack.

Pasta should ideally be made, cut, and cooked on the same day. However, you can wrap the rolled or unrolled dough in plastic and refrigerate it overnight or for a couple of days. Bring the dough to room temperature before rolling it through the machine. Pasta that has been rolled and cut can also be refrigerated; layer the strands or the filled shapes between dish towels or waxed paper, sprinkling each layer with a little coarse cornmeal before adding the next. The cornmeal will prevent the pasta from sticking together. To freeze cut pasta, spread the strands or shapes out on a cookie sheet and let them dry slightly. Put the cookie sheet into the freezer until the pasta is frozen solid. Remove the frozen pasta from the sheet and put it into a plastic bag or wrap well in plastic until you are ready to use it. It is unnecessary to thaw frozen pasta. Just cook it a bit longer than the time suggested for fresh.

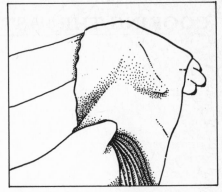

When the dough is ready to cut, it should be smooth and thin.

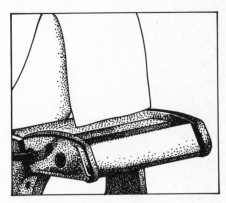

Be careful to hold the dough straight while you feed it into the pasta cutters.

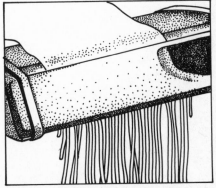

Hold the dough at a 45-degree angle when cutting it.

COOKING THE PASTA

All pasta (strands, sheets, and filled) should be cooked in a large pot of boiling well-salted water. You can add a tablespoon of cooking oil to the water to prevent the pasta from sticking together. Once the pasta has been added to the water, give it a good stir. Fresh pasta strands will cook in two to three minutes, while dry varieties will take longer. Perfectly cooked pasta should be *al dente*, literally "to the tooth." This means that the cooked strands or pockets should offer a little bit of resistance to the bite; yet the center should not be doughy, and there should be no taste of raw flour. Cooking times should be used only as a guide, and taste should be the ultimate determinant. When cooking pasta sheets that will be filled and baked, such as for the Cannelloni with Sun-Dried Tomato Sauce in this chapter, it is best to remove them from the pot *before* they are *al dente*; they will continue to cook in the oven.

As soon as the pasta is done, remove the pot from the heat and drain the contents in a colander. Pasta should be sauced and served immediately, since it cools rapidly and the strands or pockets begin to stick together. The sauce, garnishes, and accompaniments should all be ready when the pasta is cooked. Do not rinse the pasta. It is a good idea to heat the serving bowl and plates for a warm pasta dish. Remember that there should always be enough sauce to coat the pasta but never so much as to drown it.

SHRIMP AND FENNEL TRIANGLES

For this recipe and the Green Pepper Cappelletti with Red
Pepper Sauce, there are two things you should note about
filled pastas. When enclosing the fillings, make sure that the
dough edges do not quite meet. If they are sealed with one
edge slightly inside the other, they are less likely to split open
during cooking. If the dough has dried somewhat and does
not adhere properly, brush the edges with a little cold water.

1. Remove the stalks from the fennel. Reserve enough
   feathery leaves to make 2 tablespoons chopped greens.
   Chop and set aside. Cut the bulbs in half and cook
   them in a large pot of boiling water until tender, 6
   to 8 minutes. Drain well, mince, and set aside.
2. In a large frying pan, heat the butter. Sauté the shrimp
   just until they turn pink, 1 to 1½ minutes. Add the
   Madeira and cook on high heat 30 seconds. Remove
   from heat, cover, steep for 3 minutes, and uncover.
3. When the shrimp are cool enough to handle, peel,
   devein, set aside, and return the shells to frying pan.
   Pour heavy cream over the shells and cook gently
   until reduced to 1 cup, 5 to 10 minutes. Strain the
   liquid into a pot and discard the shells. Add the tomato paste and season with salt and pepper to taste.
   Simmer for 15 minutes. Set aside.
4. Mince the reserved shrimp and combine with the
   minced fennel bulbs and egg yolk. Season to taste
   with salt and pepper.
5. Roll the pasta dough as thin as possible. Cut into
   2″ - × - 2″ squares. Put a scant teaspoon of filling in
   the center of each square. Fold diagonally to form
   triangles with edges not quite meeting and seal with
   your fingers. Transfer them to a lightly floured towel
   in 1 layer, not touching each other.
6. Add the oil to a large pot of salted water and bring
   to a boil. Add the triangles and cook until *al dente*,
   about 3 minutes. Gently reheat the sauce. You may
   need to add a few tablespoons of cream to thin it.
   Drain the pasta well and toss with the sauce. Sprinkle
   with the reserved fennel greens and serve.

1 to 2 bulbs (about ½ pound) fennel
3 tablespoons unsalted butter
½ pound shrimp in shells
¼ cup Madeira
1½ cups heavy cream, plus more if
    necessary
1 tablespoon tomato paste
    Salt and black pepper
1 egg yolk, lightly beaten
1 recipe Egg Pasta (see recipe, this
    chapter)
2 tablespoons olive oil

Yield: 4 servings

EGG PASTA

1¼ to 1½ cups all-purpose flour
½ teaspoon salt
2 eggs

1. On a work surface, sift the flour and salt in a mound. Make a well in the center and break the eggs into it.
2. Beat the eggs with a fork until well mixed. Gradually incorporate the flour, using the fork to draw small amounts of it into the center of the well. Use your free hand to keep the flour wall from breaking. When the dough begins to mass together, use your hand to incorporate the remaining flour. The dough will be soft but should not stick to your finger when poked.

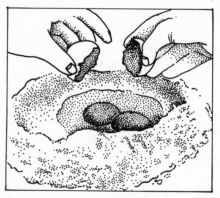

Break the eggs directly into the well in the middle of the mound of flour.

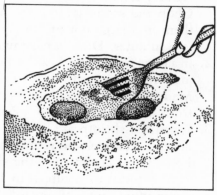

Gently mix the eggs with a fork or your fingers.

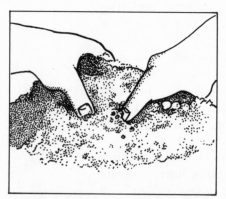

Incorporate the flour and the eggs with your hands, working from the inside of the well to the outside edges of the flour. Try to keep the well intact until enough flour has been incorporated to prevent the egg mixture from seeping out.

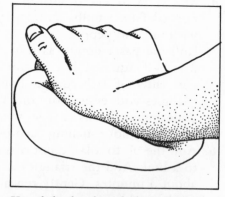

Knead the dough with the heel of your hand until it's smooth and cohesive, dry but not crumbly.

3. When the eggs have absorbed as much flour as possible, clean your hands and the work surface. Knead the dough for 8 to 10 minutes, adding more flour if necessary to keep the dough smooth. Set the dough aside under a bowl or in plastic wrap until ready to use.

Yield: about ¾ pound

Variation: For *Spinach Pasta*, beat in 1½ tablespoons cooked, well-drained, minced spinach with the eggs.

GRILLED SHRIMP WITH PASTA

Fedelini is a fine cylindrical pasta, similar to vermicelli. If you cannot find it, any very thin pasta, such as capelli di angelo, can be substituted.

1. Peel and devein ¾ pound of the shrimp, leaving ¼ pound with the shells intact. Set aside in the refrigerator.
2. Toss the tomatoes in a bowl with olive oil, vinegar, shallot, and salt and pepper to taste.
3. Heat a charcoal grill or the broiler.
4. Brush the shrimp with olive oil, season with salt and pepper, and grill or broil 4 inches from the heat source, about 2 minutes per side for unshelled shrimp, about 1½ minutes per side for shelled shrimp. Remove the shrimp and squeeze lime juice over them.
5. In a large pot of boiling salted water, cook the fedelini until *al dente* and drain.
6. In a large bowl, toss the pasta with the shelled grilled shrimp and tomato mixture. Sprinkle with coriander leaves. Garnish with the unshelled grilled shrimp and serve.

Yield: 4 servings

1 pound (26 to 30) large fresh shrimp
4 large tomatoes, peeled (see illustrations, Chapter 16, Chili Sauce), seeded, and chopped
½ cup virgin olive oil, plus more for brushing shrimp
2 tablespoons balsamic vinegar or red wine vinegar
1 shallot, minced
 Salt and black papper
 Juice of 1 lime
½ pound fedelini
 Leaves from 1 bunch coriander

PASTA WITH PEAS AND STRING BEANS

¾ *cup shelled peas (¾ pound in shell)*
¼ *pound snow peas, trimmed*
½ *pound young string beans, trimmed*
2 *tablespoons unsalted butter*
¼ *cup dry white wine*
1 *cup Chicken Stock (see recipe,*
    Chapter 3)
¾ *cup heavy cream*
    Salt and black pepper
½ *pound thin spaghetti*

1. In a small saucepan, cook the shelled peas in boiling lightly salted water to cover, 3 to 5 minutes. Drain and set aside.
2. In a saucepan, blanch the snow peas in boiling lightly salted water to cover, about 1 minute. Drain the peas, cut each in half diagonally, and set aside.
3. Blanch the string beans in salted boiling water to cover, 1 to 2 minutes. Drain the beans, halve diagonally, and set aside.
4. In a large frying pan, melt the butter and add the wine. Cook over medium heat until reduced to about 3 tablespoons, 3 to 4 minutes. Add the chicken stock and cream and reduce over medium heat until mixture thickens enough to coat the back of a spoon, 7 to 10 minutes. Add salt and pepper to taste.
5. Cook the spaghetti in boiling salted water until *al dente*, and drain.
6. Add the reserved vegetables to the sauce and heat through. Add the pasta and toss well. Serve hot.

Yield: 4 servings

CANNELLONI WITH SUN-DRIED TOMATO SAUCE

When preparing cannelloni, or any other pasta that will be cooked twice, remember to undercook it slightly to avoid overcooking in the end.

Béchamel

3 *tablespoons unsalted butter*
3 *tablespoons flour*
2 *cups milk*
¼ *teaspoon salt*
    Pinch of black pepper

1. For the béchamel, melt the butter in a pot. Whisk in the flour. Cook over medium-low heat without allowing it to color, 3 to 4 minutes. Remove from heat and gradually whisk in the milk. Return to medium heat, add salt and pepper, and bring to a boil, whisking constantly. Reduce heat and simmer for 10 minutes. Set aside.

2. For the filling, put the spinach into a large pot. Add salt to taste and cook, covered, just until leaves wilt, about 5 minutes. Drain the spinach, squeeze dry, and chop well. You should have 1 cup.

3. In a large frying pan, heat the oil. Add the onion and cook until softened, 5 to 10 minutes. Add the spinach and cook over medium–high heat, stirring constantly, for 2 minutes.

4. Transfer the onion-spinach mixture to a large bowl. Add the remaining ingredients, season with salt and pepper, mix well, and set aside.

5. For the sun-dried tomato sauce, heat the oil in a saucepan and sauté the onion until golden, 8 to 10 minutes. Add the sun-dried tomatoes and plum tomatoes, and salt and pepper to taste. Simmer gently, stirring occasionally, for 20 minutes. Set aside.

6. For the cannelloni, roll the egg pasta dough about ⅛-inch thick. Cut into sixteen 4″- × -5″ rectangles. Add the oil to a large pot of salted water and bring to a boil. Add the pasta rectangles a few at a time, stir them all well to keep from sticking, and cook for 2 minutes. Plunge the cooked pasta rectangles into cold water and then lay them flat on a dampened towel, keeping them separated.

7. Heat the oven to 375°F. Butter a 9″- × -14″ baking dish.

8. Reheat the béchamel and spread a thin layer on the bottom of the prepared baking dish. Spread 2 to 3 tablespoons of filling at one end of each pasta rectangle, leaving a ½-inch border. Roll the pasta loosely around the filling and lay the cannelloni seam-side down in the baking dish in 1 layer. Spread remaining béchamel over the cannelloni. Cover with the tomato sauce and sprinkle with Parmesan cheese. Bake in the preheated oven until hot and bubbly, 15 to 20 minutes. Cool for 10 minutes before serving.

Yield: 4 servings

Notes: Sun-dried tomatoes are available at specialty stores and may be sold dry or in oil. If in oil, drain before using here.

Mortadella is an Italian, pork-based cold cut much like bologna.

Filling

1 pound spinach, well rinsed but not dried
Salt and black pepper
2 tablespoons olive oil
½ onion, minced
½ cup sun-dried tomatoes, cut into large dice (see Notes)
¼ pound mortadella, chopped (see Notes)
1½ cups whole-milk ricotta cheese
¼ cup grated Parmesan cheese
1 egg, lightly beaten

Sun-Dried Tomato Sauce

3 tablespoons olive oil
1 small onion, chopped
3 tablespoons chopped sun-dried tomatoes
1½ cups fresh or canned plum tomatoes, peeled, chopped, with juices reserved
Salt and black pepper

1 recipe Egg Pasta (see recipe, this chapter)
2 tablespoons olive oil
½ cup grated Parmesan cheese

FETTUCCINE WITH SHELLFISH CUSTARD SAUCE

1 *recipe Egg Pasta (see recipe, this chapter)*
7 *tablespoons unsalted butter*
½ *small rib celery, chopped (about ¼ cup)*
2 *shallots, chopped*
1 *tablespoon chopped parsley stems*
2 *large cloves garlic, chopped*
1 *pound fresh shrimp, shelled and deveined, shells reserved*
1 *cup dry white wine*
2 *tablespoons lemon juice, plus more for shrimp*
4 *cups Chicken Stock (see recipe, Chapter 3)*
2 *small leeks, white parts only, cut in half lengthwise and cut into 1-inch-long julienne strips (about 1 cup)*
2 *carrots, peeled and cut into 1-inch-long julienne strips (about 1 cup)*
1¼ *cups heavy cream*
¾ *pound bay scallops*
Salt and black pepper
6 *egg yolks*

1. Roll the pasta about ¹⁄₁₆ inch thick and cut into approximately ¼-inch strips. Set aside on a lightly floured surface.
2. Melt 1 tablespoon butter in a large frying pan. Add celery, shallots, parsley stems, garlic, and shrimp shells. Sauté over medium heat for 1 minute. Add wine, lemon juice, and chicken stock. Reduce over medium-low heat to 1½ cups, about 30 minutes. Strain the stock into a bowl through a fine sieve, pressing hard to extract all liquid, and set aside. Discard shells and vegetables.
3. In the same frying pan, melt 3 tablespoons butter. Add the leeks and carrots and sauté gently for 3 minutes. Add the strained stock and simmer until the vegetables are tender and the mixture has reduced by half, about 10 minutes. Remove from heat and stir in 1 cup cream.
4. In another large frying pan, melt 1½ tablespoons butter over medium heat. When butter begins to foam, add the scallops and sauté until nearly done, about 2 minutes. Add the scallops to the vegetable mixture. Melt remaining 1½ tablespoons butter in the same pan and sauté the shrimp until nearly done, about 3 minutes. Add the shrimp to the vegetable mixture. Season with salt and pepper and a little lemon juice to taste.
5. In a small bowl, whisk the egg yolks with the remaining ¼ cup cream. Stir a little of the warm seafood-vegetable liquid into the beaten yolks and then add this mixture to the seafood-vegetable mixture itself. Stir over medium heat until the sauce thickens, about 3 minutes. Be careful not to boil the sauce or the yolks will curdle.
6. Cook the fettuccine in rapidly boiling salted water until *al dente* and drain. Toss the hot fettuccine with the sauce, adjust seasoning, and serve immediately.

Yield: 4 servings

SALMON AND PASTA SALAD WITH
LEMON-DILL VINAIGRETTE

1. Roll the pasta about ¹⁄₁₆ inch thick and cut into approximately ¼-inch strips. Set aside on a lightly
   floured surface.
2. Heat the oven to 400°F.
3. Arrange the salmon in a shallow baking dish with
   enough water to half cover. Add the lemon-dill vinegar and season lightly with salt and black pepper.
   Bake the salmon until it tests done, 10 to 12 minutes.
   Remove from the oven and cool to room temperature
   in the baking dish.
4. For the vinaigrette, whisk together the mustard,
   lemon-dill vinegar, and salt and pepper in a small
   bowl. Add the oil in a slow stream, whisking until
   all the oil has been incorporated. Adjust the seasonings and set aside.
5. Cook the fettuccine in boiling salted water until *al
   dente* and drain. Plunge the fettuccine into cold water
   to cool and drain again.
6. In a large bowl, gently toss the pasta with half of the
   onion, ¼ cup dill, and half the lemon-dill vinaigrette.
   Season with salt and pepper.
7. Drain the salmon and pat dry. Remove the skin and
   any bones. Flake the fish into a bowl and add remaining onion, dill, ½ cup of the vinaigrette, and
   salt and pepper. Toss gently.
8. Arrange the pasta on a serving platter or individual
   plates and mound the salmon in the center. Drizzle
   with the remaining vinaigrette just before serving.

Yield: 4 servings

1 recipe Spinach Pasta (see Egg Pasta,
   Variation, this chapter)
1½ pounds salmon steak or fillet
¼ cup Lemon-Dill Vinegar (see recipe,
   Chapter 16)
   Salt and black pepper
2 small red onions, diced
½ cup chopped fresh dill

Lemon-Dill Vinaigrette

1 tablespoon Dijon mustard
½ cup Lemon-Dill Vinegar (see recipe,
   Chapter 16)
   Salt and white pepper
1 cup peanut or safflower oil

CAPELLINI WITH SMOKED SALMON AND BLACK CAVIAR

Capellini is a very fine cylindrical pasta. If unavailable, use another thin pasta.

　2　*tablespoons unsalted butter*
　3　*whole scallions, minced*
　2　*ounces mushrooms, sliced thin (about*
　　　¾ cup)
　1　*tablespoon lemon juice*
　　　Salt and white pepper
　¼　*cup dry white wine*
1½　*cups heavy cream*
　½　*pound capellini*
　3　*ounces smoked salmon, sliced thin and*
　　　cut into ¼"- × -2" strips
　½　*pound fresh peas, shelled, or 4 ounces*
　　　frozen peas, thawed
　½　*cup American black caviar*
　2　*tablespoons minced fresh parsley*

1. In a large frying pan, melt the butter and sauté the scallions for 2 to 3 minutes. Add the mushrooms, lemon juice, and salt and white pepper. Sauté for 5 minutes more and add the wine. Reduce over high heat until the liquid is syrupy, about 5 minutes. Add the cream and reduce by half, or until the cream is quite thick, about 10 minutes.
2. Cook the capellini in boiling salted water until *al dente* and drain.
3. Add the capellini and smoked salmon to the frying pan, toss gently, and heat.
4. In a saucepan, cook the peas in rapidly boiling water for 1 minute. Drain the peas and add them to the pasta. Season to taste with salt and white pepper.
5. Just before serving, garnish each serving with 2 tablespoons caviar, either scattered over the top or in little mounds. Sprinkle with parsley.

Yield: 4 servings

FEDELINI WITH DUCK, GRAPES, AND CRACKED PEPPERCORNS

Duck and Duck Stock

　1　*5-pound duck with giblets*
　　　Salt and black pepper
　½　*cup red wine*
　1　*onion, chopped*
　1　*small carrot, chopped*
　6　*cups veal or chicken stock (see recipe,*
　　　Chapter 3) or a combination of
　　　stock and water

1. Heat the oven to 450°F.
2. To prepare the duck, remove the giblets and set them aside. Cut off the last 2 wing joints and put them into a roasting pan with the duck neck. Dry the duck with paper towels and prick all over with a knife. Rub inside and out with salt and pepper. Put on top of the wing joints and necks. Roast in the preheated oven for 20 minutes. Reduce heat to 300°F and continue roasting for 2 hours, straining off fat as it accumulates. Remove the duck from the oven and set aside to cool on a rack.

3. For the duck stock, remove all the meat and skin from the duck and set aside. Chop the carcasses, including the necks and wing tips, into large pieces and put into a stockpot.

4. Pour off the fat from the roasting pan and set it over high heat. Add the wine, scraping the bottom of the pan with a wooden spoon to deglaze. Add this liquid to the stockpot with the onion, carrot, and veal or chicken stock or stock-water mixture. Bring to a boil and simmer, skimming as necessary, until reduced to 3 cups, 2 to 3 hours. Strain and skim well to degrease. Reduce over medium heat to about 2 cups, 15 to 20 minutes. Set aside.

5. For the sauce, melt the butter in a large frying pan. Add the shallots, cook over low heat for 3 minutes, and add wine. Turn heat to high and reduce to 2 to 3 tablespoons, about 10 minutes. Add the reserved duck stock, jelly, port, and orange and lemon juices. Continue to boil gently until the liquid reduces by half and becomes slightly syrupy, 20 to 25 minutes.

6. Heat the oven to 350°F. Put the reserved duck skin on a baking sheet and cook in oven until browned and crisp, about 30 minutes. Sprinkle with salt, drain on paper towels, and cool. Break into small pieces. Cut the reserved duck meat into strips 1½ inches long and ¼ inch thick.

7. In a large pot of boiling salted water, cook the fedelini until *al dente* and then drain. Toss with the oil.

8. Add the duck strips and fedelini to the sauce and toss gently. Cook until just heated through, 3 to 5 minutes. Add the crushed peppercorns, grapes, and mustard. Season with salt and toss well. Serve immediately, sprinkled with the crisp skin.

Yield: 4 servings

Sauce

- 1 tablespoon unsalted butter
- 2 shallots, minced
- ¼ cup red wine
- 1½ tablespoons red-currant jelly
- 1 tablespoon port
- 2 tablespoons orange juice
- 2 tablespoons lemon juice
- ½ pound fedelini (Grilled Shrimp with Pasta, headnote, this chapter)
- 1½ tablespoons vegetable oil
- 1 tablespoon crushed black peppercorns
- 1 cup halved seedless green grapes
- 2 tablespoons Dijon mustard
  Salt

HAM AND THREE-CHEESE PASTA ROLL

Tomato Sauce

- 1 16-ounce can Italian plum tomatoes, drained
- ¼ cup chopped fresh parsley
- 2 cloves garlic, halved
- 2 tablespoons minced fresh basil, or 2 teaspoons dried basil
- 3 tablespoons unsalted butter

Filling

- 2 tablespoons unsalted butter
- 4 scallions, minced
- 2 ounces smoked ham, cut into ⅛-inch dice (about ½ cup)
- ½ pound cream cheese, softened
- ½ cup whole-milk ricotta cheese
- 1 egg
- ¼ cup grated Parmesan cheese
- ½ teaspoon black pepper

- 1 recipe Spinach Pasta (see Egg Pasta, Variation, this chapter)
- ½ pound smoked ham, cut in ⅙-inch-thick slices

1. For the tomato sauce, in a saucepan, simmer all the ingredients except the butter, uncovered, until reduced by one-third, 30 to 40 minutes. The sauce should be thick and strongly flavored. Put through a medium strainer and press firmly to get all the sauce. Return to the saucepan.

2. For the filling, melt the butter in a frying pan. Add the scallions and cook over low heat until soft, 1 to 2 minutes. Add the diced ham and cook over medium heat for 1 to 2 minutes. Set aside.

3. In a bowl, beat together the cream cheese and ricotta until smooth. Add the egg and beat well. Stir in the Parmesan cheese, ham mixture, and pepper. Mix well and refrigerate.

4. Roll the pasta out into four 12"-×-4" sheets. Lay 2 pasta sheets side by side, lengthwise. Score 1 long edge with short diagonal strokes using the dull side of a knife. Brush water over scoring. Lay the second sheet over the moistened edge to overlap by ½ inch. Press along the seam so that sheets adhere.

5. Remove the filling from the refrigerator and spread half of the mixture over the assembled sheets of pasta, leaving a ½-inch uncovered border all the way around. Cover the cheese mixture with a layer of half the sliced ham. Beginning at one of the short ends, roll up the pasta, jelly-roll style. Do not roll too loosely or water may seep in as it poaches. Repeat the entire procedure with the remaining pasta, filling, and ham, making 2 completed rolls. Wrap each roll in a double thickness of cheesecloth and tie each end securely with string.

6. Bring a large pot of salted water to a boil and add the pasta rolls. Reduce heat and simmer the rolls, turning them occasionally, for 25 minutes. Drain, cool slightly, and remove the string and cheesecloth.

7. Warm the tomato sauce and swirl in the 3 tablespoons butter.
8. Cut each roll into ½-inch-thick slices and arrange on plates. Pour a bed of tomato sauce onto each plate and top with the slices. Serve warm.

Yield: 4 servings

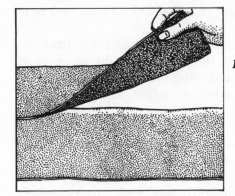

Lay one sheet of pasta over the moistened edge of the other.

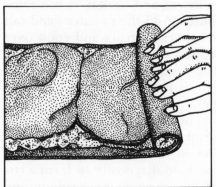

Lay the ham over the cheese mixture and roll the pasta.

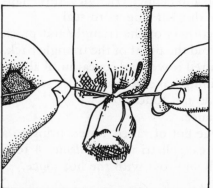

Wrap the pasta roll in cheesecloth and tie each end.

GREEN-PEPPER CAPPELLETTI
WITH RED-PEPPER SAUCE

Pasta

1 green pepper, skin, seeds, and ribs
    removed
1½ to 1¾ cups all-purpose flour
½ teaspoon salt
1 egg

Filling

½ pound sweet Italian sausage
1 tablespoon olive oil
½ pound ground veal
1 egg, lightly beaten
3 tablespoons grated Parmesan cheese
½ teaspoon salt
⅛ teaspoon black pepper

Sauce

3 tablespoons olive oil
2 cloves garlic, minced
4 red peppers, quartered, skin, seeds,
    and ribs removed
1 cup chopped fresh or canned plum
    tomatoes with juices
    Salt and black pepper

2 tablespoons olive oil

*After filling, fold diagonally and seal.
Pinch the ends of the slanted sides
together and bend the point back.*

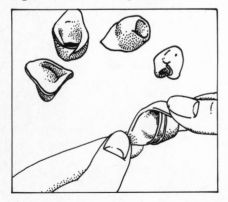

1. For the pasta, puree the green pepper in a food processor until liquefied, about 1½ minutes. Follow the basic method for making Spinach Pasta dough (see Egg Pasta, Variation, this chapter), substituting pureed pepper for the spinach.
2. For the filling, remove the sausage meat from its casing and break up the meat. Heat the olive oil in a large frying pan and sauté the meat over medium-high heat until color begins to fade, about 5 minutes. Add the veal and cook until meats are no longer pink, about 5 minutes. Remove from heat, pour off excess fat, and cool the meat mixture slightly. Blend in the egg, cheese, and salt and pepper. Set aside.
3. For the sauce, heat the oil in a large frying pan and cook the garlic until lightly browned, 2 to 3 minutes. Add the red peppers, cover, and cook over medium-low heat for 10 minutes. Add the tomatoes and salt and pepper to taste. Cover partially and cook over low heat until the peppers are soft, about 40 minutes. Puree in a food processor. Strain and press hard on the vegetables to get all the sauce. Adjust the seasonings and set aside.
4. Roll the pasta by hand or machine as thin as possible. You may need to sprinkle with more flour. Cut into 1½-inch squares. Put ¼ teaspoon of filling in the center of each square. Fold diagonally to form a triangle with edges not quite meeting (see headnote and illustrations, Shrimp and Fennel Triangles, this chapter). Press firmly with your fingers to seal.
5. Join the 2 bottom corners of the triangle and pinch securely together. Fold the point of the triangle back. Put on a lightly floured towel and repeat until all the pasta squares and filling have been used. Be sure the formed cappelletti do not touch.
6. Gently reheat the sauce.
7. Add the oil to a large pot of salted water, bring to a boil, and cook the cappelletti until *al dente*, 4 to 5 minutes. Drain well and toss with the hot sauce.

Yield: 4 servings

Chapter

10 | Vegetables and Herbs

N early every kind of vegetable known to human beings can be grown success-fully somewhere in North America. Yet despite this abundance of vegetables of practically all kinds, we're just now de-veloping a varied repertoire of vegetable cookery to match the possibilities of our vegetable growing.

It has never been lack of technique that has caused our failure to cook vegetables properly; cooking vegetables, in fact, is one of the simplest of processes. Rather, the great stumbling blocks have been conceptual. In the past, two imperatives dominated our attitudes toward vegetables: One was a desire to make vegetables into year-round products. Consequently, much of our in-terest in vegetables over the last one hundred years has been devoted to learning how to can, freeze, and grow them, factory style, year-round in Texas, California, and Florida. And as we became mesmerized by our success, we forgot to ask a simple question: Does it taste good?

The second factor that has clouded our thinking about vegetables has also been partly responsible for our failure to ask the flavor question. For too long vegetables were part of the spinach syndrome. The good boy or girl ate his or her vegetables because it was a duty; it was good for you. We won't explore the cultural origins of this idea, but it is one that led generations of Americans to adopt a sulky hostility toward most vegetables and helped us to accept the standardized canned or frozen pap the distributors gave us twelve months a year. Too few of us believed vegetables could taste good anyway.

Now, however, eating what's good for you is in fashion, and we have begun to think seriously about vegetables and how to cook them. Our contemporary fascination with the health value of foods, if occasionally excessive, has been a positive factor in new American culinary attitudes toward vegetables. One result is that the trend toward the disappearance of fresh vegetables from our markets in favor of frozen ones has been reversed. Recent figures indicate we've increased our purchases of fresh vegetables and decreased our reliance on the frozen varieties. There's ample evidence of this consumer inclination in supermarkets, where the vegetable shelves have taken on a new allure. In large cities, Oriental greengrocers have moved into the retail end of the vegetable distribution chain and brought with them an attention to presentation, variety, and quality. And farmers' markets are now part of the yearly ritual of summer and fall in most areas of the country.

To our concern for freshness can be added several other new developments that point toward the emergence of a stylistic revolution in American vegetable cookery. First, we're rediscovering the variety of vegetables that can be grown in this country. Gone are the predictable days when peas, carrots, green beans, and potatoes were nearly the only vegetables we cared to cook or serve. Now our cooks are fascinated with forgotten traditional favorites like kale and sweet potatoes and enamored of newly available vegetables such as sugar snap peas. And we've found that vegetables don't always have to be baked, boiled, or fried. Sautéed, stir-fried, stewed, steamed, and grilled vegetables can all be found in restaurants and at home. Our attitude has changed— creating vegetable dishes can be fun!

In addition, the French nouvelle cuisine and the Oriental cooking traditions have taught us the importance of vegetables to the presentation of a dish. For decades, traditional restaurant garnish for most plates was a sprig of parsley or, for the more adventurous chef, perhaps a grilled tomato half. But now American cooks have become aware of the value of the colors that vegetables offer. From a variety of shades of green through yellow, red, white, and even purple, vegetables give a chef the chance to create an appealing arrangement as well as a flavorful one.

KINDS OF VEGETABLES

While vegetables can be classified by several methods from their botanical family to the part of the plant that is eaten (bulb, root, stem, fruit, leaf, or seed), the system that is most useful to a cook is one that arranges them according to their high season. Buying seasonal vegetables is not a guarantee that you'll get good-quality locally grown produce, but it is the first step, and increasing numbers of serious cooks are planning menus around what's best at the time of the year.

Winter Vegetables

It's no accident that in Germany sauerkraut and other forms of cabbage are king. There the gastronomic blessing is an abundance of sausage, fish, pork, and veal, and wine and beer, while vegetables have traditionally been hard to come by. Even the peak summer growing season is not really long enough or sunny enough to produce much variety, and so the Germans learned early to get the most out of those vegetables that thrive in a cooler climate. Contrary to what most people imagine, there are such "winter" vegetables, and in the United States they are at their peak during the winter months, especially January and February. Broccoli and Brussels sprouts are well-known winter vegetables. Look also for savoy cabbage, celery and celeriac or celery root, collards, Jerusalem artichokes, kale, leeks, parsnips and turnips, rutabaga, and Belgian endive (though still little grown in this country and consequently often quite expensive even during its season). For those who are interested and can afford them, imported black truffles are also in season during the winter.

Spring Vegetables

The happiest sign of spring for the gastronome has to be the arrival of the first local asparagus in the markets. Asparagus is the quintessential spring vegetable, but peas are also especially notable. If you've only eaten frozen or canned peas, fresh seasonal peas are a revelation. From March through mid-June look also for dandelion greens, fava and snap beans, artichokes, fiddlehead ferns, sorrel, radishes, watercress, arugula, Vidalia onions, new potatoes, snow peas, the last of the leeks, and the earliest sweet corn and peppers. Some mushroom varieties, especially morels, which have a short harvest from late April into May, are a seasonal treat.

Summer Vegetables

In summer the vegetable is in its glory. Even the most jaded eater is excited by those tantalizing weeks when really ripe, flavorful red tomatoes arrive by the bushel in nearly every market and when the ears of white and yellow sweet corn lie in heaps upon the counter ready to be taken home, shucked, and quickly boiled or grilled. Besides these vegetables, the summer provides us with the best eggplant and the most delicious red, yellow, and green bell peppers. You will also find lima beans; zucchini; pattypan, yellow, and spaghetti squash; okra; watercress; radishes; and the sweet northwestern Walla Walla onions.

Fall Vegetables

Just as the growing season begins to dim and we look toward the winter, there comes a final burst of vegetable brilliance. The fall vegetables have neither the anticipation of spring nor the fullness of summer to offer, but they bring a kind of melancholy delight of their own. Pumpkin, sweet potatoes, acorn and butternut squash are a rich summation of the year's harvest. You'll also find salsify, fennel, Jerusalem artichokes, mushrooms, cauliflower, and, in November into December, leeks, broccoli, and turnips.

Year-Round Vegetables

These are vegetables whose supply and quality stay nearly constant most of the year. They are well adapted to constant cropping in the South and West or suffer little when stored and shipped around the country. Among these vegetables are potatoes, onions, many varieties of lettuce, and cultivated mushrooms. Broccoli and artichokes also are now available practically year-round.

HERBS

The most common herbs are really not much different from leafy vegetables, and strict lines of demarcation are difficult to draw. From a culinary standpoint, herbs are normally used to flavor or garnish dishes rather than to be served by themselves. However, some herbs— parsley and sorrel, for instance—can be cooked as vegetables. See, for instance, our recipe for Steamed Parsley. As with vegetables, many more kinds of herbs are now commercially available than before, and American cooks are becoming more and more sophisticated about their use. Even supermarkets often have dill, basil, thyme, sorrel, sage, chives, and mint. More exotic herbs, such as coriander, rosemary, tarragon, marjoram, oregano, and chervil, show up increasingly. The growth of interest in vegetables and herbs has led to many wonderful new vegetable dishes that are marriages of the two.

The best way to ensure yourself of a supply of fresh herbs is still by growing your own in an herb garden. Herbs are either perennial or annual. The basic annuals, which must be replanted each year, are basil, chervil, dill, and savory. Chives, lovage, mint, marjoram, oregano, rosemary, sage, sorrel, thyme, and tarragon are all perennials. Once planted, they should return each growing year. Parsley is a biennial.

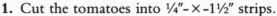

SAUTÉ OF JULIENNED TOMATOES WITH CREAM AND HERBS

More wasted energy has been expended on producing the standard, year-round, supermarket tomato than on any other gastronomic project. But if the firm-textured, thick-skinned, flavorless tomato of the scientists is a culinary disaster, the locally grown, vine-ripened beauty of late summer is a miracle. Our best advice on fresh tomatoes is to eat them every way possible from the beginning of the season until the end.

8 large (about 3 pounds) ripe plum
    tomatoes, peeled (see illustrations,
    Chapter 16, Chili Sauce), halved,
    and seeded
4 to 5 tablespoons unsalted butter
    Salt and white pepper
1 cup heavy cream
4 teaspoons chopped fresh basil, parsley,
    or chervil leaves, or a mixture

1. Cut the tomatoes into ¼"-×-1½" strips.
2. Melt the butter in a frying pan over medium-high heat. Add the tomato strips and sauté, tossing, until just cooked, 4 to 5 minutes. Season to taste with salt and white pepper. Drain in a colander, reserving the juices.
3. Return the reserved juices to the pan and add the cream. Cook until the sauce thickens enough to coat a spoon, about 5 minutes.
4. Add the herbs and remove from heat for 1 to 2 minutes. Return to high heat and fold in the tomato strips. Cook until just heated through, adjust the seasonings, and serve immediately.

Yield: 4 servings

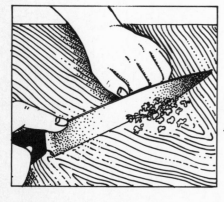

To chop parsley or other herbs, first slice through the bunch from the top down to the stems, holding the bunch together with your free hand.

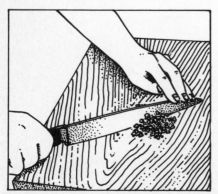

Next, gather the sliced leaves into a pile and, steadying the top of the knife with the free hand, cut repeatedly, keeping the tip on the work surface and moving the knife in an arc.

ASPARAGUS WITH LEMON BEURRE ROUGE

Asparagus isn't a native vegetable but has been grown in America since at least the eighteenth century. The late famed modern French chef Jean Troisgros considered American asparagus to be the best in the world, and our green variety is generally more tender and less bitter than the European white. Buy the freshest locally grown asparagus you can find with tight-capped heads and still-moist ends.

1. In a small, nonreactive saucepan, cook the wine with the shallot over medium heat until the shallot is soft and the wine has almost evaporated, about 3 minutes.
2. In a shallow pan large enough to hold all the asparagus lying flat, bring enough salted water to cover the asparagus to a boil. Add the spears and cook, uncovered, until just done, about 4 minutes. Remove with tongs and drain on paper towels.
3. Over the lowest possible heat, whisk the butter, a tablespoon at a time, into the wine-shallot mixture. The butter should soften to form a creamy sauce but should not melt completely. Season to taste with salt and pepper and then whisk in the lemon zest. Serve the asparagus immediately with the sauce poured over it.

Yield: 4 servings

3 tablespoons red wine
1 small shallot, minced
2 pounds asparagus, ends snapped off and stalks peeled
¼ pound unsalted butter
  Salt and black pepper
  Zest of 1 lemon, grated

Break tough ends off asparagus where the stalk snaps naturally.

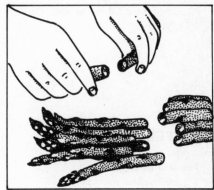

Cut the peeling from asparagus spears into thin strips starting at the base and going up to the beginning of the tip.

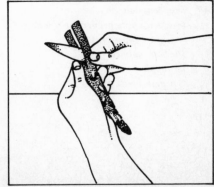

STEAMED PARSLEY SERVED WARM OR COLD

A parsley reassessment is long overdue. This most familiar of culinary herbs is too often relegated to garnish duty. Try it as the dominant seasoning on meat dishes, pizzas, or roasted poultry. A parsley-lemon butter goes well with grilled fish. And as this recipe shows, parsley is one of those herbs, like sorrel, that is suitable for cooking and serving as a vegetable side dish.

6 cups (3 ounces) loosely packed curly-
    leaf parsley, large stems removed

Warm Dressing

4 tablespoons unsalted butter
2 teaspoons lemon juice
    Salt and black pepper

Cold Dressing

3 tablespoons vegetable oil
2 tablespoons rice-wine vinegar
¾ teaspoon grated lemon zest
    Salt and black pepper
2 teaspoons toasted sesame seeds (see
    Note)

1. In a covered steamer, cook the parsley to soften, about 1 minute. Remove immediately.
2. For the warm dressing, melt the butter in a saucepan with lemon juice and salt and pepper. In a large bowl, fluff the parsley with 2 forks. Pour the butter mixture over the parsley and lightly mix with the forks, being careful not to compact the parsley. Serve at once.
3. For the cold dressing, chill the steamed parsley. In a small bowl, beat together the oil, vinegar, lemon zest, and salt and pepper. In another bowl, fluff the chilled parsley with 2 forks. Pour the dressing over and toss. Set aside for about 15 minutes, sprinkle with toasted sesame seeds, and toss again. Serve at once.

Yield: 4 servings

Note: Toast sesame seeds in a small frying pan over medium heat, stirring constantly, until honey-colored, about 3 minutes.

WINTER GRATIN

1 pound white potatoes
1 pound yellow sweet potatoes
1⅔ cups heavy cream
2 small cloves garlic, crushed
1½ teaspoons salt
¼ teaspoon white pepper, or 6 whole
    white peppercorns
    Pinch of nutmeg
1 tart apple
⅓ cup fresh bread crumbs

1. Heat the oven to 375°F. Lightly butter a 1½-quart casserole.
2. Bake the white and sweet potatoes until a sharp knife will go into the potatoes with some resistance, 20 to 25 minutes, depending on size. Cool and peel carefully.
3. Grate the white potatoes into a bowl and the sweet potatoes into another bowl.
4. In a heavy saucepan, slowly heat the cream, garlic, salt, pepper, and nutmeg to a simmer and continue simmering for 5 minutes. Strain half the hot cream

mixture over each bowl of grated potatoes and toss until well mixed. Peel, core, and grate the apple.

5. Arrange a layer of one-third of the sweet potatoes with one-third of their liquid in the prepared casserole. Add a layer of one-third of the apple, and a layer of one-third of the white potatoes with one-third of their liquid. Repeat twice more with alternate layers of potatoes with liquid and apple, ending with a layer of white potatoes. Top with the bread crumbs.

6. Put the casserole into a larger baking pan. Add water to the pan to come halfway up the sides of the casserole. Bake, uncovered, in the preheated oven until the bread crumbs are golden, about 25 minutes. Serve immediately.

Yield: 4 to 6 servings

BRAISED SPRING KALE WITH OREGANO

1. In a large frying pan over medium–high heat, warm the olive oil. Add garlic and cook until it begins to turn golden, 4 to 5 minutes. Reduce heat to low, add the kale and 1¼ teaspoons salt, and toss. Cover and cook until tender, about 10 minutes. Remove from heat and season to taste with pepper.

2. In a large bowl, toss the kale with the herbs and vinegar. Serve hot or at room temperature, garnished with kasseri cheese if desired.

Yield: 4 servings

¼ cup olive oil
4 cloves garlic, chopped
2 pounds kale, ribs removed, chopped
1¼ teaspoons salt
 Black pepper
2 tablespoons minced fresh oregano leaves, or 2 teaspoons dried oregano
2 teaspoons minced fresh thyme, or ½ teaspoon dried thyme
2 teaspoons red wine vinegar
2 ounces kasseri cheese or other mild, hard cheese, grated (optional)

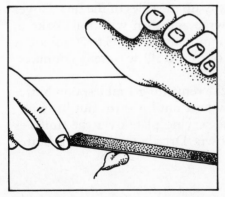

To peel garlic easily, place the flat of the knife on top of the clove with the cutting edge angled into the work surface and hit the side of the knife sharply with the palm of your hand; the skin will slide off.

BRUSSELS SPROUT TIMBALES

Brussels sprouts are really miniature cabbages and like the rest of the cabbage family can have a very strong flavor. They're most often served boiled, but we find that their assertiveness is just right cooked in timbales. Red pimientos atop the green timbales make this dish a particularly pretty addition to the holiday table.

⅔ pound Brussels sprouts, trimmed
2 ounces whole pimientos
2 tablespoons unsalted butter
1 small clove garlic, sliced
¾ cup milk
2 eggs
Salt and black pepper

1. Bring a large pot of salted water to a boil. Add the Brussels sprouts and cook until just tender. Drain thoroughly.
2. Cut four ¾-inch–long diamond shapes from the pimientos. Chop 1 tablespoon pimientos into ½-inch dice, drain well on paper towels, and set aside.
3. Place 4 outer leaves from the Brussels sprouts around the bottom of each prepared tin and 1 diamond-shaped pimiento in the center.
4. In a large, heavy pot, melt 1 tablespoon butter. Sauté the garlic over low heat until soft. Add the Brussels sprouts and sauté to evaporate excess moisture. Add the milk and simmer for 15 minutes.
5. In a food processor or blender, puree the sprouts with milk until very smooth.
6. Heat the oven to 350°F. Butter 4 muffin tins or 2- to 3-ounce baking cups.
7. In a large bowl, beat the eggs lightly. Add the sprout puree and stir together. Gently stir in the reserved drained pimiento. Season with salt and pepper. Fill tins to the top with the puree.
8. Put the tins in a baking dish and add water to the dish to come halfway up the sides of the tins. Cover first with plastic wrap and then with foil. Bake in the preheated oven until just firm, 25 to 30 minutes. Remove from the oven and allow to set 15 minutes, covered.
9. Meanwhile, melt the remaining 1 tablespoon butter and cook over low heat until it turns nut brown.
10. To serve, place the serving plate over the timbales and turn upside down. Drizzle the browned butter over the tops.

Yield: 4 servings

JERUSALEM ARTICHOKES

The Jerusalem artichoke is a native North American vegetable related to the sunflower. The flavor is vaguely reminiscent of that of artichokes, and since the plant is technically called a girasole, it was evidently described colloquially as girasole artichokes, which was corrupted to Jerusalem artichokes. A strong-flavored winter vegetable, they stand up nicely to the dill, chives, and garlic in this recipe.

1. Bring a saucepan of water to boil. Add the artichoke slices and boil for 5 minutes. Drain and return the artichokes to the saucepan. Pour the oil and vinegar or lemon juice over the artichokes and add dillseed and garlic.
2. Mix thoroughly and simmer for 10 minutes, stirring frequently. Sprinkle with chives and dill. Season to taste with salt. Serve hot or cold as a side dish or as a relish.

Yield: 4 to 6 servings

1 *pound Jerusalem artichokes, peeled and sliced*
½ *cup sunflower seed oil* or *other light oil*
½ *cup cider vinegar* or *lemon juice*
½ *teaspoon dillseed*
2 *cloves garlic, chopped*
2 *tablespoons chopped fresh chives*
2 *tablespoons chopped fresh dill*
Salt

BAKED SWEET DUMPLING SQUASH

1. Heat the oven to 350°F.
2. In a pot of rapidly boiling salted water, blanch the carrots for 4 minutes. Drain and refresh under cold water. Set aside.
3. Slice a sliver off the bottom of each squash half to prevent tipping.
4. Put a sliver of the butter and 1 teaspoon maple syrup in each squash half. Top with blanched diced carrots and raisins. Pour 1 more teaspoon maple syrup over each half and finish with another piece of butter. Season with salt and pepper to taste.
5. Put the squash halves back together and wrap tightly with foil. Place in a baking dish and bake until the flesh is soft, 35 to 45 minutes. Halfway through baking, turn the squash over.
6. To serve, unwrap the squash and place the halves upright on a platter or plates.

Yield: 4 servings

2 *carrots, cut into ⅛-inch dice*
2 *sweet dumpling squash, small turban squash,* or *acorn squash, halved and seeds removed*
1½ *tablespoons unsalted butter*
8 *teaspoons maple syrup*
2 *tablespoons golden raisins*
Salt and black pepper

GLAZED CARROTS WITH MACE AND BASIL

Basil is one of the most popular of herbs and is now quite often found in markets, especially during the summer. Most frequently paired with red, ripe tomatoes, it matches up well with carrots, too.

3 tablespoons unsalted butter
¼ cup water
   Salt
1 pound carrots, sliced diagonally
¼ teaspoon ground mace
2 teaspoons sugar
2 tablespoons minced fresh basil, or 2 teaspoons dried basil

1. In a heavy frying pan, heat 1 tablespoon butter with water and ¼ teaspoon salt until the butter is melted. Add the carrots and mix well. Cook over medium-low heat, covered, until tender, 8 to 10 minutes. Transfer to a bowl and set aside.
2. Add the remaining 2 tablespoons butter to the frying pan and heat. When butter begins to sizzle, add the mace and sugar. Shake the pan a few times and add the cooked carrots and basil. Sauté over medium heat, tossing the carrots until the seasonings are well distributed and the carrots are glazed, 3 to 5 minutes. Taste for seasoning. Serve hot or at room temperature.

Yield: 4 servings

GARLIC-HERB WHIPPED POTATOES

⅓ cup heavy cream
2 tablespoons unsalted butter
3 cloves garlic, quartered
2 pounds boiling potatoes, peeled and cut into 2-inch chunks
2 tablespoons minced fresh chives (see Note)
1 tablespoon minced fresh curly-leaf parsley
   Salt and black pepper

1. In a small saucepan, heat the cream, butter, and garlic over low heat. Bring just to a simmer, remove from heat, and let sit for at least 20 minutes.
2. In another saucepan, cover the potatoes with well-salted water and bring to a boil. Cook until tender, about 20 minutes. Remove from heat.
3. Strain the potatoes, reserving some of the liquid. Whip the potatoes until smooth. Strain the garlic cream into the potatoes and add enough reserved cooking liquid, about 1 tablespoon, to make the potatoes light and fluffy but still stiff enough to hold soft peaks. Stir in the chives and parsley. Season with salt and pepper to taste and serve immediately.

Yield: 4 servings

Note: Thyme, rosemary, or sage can be substituted for the chives. Sauté them in butter for 10 seconds, add 2 tablespoons water, boil until almost dry, and proceed as for the chives.

Chapter 11

Yeast Breads, Quick Breads, Spoon Breads, and Doughnuts

Bread is basic. From the nut-spiked fruity muffins and light doughnuts of the Northeast to the meltingly rich biscuits and airy spoon breads of the South and the crusty, tangy sourdoughs of the West, breads have long played an important role in American cuisine. And regional specialties spread around the country as easily as butter spreads on the bread. Although we strongly associate biscuits with southern culinary tradition, they were baked in all parts of the country in countless variations. Following the invention of baking powder, muffins were adopted by American cooks as the quickest and most easily varied alternative to yeast-risen breads. Though fried cakes originated in Pennsylvania Dutch kitchens, doughnuts of all shapes were soon enjoyed from coast to coast. Spoon breads, which evolved from a local Indian porridge known as *suppawn*, were prepared regularly in the kitchens at Monticello.

What do yeast breads, quick breads, spoon breads, and doughnuts have in common? They are all made by combining a milled grain or cereal with a liquid and a leavening agent, and subjecting the resulting dough or batter to manipulation and heat. Most breads begin with wheat flour, since wheat contains more gluten than any other grain or cereal. Wheat flour is often supplemented

175

or embellished with other flours or meals to give basic bread a different flavor and texture. Liquids range from water and milk to buttermilk and fruit juice. Leavening agents may be either natural or chemical. Natural leaveners include yeast in its dry or compressed (cake) form, yeast starters, and stiffly beaten egg whites. Commercially available baking powder and baking soda are the most common chemical leaveners used in home baking. Some doughs and batters require a great deal of kneading or beating and rising, while others are gently mixed together and quickly baked in the oven. The key to successful bread making is neither magic nor wizardry, but lies in an understanding of how the various ingredients combine and interact with one another.

FLOURS

Wheat kernels are made up of three parts—the germ, the bran, and the endosperm. White flour is milled from the endosperm alone, which makes up the bulk of the kernel and contains significant amounts of two proteins called gliadin and glutenin. When flour is moistened, these two proteins combine to form a protein called gluten, which in turn forms a cablelike network throughout the dough. Kneading further develops the gluten chains or strands, and they bond and stretch to form an elastic network that traps the gases and steam, thus leavening the dough and making the bread rise. Gluten also requires heat in order to develop fully, and while some is generated during kneading and rising, it is the heat of the oven that finally coagulates the gluten and sets the structure of the bread. Flours with a higher gluten content will produce breads with higher rising capacities.

In America, all nationally available brands of all-purpose flour are blended from hard and soft wheat and have the same gluten content. Hard wheat is grown in areas with short, hot summers, and it yields a flour that is high in gluten and low in starch. This makes it a good choice for yeast breads, since the gluten can support the high rise. Soft flour, by contrast, is milled from winter wheat produced in areas with long growing seasons. It is low in gluten and high in starch, which makes it ideal for tender biscuits and muffins; if used alone, it does not contain enough gluten to support a high-rise yeast dough. Bleached all-purpose flours contain less protein, hence less gluten, than unbleached varieties.

Bread flour is milled from hard wheat only, giving it a higher gluten content than all-purpose flour and making it an excellent flour for yeast breads. Whole-wheat flour is milled from the entire wheat berry; it is more nutritious than white flour, but it has a lower gluten content. Due to the oil in the bran, whole-wheat flour produces a heavier, coarser bread with a chewy crust. Cake flour is a highly refined soft flour; it is low in protein and in gluten. Cornmeal is akin to a coarse flour, milled from corn rather than wheat. Since corn contains no gluten-producing proteins whatsoever, cornmeal is unsuitable for a high-rise bread if it is used alone. Its lack of gluten makes it ideal for tender-crumbed corn bread and fluffy spoon breads.

LEAVENERS

Yeast

Yeast is the oldest known leavener. It was accidentally discovered by the Egyptians some four thousand years ago, when an unbaked portion of dough was left out in a warm place, attracted wild yeast spores, and began to bubble. Yeast is a living, single-cell fungus that floats about freely in the air. Given the right environment, yeast cells divide and multiply at a phenomenal rate. During kneading, rising, and baking, yeast cells feed on the sugars converted from the starch in flour, and they produce alcohol and carbon dioxide. These gases are captured in the elastic gluten strands in the dough. When the dough is baked or fried, the temperature rises above 120° Fahrenheit, the yeast cells die, the bread sets in its risen form, the alcohol evaporates, and the carbon dioxide is driven off.

Until the mid-nineteenth century, American bakers had to content themselves with brewers' yeast or with sourdough-type starters. These starters were made by the time-honored method of preparing a sweet, starchy dough to attract yeast spores from the air. Compressed (cake) yeast was introduced in the 1860s, and active dry yeast was developed during World War II for the armed forces overseas. Compressed yeast must be stored in the refrigerator. As the cakes age, they tend to turn brown and lose their potency. Many cooks prefer the dry variety; it does not demand refrigeration, though some brands recommend refrigerating, and it remains active for many months.

Yeast is sensitive to temperature. It is dormant below 50° Fahrenheit, and it dies at 120°. Since yeast is a living organism, it is usually "proofed" or tested in warm liquid to see if it is still active. Proofing also activates yeast so that it can begin working immediately upon contact with flour. Yeast is most active between 78° and 105° Fahrenheit, and it is therefore sprinkled or crumbled over warm liquid to dissolve or rehydrate it. Since yeast cells feed on sugars, a sweetener is often stirred into the proofing liquid to encourage yeast activity and accelerate its development. After five to ten minutes, depending on the temperature of the yeast and the liquid, the mixture should begin to bubble and foam.

Once the yeast has been proofed, flour is added and the dough is kneaded. Kneading is necessary to develop and strengthen the moisture-activated gluten proteins in the flour. Without proper and sufficient kneading, the gluten would remain underdeveloped, the gases would not be trapped in its meshwork, and the dough would not rise. Once dough has been kneaded, it is set aside to rise. Once risen, it is punched down to distribute the leavening gases evenly. During baking the dough obtains the ultimate rise. The gases continue to be released until the dough reaches 120° Fahrenheit and the yeast dies. Since the outer cells die while the inner ones continue to expel gas, pressure builds up and often causes the dough to crack. This can be avoided by slashing the dough before it is baked.

A well-baked loaf of bread should smell irresistibly inviting. The crust should be evenly browned, and the loaf should sound hollow when tapped on the bottom. Underbaked bread may have an overly yeasty flavor and a tough, heavy consistency. Overbaked bread will have a tough, heavy crust and a dry interior.

Baking Powder and Baking Soda

While yeast doughs rely on a natural fermentation process to create the leavening gases, quick breads depend on the chemical reaction between an acid and an alkali to produce carbon dioxide. Quick breads today are made with baking powder, baking soda, or a combination of the two. Before the invention of baking powder, baking soda (an alkali) was used in combination with acidic ingredients such as milk, buttermilk, vinegar, or cream of tartar to produce the leavening gas. Due to variables in the actual ingredients and the proportions in which they were used, results were both inconsistent and unpredictable. With the invention of baking powder in the mid 1800s, home bakers were finally guaranteed greater rewards for their efforts.

Baking powder is composed of sodium bicarbonate (baking soda) and an acid (usually cream of tartar). When moistened, baking powder releases carbon dioxide gas, which in turn expands to make the dough or batter rise. The most commonly available commercial baking powders today are "double acting." This means that they contain two acids, one that reacts at room temperature and a second that is activated by the heat of the oven. The inclusion of the second acid gives the baker a little more leeway after mixing and before baking. Breads made with old-fashioned baking powder had to be rushed to the oven.

Doughs and batters containing no acidic ingredients may be leavened by baking powder alone. Once an acidic ingredient is added, the acid–alkali balance is disturbed, and baking soda is needed to neutralize the excess acid. By contrast, in recipes with a high proportion of acidic ingredients, baking soda alone is sufficient as the leavening agent.

Beaten Egg Whites

Spoon breads rely on egg whites, an aerating leavener. This leavener operates on the principal that a volatile substance will produce vapors or gases that will be captured by the batter as it dries and sets during baking. Egg whites are made up of approximately 90 percent water and 10 percent protein. When beaten, the whites expand in volume because the proteins trap air in the foam. The foamy egg whites are then gently folded into the batter. As the spoon bread bakes in the oven, the moisture in the foam turns to water vapor (steam) expanding the batter further, the protein holds the batter in suspension, and the heat firms the structure.

Needless to say, one of bread's greatest virtues is its versatility. With the infinite range of basic ingredients and the various methods of producing and cooking specific doughs and batters, there is, without a doubt, a bread to suit every person and any occasion. While yeast breads require a bit more time and patience, a batch of fresh muffins can be quickly mixed and baked to order. Hearty loaves stand up to soups and are ideal for sandwiches, while hot biscuits and spoon breads provide perfect side-dish accompaniments to many meals.

OATMEAL BREAD

1. In a saucepan, scald the milk. Pour it into a large mixing bowl and add the oatmeal, sugar, salt, and butter. Stir to melt the butter. Cool to lukewarm.
2. In a small bowl, dissolve the yeast in lukewarm water. Let stand until foamy, about 5 minutes. Add to the milk mixture. Add about 4 cups flour and mix well with a wooden spoon or heavy-duty mixer. Set aside, covered, until doubled, about 1 to 1½ hours.
3. Butter a baking sheet.
4. Punch the dough down and turn it out onto a floured work surface. Knead until elastic, about 8 minutes, adding more flour as necessary so that the dough doesn't stick to the work surface. Form into 2 round loaves and put on the prepared baking sheet. Cover lightly and set aside to rise until doubled in bulk, 45 to 60 minutes.
5. Heat the oven to 375°F.
6. Brush the surface of the loaves with the egg-white glaze. Sprinkle the loaves with the uncooked oatmeal. Bake in the preheated oven until the loaves sound hollow when tapped on the bottom, about 40 minutes.

Yield: 2 loaves

Note: The dough may be formed into small round rolls and baked in a preheated 400°F oven for about 20 minutes. Makes about 2 dozen rolls.

2 cups milk
2 cups uncooked oatmeal, plus more for sprinkling
2 tablespoons dark-brown sugar
1 tablespoon salt
2 tablespoons unsalted butter
1 package yeast
¼ cup lukewarm water
4½ to 5 cups all-purpose flour
1 egg white, beaten with 1 tablespoon water

WHEAT-KERNEL ROUND LOAF

This even-textured, hearty loaf is produced by what is known as the "short-rise method." Short-rise breads require extra yeast, flour high in gluten, and thorough kneading. The rising time of these breads is cut by almost half as compared to traditional yeast breads, which require two full rising periods.

For this short-rise bread, proof the yeast in 105°F water in order to accelerate its growth. Combine the yeast mixture with bread flour and vigorously knead the dough for a full 20 minutes by hand or for 10 minutes with an electric dough hook. After a 15-minute rest, shape the dough into loaves and let them rise in a warm place. In less than 1 hour, the loaves will have doubled in size. Score the tops of the loaves just before baking; this will prevent a buildup of pressure within the bread, which would result in a heavy, cracked loaf.

¾ *cup whole-wheat kernels (see Note)*
1½ *cups water*
3½ *teaspoons salt*
2½ *cups warm water*
1½ *packages yeast*
1 *tablespoon sugar*
1 *tablespoon unsalted butter*
3 *tablespoons dry milk*
4½ *to 5½ cups bread flour, plus more for coating*

1. In an ovenproof dish, combine kernels, water, and ½ teaspoon salt. Cover and put into a cold oven. Heat the oven to 400°F. When the oven reaches the correct temperature, cook the kernels for 10 minutes. Turn off heat and leave the kernels in the oven for 8 hours or overnight.

2. In a large mixing bowl, combine warm water, yeast, sugar, butter, and dry milk. Proof until the mixture bubbles and foams, about 5 minutes. Add the remaining 3 teaspoons salt, wheat kernels, and enough flour to make a soft, but not sticky, dough. Turn out onto a lightly floured work surface and knead for 20 minutes by hand, or in a mixer for 10 minutes. Set aside for 15 minutes.

3. Divide the dough into 3 portions. Shape each portion into a ball and set aside for 5 minutes.

4. Butter 3 baking sheets or cake pans.

5. Form each ball of dough into a rounded loaf. Roll the top of the loaf in a generous amount of flour, Put the loaves on the prepared baking sheets or in cake

pans and let them rise in a warm area until very light and nearly doubled in bulk, 45 to 60 minutes.

6. Heat the oven to 375°F.

7. Score the loaves with evenly spaced cuts across the top of the bread or in a starburst pattern. Bake in the preheated oven until the loaves sound hollow when tapped, 35 to 45 minutes. Cool on racks.

Yield: 3 6½- to 7-inch round loaves

Note: Wheat kernels are available in health-food and specialty stores.

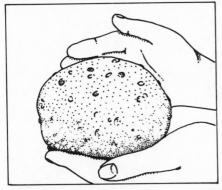

Form each ball of dough into a rounded loaf and roll the top in flour.

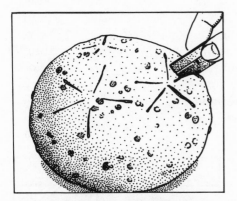

After the loaf has risen until it's very light and doubled in size, score with a razor or sharp knife in a starburst pattern.

SAN FRANCISCO–STYLE SOURDOUGH BREAD

Breads made with sourdough starters require more patience than other yeast-leavened breads, but the wait is well worth it. The sourdough method produces pungent, aromatic loaves that keep well. To begin the process, a room-temperature starter is combined with flour to form a "sponge." This sponge is left to ferment and bubble for anywhere from 4 to 12 hours or even more; the longer it stands, the more sour the finished bread will be. Salt, sugar, and additional flour are added to the sponge, and the dough is kneaded and left to rise for 2 hours. This kneading and rising is repeated two more times before the dough is baked. The lengthy risings are necessary for the full fermentation that gives sourdough bread its characteristic flavor.

Commercially prepared starters and dried starter crystals are available at specialty food shops, but there are two easy methods of preparing starters at home: One method uses regular dry yeast, and the other relies on wild yeast spores from the air. The recipes for these follow.

A starter should be kept in the refrigerator in a loosely covered, nonmetallic container. If it is used infrequently, it can also be frozen in plastic containers or bags. In either case, the starter must be brought to room temperature before it is used. To replenish your starter, simply replace what you have removed with equal parts of flour and water or milk. If your starter supply seems to be running out, you can expand it: Mix the starter with equal amounts of flour and water or milk and let it stand at room temperature for 4 hours or until it bubbles. An ignored starter will develop a strong, sour smell and a darkish color, but it can, in most cases, be revived. Try adding about ¼ cup each of flour and water and letting the mixture stand at room temperature for a few hours; if it bubbles, all is not lost.

A ripened starter is frothy and smells slightly sour.

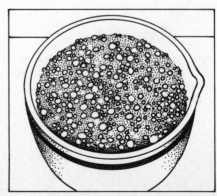

1. In a large bowl, mix the sourdough starter with water and 3 cups flour. Beat with a wooden spoon until smooth. Cover loosely with a towel or plastic wrap and set aside in a warm (85°F) place for 10 to 12 hours. The longer the sponge stands, the more sour the bread.
2. Add sugar and salt to the starter and work in as much more flour as necessary to make a soft, but not sticky, dough. Turn the dough onto a heavily floured work surface and cover with a cloth. Let rest for 15 minutes.
3. Knead the dough until it is smooth and elastic, 5 to 10 minutes, adding as much flour as necessary to avoid sticking.
4. Butter a large bowl. Put the kneaded dough into the bowl and turn once so that the top of the dough is buttered. Cover with a cloth and allow to rise in a warm place until doubled, about 1½ hours.
5. Turn the dough out onto a floured work surface and gently knead the dough 10 or 15 times. Form it into a ball again and return it to the buttered bowl to rise again until almost doubled, about 1½ hours.
6. Sprinkle a cookie sheet with cornmeal.
7. Shape the dough into a large round loaf and put it on the prepared cookie sheet. Arrange a cloth tent over the loaf: Prop the cloth on glasses or pans so that the loaf is covered but the cloth is not resting directly on the dough. Set aside in a warm place until the loaf is doubled in bulk, 1 to 1½ hours. If a crust forms during rising, brush the surface with warm water.
8. Heat the oven to 450°F. Put a pan of boiling water on the bottom rack (see Note).
9. With a razor blade or sharp knife, slash the top of the loaf in a tic-tac-toe pattern. Bake until the bread is golden brown and sounds hollow when tapped on the bottom, 45 to 50 minutes. Cool completely on a rack before cutting.

Yield: 1 large loaf

Note: You can spray water onto the loaf 2 or 3 times during the first 10 minutes of baking rather than cooking it with a pan of boiling water.

½ cup sourdough starter (recipes follow), room temperature
2¼ cups lukewarm water
6 to 7 cups unbleached flour
1 tablespoon sugar
1 tablespoon salt
Cornmeal

DRY YEAST STARTER

1 package yeast
2 cups unbleached flour
1½ cups warm water or milk
1 tablespoon honey

1. In a nonreactive container large enough to allow the mixture to triple in volume, stir together all the ingredients. Set aside at room temperature, loosely covered, until it is frothy and smells slightly sour. Bubbles will begin to form in 3 to 4 hours. Fermentation and sourness could take as much as another day.
2. Stir the mixture down and age in the refrigerator for at least 3 days, loosely covered, before bringing again to room temperature and using.

Yield: about 2 cups

WILD YEAST STARTER

2 cups unbleached flour
1 teaspoon salt
1 tablespoon honey
2 cups potato water (see Note)

1. In a nonreactive container large enough to allow the mixture to triple in volume, mix all the ingredients. Set aside in a warm place, loosely covered, for 2 to 3 days. The mixture will either bubble and grow or mold and smell rotten. If it molds, discard it and try again. If it bubbles and smells pleasantly sour, it is successful.
2. Refrigerate, loosely covered, for at least 3 days before bringing again to room temperature and using.

Yield: about 2 cups

Note: Potato water is simply the water in which peeled potatoes have been cooked.

BISCUITS
Biscuits are dough quick breads (as opposed to batter quick breads). They are made with a much higher proportion of flour to liquid than muffins, and the dough is kneaded gently to form a soft, smooth, homogenous mass. Although the legendary biscuits of the South are made with soft, low-gluten flour, delicious light, flaky biscuits can be successfully prepared with all-purpose flour as well.

For extra-light biscuits, sift the flour before measuring and then once again with the other dry ingredients. Check the date on your baking powder to make sure that it is fresh. Cut cold butter into pieces and add to the dry ingredients. Cut in the butter with a pastry blender or two knives or rub in lightly with your fingers until the mixture resembles coarse meal; this process guarantees a flaky biscuit. As the dough bakes, the moisture in the butter vaporizes to form the light, flaky layers characteristic of biscuits. Add enough liquid to form a soft, workable dough. Knead the dough on a lightly floured surface for about half a minute.

Roll the dough or pat it out with your hands to a ½-inch thickness. With the rim of a glass or a floured biscuit cutter, stamp out round biscuits, cutting them as close together as possible. Press down firmly when cutting the dough; if you twist the glass or cutter, the biscuits may turn out lopsided. For biscuits with soft sides, arrange the rounds on the baking sheet so that they almost touch; for crustier biscuits, space them about 1 inch apart.

To reheat a batch of baked biscuits, wrap them in aluminum foil and heat in a 300°F oven for 10 to 12 minutes. Or try an old trick: quickly dip each biscuit into hot milk or water and bake at 450°F for 4 minutes.

BUTTERMILK BISCUITS

1¾ cups all-purpose flour, sifted before
    measuring
  1 teaspoon salt
  2 teaspoons baking powder
  1 teaspoon sugar
  ½ teaspoon baking soda
  5 tablespoons unsalted butter
  ⅔ to ¾ cup buttermilk

1. Heat the oven to 450°F.
2. In a mixing bowl, combine the flour, salt, baking powder, sugar, and baking soda. Cut in the butter until the mixture resembles coarse meal. Add ⅔ cup buttermilk all at once and then more as necessary to form a soft dough.
3. Turn the dough out onto a floured work surface and knead for about ½ minute. Pat or roll out to ½-inch thick. Cut out 1½-inch rounds with a floured biscuit cutter or the rim of a glass. Put the rounds on an ungreased baking sheet and bake in the preheated oven for 10 to 12 minutes.

Yield: 2 dozen biscuits

Cut cold butter into the flour until the mixture resembles coarse meal.

SWEET POTATO–PECAN BISCUITS

  ¾ cup mashed sweet potatoes
  4 ounces unsalted butter, melted
1½ tablespoons brown sugar
  2 cups all-purpose flour, sifted before
    measuring
  1 teaspoon salt
  4 teaspoons baking powder
  ½ cup milk
  ½ cup finely chopped pecans, mixed with
    1 tablespoon flour

1. Heat the oven to 400°F. Lightly butter a baking sheet.
2. In a mixing bowl, combine the sweet potatoes, butter, and brown sugar and beat until smooth. In a separate bowl, combine the flour, salt, and baking powder and add to the sweet potatoes along with the milk. Stir until just mixed. The dough will be quite soft and spongy. Add the pecans.
3. On a lightly floured work surface, knead the dough for about ½ minute. Roll the dough out to ½-inch thickness. Cut into 2-inch rounds. Put on the prepared baking sheet and bake in the preheated oven for 12 to 15 minutes.

Yield: 2 dozen biscuits

MUFFINS
Muffins are batter quick breads, as opposed to biscuits, which are classified as dough quick breads. Muffins are made with melted butter and a proportion of about two parts flour to one part liquid. The dry ingredients are sifted together and combined with the liquids in a few swift strokes. The resulting batter is spooned into buttered tins and immediately baked in the oven.

The most important step in muffin making is the stirring process. Generally, the liquid and dry ingredients are stirred together just enough to form a thick, lumpy batter; fifteen to twenty strokes should be sufficient to moisten the dry ingredients and to develop gluten strands to trap the carbon dioxide released by the leavening agent. Overmixing will result in a tough muffin with a peaked dome and a tunneled interior. Undermixing, on the other hand, yields crumbly muffins with poor volume and lumps of raw flour. A perfectly made muffin will have a rounded dome and a light, slightly coarse but even texture.

Once the batter has been made, it must be spooned into prepared muffin tins as gently as possible. Rough handling at this point could deflate the batter and overactivate the gluten. No matter what size your muffin tin may be, each cup should be two-thirds full of batter. Bake the muffins in the middle of a preheated oven and cool them in their cups for 3 to 4 minutes before serving. Muffins are best eaten when just made.

HERBED RICE MUFFINS

1. Heat the oven to 425°F. Butter standard-size muffin tins.
2. In a large mixing bowl, sift together the flour, sugar, baking powder, and salt.
3. In another bowl, lightly beat the egg. Add the milk, melted butter, rice, and herbs.
4. Make a well in the dry mixture, pour the liquid in all at once, and mix the batter until no dry flour is visible. A few lumps may remain. Fill the prepared tins two-thirds full and bake in the preheated oven until the muffins turn pale golden brown and a skewer comes out clean, 20 to 25 minutes.

Yield: 16 muffins

1¾ cups all-purpose flour
1 tablespoon sugar
4 teaspoons baking powder
½ teaspoon salt
1 egg
1¼ cups milk
4 tablespoons unsalted butter, melted
1 cup cooked brown or white rice, cooled
¼ cup each minced fresh parsley, scallions, and dill or basil, mixed together

PUMPKIN-GINGERBREAD MUFFINS

1½ cups all-purpose flour
½ teaspoon salt
½ teaspoon baking soda
2 teaspoons baking powder
¾ teaspoon ground ginger
⅛ teaspoon ground cloves
½ teaspoon ground cinnamon
6 tablespoons unsalted butter, softened
⅓ cup dark-brown sugar
⅓ cup granulated sugar
1 egg
½ cup canned or fresh pumpkin puree
½ cup milk
1 cup currants (optional)
2 tablespoons sugar mixed with 1
    teaspoon cinnamon

1. Heat the oven to 350°F. Butter standard-size muffin tins.
2. In a bowl, sift together the first 7 dry ingredients.
3. In a large mixing bowl, cream the butter with both sugars until light and fluffy. Beat in the egg and pumpkin puree. Add the dry ingredients alternately with the milk. Beat more thoroughly than usual for muffins so that the batter is well mixed and falls smoothly when the spoon or beater is lifted. Stir in the currants, if using.
4. Fill the prepared muffin tins two-thirds full. Sprinkle with the sugar-cinnamon mixture. Bake in the preheated oven until a skewer inserted in the center comes out clean, 25 to 28 minutes.

Yield: 1 dozen muffins

CORN BREAD LOAF

The meal for corn bread should be stone-ground or water-ground. The flavor and texture are far superior to those of the fine-milled, supermarket variety. Though some areas of the country cling to a preference for white cornmeal over yellow, there is virtually no difference in taste between them, and yellow stone- or water-ground meal can be substituted in this recipe.

2 cups white cornmeal
1 teaspoon salt
1 teaspoon baking powder
1 cup all-purpose flour
1 teaspoon baking soda
2 tablespoons bacon drippings or
    vegetable shortening, melted
2 cups buttermilk

1. Heat the oven to 350°F. Butter an 8″-×-4″ loaf pan.
2. In a bowl, combine the dry ingredients. Add the drippings and buttermilk and stir only until the batter is smooth, being careful not to overmix. Pour into the prepared pan and bake in the preheated oven until the top is golden brown, 50 to 60 minutes. Turn out and serve immediately or cool on a rack.

Yield: 1 loaf

SPOON BREAD   Spoon breads have been appearing

on American tables since colonial times. Until the nineteenth century, spoon bread was considered strictly a bread; eventually, it came to be served as a side-dish substitute for potatoes or rice. Topped with a tangy, savory sauce, spoon bread can also make a light first course or lunch; accompanied by fruit preserves or honey, it makes a good breakfast or brunch dish. Spoon bread's mild flavor welcomes the addition of other ingredients, from fresh corn kernels and spices or chopped peppers and herbs, to crumbled bacon or sausage or ground ham.

Spoon bread has the consistency of a firm pudding and a composition somewhere between that of corn bread and a soufflé. It is based on cornmeal, milk, and egg yolks, which are cooked together to form a thick base known as a rick. Stiffly beaten egg whites are folded into the rick, and the mixture is baked in the oven until puffed and golden.

For traditional richness, whole milk should be used in spoon breads, as opposed to skimmed or low-fat varieties. For an extra-rich spoon bread, light cream or half and half can be substituted for some of the milk. Buttermilk will give the spoon bread an extra tang. Both yellow and white cornmeal work well. There is now little difference between them beyond color. Stone-ground or water-ground cornmeals, in either color, still contain the germ, and will produce a more flavorful spoon bread.

BASIC SPOON BREAD

6 *tablespoons unsalted butter*
3 *cups milk*
1 *cup white* or *yellow cornmeal*
1½ *teaspoons salt*
½ *teaspoon black pepper*
3 *eggs, separated, room temperature*
  Pinch of salt
  Fresh Tomato Sauce (recipe follows)

1. Heat the oven to 350°F. Butter the sides and bottom of a 1½-quart casserole with 1 tablespoon butter.
2. In a large, heavy saucepan, bring the milk almost to a boil over medium heat. Gradually add the cornmeal, stirring to blend. Continue stirring over reduced heat until thick, about 2 minutes. Add the remaining 5 tablespoons butter, salt, and pepper. Mix well and cook for 2 minutes longer. Remove the saucepan from heat.
3. In a small bowl, lightly beat the egg yolks. Add the yolks to the cornmeal and mix to incorporate.
4. In another bowl, beat the egg whites with a pinch of salt until stiff but not dry. Fold into the yolk-meal mixture.
5. Pour the batter into the prepared casserole, spreading it evenly and smoothing the top with a spatula. Bake in the preheated oven, uncovered, until puffed and browned, 30 to 40 minutes. Serve immediately with fresh tomato sauce on the side.

Yield: 4 servings

FRESH TOMATO SAUCE

2 *tablespoons olive oil*
2 *onions, diced*
3½ *pounds tomatoes, chopped*
3 *cloves garlic, crushed*
2 *teaspoons chopped fresh parsley*
2 *teaspoons each chopped fresh basil,*
  marjoram, and thyme, or ⅔
  teaspoon each dried
2 *teaspoons sugar (optional)*
  Salt and black pepper

1. Heat the oil in a large, nonreactive saucepan, and sauté the onions until soft, 5 to 7 minutes. Add the tomatoes, garlic, parsley, mixed herbs, and sugar as needed. Simmer, stirring, until the tomatoes have reduced to a thick pulp, 40 to 50 minutes.
2. Strain the mixture through a sieve, and return to the saucepan. Reduce the sauce further over low heat to reach the desired consistency. Season with salt and pepper to taste.

Yield: about 4 cups

SPOON BREAD WITH CORN

1. Heat the oven to 350°F. Butter the bottom and sides of a 1½-quart casserole with 1 tablespoon butter.
2. In a large, heavy saucepan, over medium heat, bring the corn and milk to a boil. Add the cornmeal slowly, stirring to blend. Simmer, stirring, until thick, about 2 minutes. Remove the pan from heat and immediately add the remaining 6 tablespoons butter, salt, sugar, nutmeg, and cayenne. Mix well.
3. In a small bowl, lightly beat the egg yolks. Add the yolks to the saucepan and incorporate.
4. In another bowl, beat the egg whites with a pinch of salt until stiff but not dry. Fold into the cornmeal mixture.
5. Pour the batter into the prepared casserole, spreading it evenly and smoothing the top with a spatula. Bake in the preheated oven, uncovered, until puffed and golden, 30 to 40 minutes.

Yield: 4 servings

7 tablespoons unsalted butter
1½ cups white corn kernels (cut from about 3 ears)
3 cups milk
1 cup white or yellow cornmeal
2 teaspoons salt
1 tablespoon sugar
¼ teaspoon nutmeg
¼ teaspoon cayenne
3 eggs, separated, room temperature
Pinch of salt

DOUGHNUTS
Americans have been eating doughnuts of all shapes for more than three centuries, but the traditional ring shape did not appear until the late 1840s. Until then, otherwise perfectly fried doughnuts often had heavy, soggy centers. An experiment proved that by stamping out and removing the centers of the dough, heat could penetrate evenly during frying, resulting in perfect doughnuts every time. Most of today's commercially available doughnuts have been mass produced and cannot begin to rival the taste and alluring aroma of just-fried, homemade cakes. Doughnuts are not difficult to make and take surprisingly little time.

Homemade doughnuts can be leavened with yeast or with baking powder. White flour is most commonly used, but it can be mixed with whole-wheat flour, mashed potatoes, or even rice. Rich in eggs, sugar, and butter, doughnut doughs should be handled gently during rolling, cutting, and frying. Doughnuts can be served plain, dusted with sugar, or glazed; they can be filled with pastry cream, thick jam or marmalade, or fruit preserves.

Frying is the most crucial step in producing perfect doughnuts. Maintaining the correct oil temperature and carefully monitoring frying times are the two keys to success. The oil should be heated to 375°F for unfilled doughnuts and 370°F for filled varieties. If the oil is too hot, the outside of the dough will burn before the inside has had a chance to cook. When doughnuts are lowered into heated fat, the moisture in the dough vaporizes, and the steam causes the dough to sizzle and inflate. As long as the steam bubbles out, oil is prevented from seeping in. When all of the moisture has been released, the steam barrier is no more, but by then a protective crust has formed.

In order to maintain a constant oil temperature, fry only a few doughnuts at a time. Replace cooked doughnuts with uncooked dough as you fry, without waiting for the entire batch to be done. Try to turn the doughnuts only once during frying to reduce the risk of puncturing the dough and allowing oil to seep in. Drain fried doughnuts on paper towels to remove excess oil.

Pinto Bean and Parsley Salad, p. 140

Lamb and White-Bean Salad, p. 138

Cannelloni with Sun-Dried Tomato Sauce, p. 154

Two-Chicken Balsamico, p. 144

Steamed Parsley Served Warm or Cold, p. 170

Green-Pepper Cappelletti with Red-Pepper Sauce, p. 162
Ham and Three-Cheese Pasta Roll, p. 160

Best Strawberry Shortcake, p. 216

Pecan-Pie Ice Cream and Pie-Pastry Cookies, p. 254
Fudge Cake with Milk-Chocolate Frosting, p. 210

Steamed Brownie Pudding, p. 226

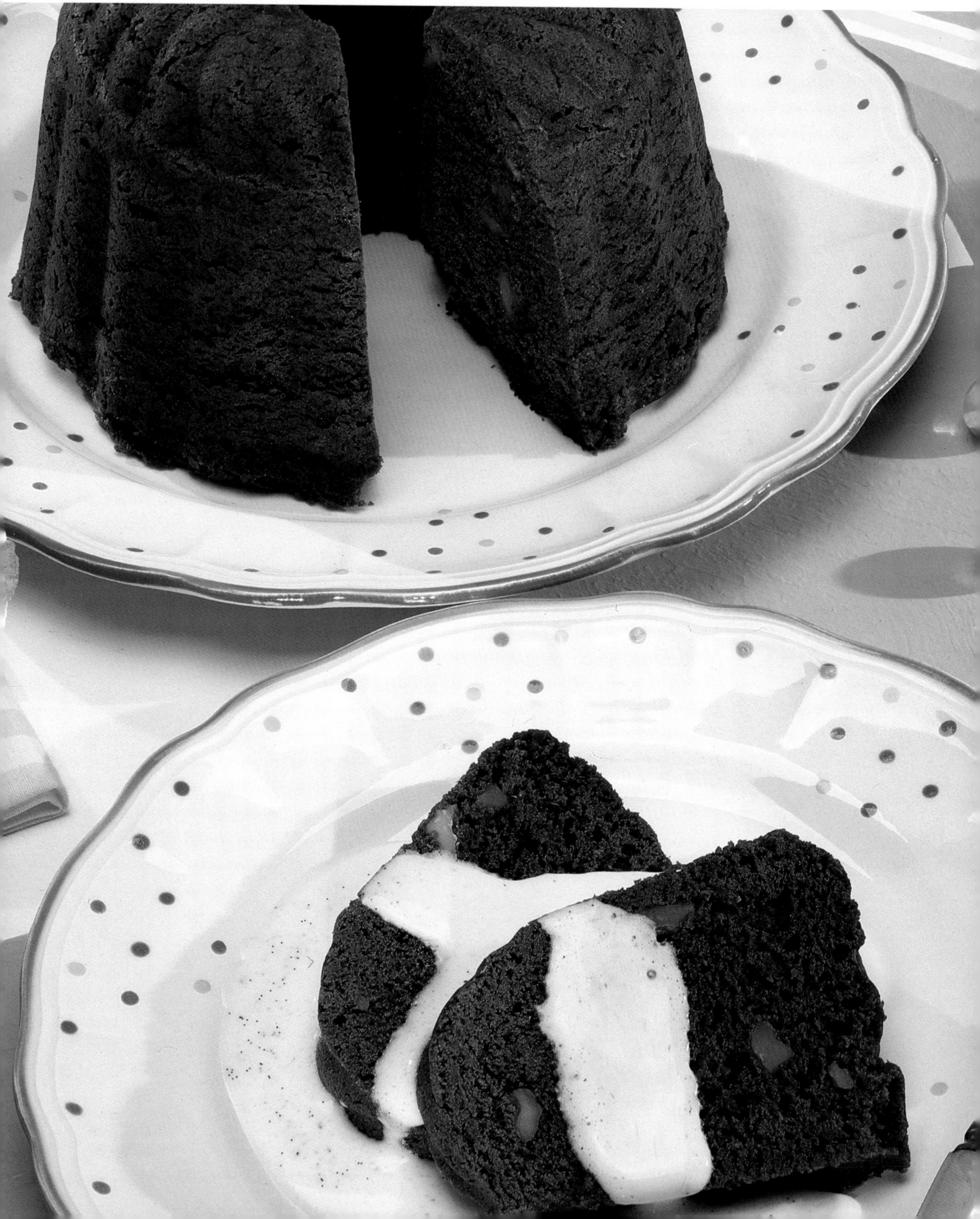

Raspberry-Peach Cobbler, p. 230

SPUDNUTS

1. For the doughnuts, put the yeast, milk, and ½ teaspoon sugar in a small bowl and let it stand until foamy, about 5 minutes.
2. In a large bowl, beat the potatoes, butter, remaining sugar, and salt until well blended and smooth. Add the yeast mixture, vanilla extract, and egg.
3. In another bowl, sift together the cake flour and all-purpose flour. Beat the sifted flours into the potato-yeast mixture, 1 cup at a time, to make a soft, smooth dough. If the dough is too sticky, add as much as ½ cup additional flour but make sure the dough remains soft. Cover the dough and let rise in a warm place until doubled in bulk, 1 to 1½ hours.
4. Lightly flour a baking sheet.
5. Turn the dough onto a lightly floured work surface and roll to ½-inch thickness. Cut into rounds with a 2½- to 3-inch doughnut cutter. Separate the doughnuts from the holes and put all on the prepared baking sheet. Let rise in a warm place, loosely covered, until nearly doubled, about 1 hour.
6. Heat 2 to 3 inches of oil to 370°F in a deep fryer.
7. Fry the doughnuts and then holes, a few at a time, turning once, until golden, about 2 to 3 minutes per side. (The holes will take less time than the doughnuts.) Drain on paper towels.
8. For the glaze, beat sugar, milk, and vanilla in a large bowl until smooth. Beat in enough hot water to make a thin glaze.
9. Dip the warm doughnuts into the glaze to coat completely and allow the excess glaze to drip back into the bowl. Put the doughnuts onto a rack until the glaze is set. Serve warm or at room temperature.

Yield: about 1 dozen doughnuts and 1 dozen holes

Doughnuts

- 1 package yeast
- 1 cup warm milk
- ¼ cup sugar
- ½ cup warm, mashed potatoes
- 4 tablespoons unsalted butter, softened
- ½ teaspoon salt
- ½ teaspoon vanilla extract
- 1 egg, lightly beaten
- 1½ cups cake flour
- 1½ cups all-purpose flour, plus more if necessary

Glaze

- 2 cups confectioners' sugar
- 3 tablespoons milk
- 1 teaspoon vanilla extract
- 3 tablespoons (approximately) hot water

Oil

Roll the dough to about ½-inch thickness and cut into rings with a doughnut cutter.

Fry the doughnuts a few at a time, turning once.

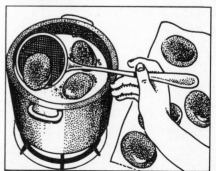

BOSTON CREAM DOUGHNUTS

Doughnuts

1 *package yeast*
½ *cup sugar*
¼ *cup warm water*
1 *cup milk*
4 *tablespoons unsalted butter, cut into bits*
½ *teaspoon salt*
¼ *teaspoon vanilla extract*
2 *egg yolks, lightly beaten*
3 *to 3½ cups flour*

Pastry Cream

1 *cup milk*
⅓ *cup sugar*
3 *tablespoons flour*
3 *egg yolks*
¾ *teaspoon vanilla extract*
1 *tablespoon unsalted butter, cut into bits*

1 *egg white beaten with 1 teaspoon water*
Oil

Chocolate Glaze

1 *ounce bittersweet chocolate, broken into bits*
1 *ounce unsweetened chocolate, broken into bits*
1 *tablespoon unsalted butter*
1½ *cups confectioners' sugar*
½ *teaspoon vanilla extract*
¼ *cup (approximately) boiling water*

1. For the doughnuts, rinse a large mixing bowl with warm water. Combine the yeast, ½ teaspoon sugar, and warm water and set aside until foamy, about 5 minutes.

2. Scald the milk in a saucepan with the butter, remaining sugar, and salt, stirring to dissolve the sugar. Cool to lukewarm.

3. Pour the milk mixture into the proofed yeast and add vanilla, egg yolks, and 2 cups flour. Beat until smooth and add enough additional flour to make a soft dough. Turn the dough out onto a lightly floured work surface and knead until smooth, about 3 minutes.

4. Lightly butter a large bowl.

5. Put the dough into the prepared bowl, turning to coat the top of the dough with butter. Let rise in a warm place, lightly covered, until doubled in bulk, about 1½ hours.

6. While the dough is rising, scald milk in a saucepan for the pastry cream.

7. In a bowl, beat the sugar, flour, and egg yolks until light and the mixture trails in a ribbon from beater. Whisk about half the hot milk into the egg mixture and then pour the milk-egg mixture into the milk remaining in the saucepan. Cook, whisking constantly, until the mixture is thick and nearly boiling. Continue cooking just under the boiling point for about 2 minutes. Remove from heat and stir in the vanilla and butter. Cool and refrigerate the cream until needed.

8. Punch down the dough and put onto a lightly floured work surface. Roll to a ¼-inch thickness. Cut into rounds with a 2½-inch pastry cutter. Put 2 teaspoons of the pastry cream in the centers of half of the rounds. Moisten the edges liberally with the egg-white wash and top each with an unfilled round. Firmly press the edges together to seal. If necessary, recut the rounds with a pastry cutter to trim evenly.

9. Lightly flour a baking sheet.

10. Put the rounds on the prepared baking sheet and

allow to rise in a warm place until nearly doubled in bulk, about 1 hour.

11. Heat 2 to 3 inches of oil to 375°F in a deep fryer.
12. Fry the doughnuts, a few at a time, turning once, until golden, about 2 minutes per side. Drain on paper towels and let cool.
13. For the chocolate glaze, melt both chocolates and butter in the top of a double boiler over hot water, stirring until smooth.
14. Add the confectioners' sugar and vanilla and whisk in enough hot water to make a thin icing. Cool slightly. If the glaze sets before you are ready to use it, rewarm over hot water.
15. Drizzle the chocolate glaze over the doughnuts or dip the tops directly into the glaze. Let the glaze set. Serve at room temperature.

Yield: 2 dozen doughnuts

Note: These doughnuts are best eaten quickly, but if they must be kept for more than a few hours, they should be stored in the refrigerator.

MOLASSES–SPICE CAKE DOUGHNUTS

2 *eggs*
¾ *cup sugar, plus sugar for rolling, if desired*
½ *cup dark molasses*
¾ *cup buttermilk*
2 *tablespoons unsalted butter, melted*
1 *tablespoon orange juice*
2 *teaspoons grated orange zest*
4 *cups all-purpose flour, plus more if necessary*
2 *teaspoons baking powder*
1 *teaspoon baking soda*
¼ *teaspoon salt*
½ *teaspoon ground cinnamon*
½ *teaspoon grated nutmeg*
1 *teaspoon ground ginger*
⅛ *teaspoon ground cloves*
  Oil

1. In a mixing bowl, beat the eggs with sugar until light.
2. In another bowl, combine the molasses, buttermilk, melted butter, orange juice, and zest.
3. In a third bowl, sift together the flour, baking powder, baking soda, salt, cinnamon, nutmeg, ginger, and cloves.
4. Stir the buttermilk mixture into the egg-sugar mixture, alternating with the dry ingredients. The dough should be smooth and very soft. If it is too sticky, add up to ¼ cup more flour. Cover and refrigerate for 1 to 2 hours.
5. Line 3 baking sheets with waxed paper or foil.
6. On a lightly floured work surface, roll one-quarter of the dough to ½-inch thickness. Keep the remaining dough in the refrigerator, covered. Cut the rolled-out dough into rounds with a 2½-inch doughnut cutter and separate the doughnuts from the holes. Chill the doughnuts and holes on the prepared baking sheets for 20 to 30 minutes. Repeat with the remaining dough, one-quarter at a time.
7. Heat 2 to 3 inches of oil to 370°F in a deep fryer.
8. Fry the doughnuts and then the holes, a few at a time, turning once, until deep golden brown, 1 to 2 minutes per side. (Holes will take less time.) Drain on paper towels. Roll in granulated sugar, if desired, and serve warm.

Yield: about 2 dozen doughnuts and 2 dozen holes

Chapter

12 | Pies, Cakes, and Shortcakes

From early times, Americans have had a hunger for sturdy, no-nonsense desserts like cakes and pies. With just two eggs, one cup of sugar, a quarter cup of butter, and a few other less expensive ingredients, the frugal cook could turn out a perfectly respectable "plain cake." A basic pastry dough held just about anything from leftover venison to just-picked berries or green tomatoes and was likely to turn up at any meal, including breakfast.

Modern cooks don't know how good they have it. Calibrated ovens have taken the place of the wood-fired variety, thus removing one of the major contributions to the mortality rate in colonial America—culinary burns. In addition to their perilous nature, early ovens were erratic; making a light cake or a perfectly baked pie was indeed the mark of a good cook. Today we have self-cleaning and microwave ovens, but because of the equally handy mass-produced baked goods made with questionable ingredients, a fine pie or cake still points to a proficient cook. The ingredients available to the home cook are, like the ovens, dependable and come in great variety.

FLOURS

Cake flour, pastry flour, all-purpose flour, whole-wheat flour, unbleached flour—the profusion can be confusing. Any cook can make excellent pies and cakes with nothing more than standard all-purpose flour in the larder, or can use the more natural unbleached flour as the household all-purpose flour. The other types are interesting to work with, though, and have their advantages.

Whole-wheat flour makes an earthier piecrust; up to half the all-purpose flour can be replaced by whole-wheat in the pastry recipes in this chapter. You may need slightly less water when using whole-wheat flour. You can also substitute oatmeal or cornmeal for a portion of the all-purpose—use one part to three parts all-purpose flour. These substitutions will require slightly *more* water. Nuts, such as ground filberts or almonds, in proportions similar to those for oatmeal will enhance flavor, but avoid oily varieties, such as cashews or peanuts, which will produce a sticky, unworkable dough.

Pastry flour is softer than all-purpose and ideal for all-butter crusts, which can be too brittle when made with standard flour, but pastry flour is not nearly so available as the other types. The usual American solution to this problem is to cut the butter with vegetable shortening. If you prefer to experiment with altering the flour rather than the fat, we recommend four parts all-purpose to one part cake flour.

Cake flour is the softest of all. It makes a tender cake and is often called for in high-rising layer cakes such as our Fudge Cake with Milk Chocolate Frosting. We recommend using part cake flour in our shortcake recipes too, for a melt-in-your-mouth result. If only all-purpose flour is on hand, substitute by mixing ¾ cup all-purpose flour with 2 tablespoons cornstarch for each cup of cake flour indicated in the recipe.

SHORTENING

Shortening is a key ingredient in any pie or cake. The three obvious choices are butter, vegetable shortening, and lard. When making pie pastry, most recipes call for a combination of butter and vegetable shortening: The butter is added for taste; the vegetable shortening makes the dough easier to work and the final baked product flakier.

Many cooks swear by lard for making pie pastry; it boasts rich flavor and yields very flaky pastry. It is often combined with butter, however, to soften its flavor. Margarine can be used for those concerned with dietary restrictions. Use a solid-stick type and chill it thoroughly before using.

In cakes, fats play a critical role by trapping air bubbles in the batter. When baked, the carbon dioxide released by baking powder attaches itself to these bubbles in the batter and enlarges them. After five minutes in the oven, the fat melts, and the air is released into the mixture. This is very important to keep in mind when choosing a fat to use when baking cakes. Oils are a poor choice because they don't trap air bubbles well. Vegetable shortening does the best job but lacks flavor. Butter, the most frequently used alternative, provides rich flavor and can be mixed with vegetable shortening to provide a finer crumb.

MAKING AND BAKING A CAKE

Two steps are crucial in making light cakes: creaming the butter or other shortening with the sugar and adding the eggs. Butter can be creamed from the solid state by hard beating, but if you have the time, it's much easier to allow it to come to room temperature first. Don't let it melt, or you won't be able to incorporate air. Beat until soft and light, adding the sugar gradually.

The classic American layer cake is made by separating eggs and folding the whites in at the end. This is the best method for light, well-risen cakes when preparing them by hand. However, most modern recipes assume the availability of an electric mixer, and with its powerful beating, the eggs can be added whole. The way they're incorporated is still important. They should go in one at a time with thorough beating between each addition. Of course, airiness is not the aim in every cake, and the treatment of eggs is not so important in denser ones such as the Mississippi Mud Cake in this chapter.

Fill the cake pans no less than half and no more than two-thirds with batter. Place them in a preheated oven that is no cooler than 350° Fahrenheit and no hotter than 375°—if heat penetration is too slow, the texture of the finished cakes will be coarse, and if it is too fast, they will burn on the outside and crack. The cakes should be baked as close to the center of the oven as possible and positioned so that air can circulate all around the pans; do not let them touch each other or the sides of the oven. For even baking, turn the pans around halfway through baking.

HOW TO MAKE A PIECRUST

Success with pie pastry has a lot to do with gluten, a protein found in flour. When preparing pie pastry, keep in mind that the softer the flour, the less gluten, and that moisture, manipulation, and heat all help develop gluten, a great thing for bread but bad for pastry. The shortening and liquid should be cold, the dough should be handled as little as possible, and only enough liquid should be added to make the dough hold together. Allowing the dough to rest in the refrigerator before rolling out will also contribute to a tender crust. If you're having trouble with tough crusts, try using a teaspoon of lemon juice or other acidic ingredient, which will soften the gluten, for part of the liquid.

Work the shortening into the flour using your fin-

Flute the edges together using your left thumb and forefinger and the knuckle of right forefinger.

Edges can be crimped with a fork. For a scalloped edge, indent the dough with your thumb between sets of tine marks.

For a simple scalloped edge, squeeze the edges of the dough together with your thumb and forefinger.

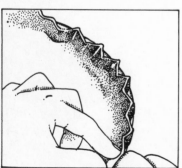

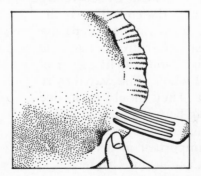

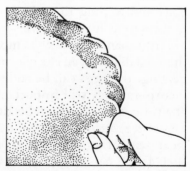

gertips, a pastry blender, two knives, or a food processor. The final texture should resemble coarse meal with
a few pea-size pieces left. Larger pieces of butter will
create a flakier, more layered pastry caused by the action
of the steam that results from the moisture in the butter.
Sprinkle the cold liquid over the mixture, tossing with
a fork. The amount of liquid required will vary depending on humidity and the condition of the flour.
Work quickly in order to prevent the shortening from
softening. If you use a food processor, which we think
makes an excellent pastry, be careful not to overprocess
the dough. This will yield a tough crust.

Refrigerate the dough for at least half an hour. If the
dough has been thoroughly chilled, allow it to warm
up until soft enough to roll.

PREBAKING

Prebaking piecrusts can be one of the most frustrating
techniques for beginners. The following suggestions should
help: Ease the pastry into the pan allowing plenty of slack.
Stretched dough shrinks. Push some of the excess dough
from the edge down the sides of the pan so that the sides are
somewhat thicker than the bottom. The crust is less likely to
shrink this way, and also the sides cook more quickly than
the bottom.

If you're using an American pie pan, flute or crimp the
border, bringing some of the dough over the edge of the pan
to hold the crust in place. When using a tart pan, cut the
dough off level with the top of the pan and then, using your
thumbs, push the dough back up slightly above the rim to
allow for shrinkage. Prick the shaped dough thoroughly so
that the crust won't bubble up, and press a double thickness
of buttered aluminum foil into the pan to hold the dough in
place until it is set. Freeze for fifteen to thirty minutes to
firm. Pop it directly into a preheated oven at high heat to set
the crust. Reduce the heat and, once the pastry is firm,
remove the foil and continue baking until done.

FREEZING

Undecorated cakes can be frozen for two to three months. Wrap the cooled layers first in plastic wrap and then in foil. Thaw without unwrapping. You can freshen the thawed cake in a 350° Fahrenheit oven for ten minutes.

Pie pastry can be frozen either unrolled or shaped in a pie tin. If already shaped, there's no need to thaw before baking.

SHORTCAKES

Shortcakes can be viewed as combining the best of both worlds: a sweet, cakey biscuit that's as rich as pastry and filled with luscious, ripe fruit topped off with whipped cream. In season, nothing is better than our traditional Best Strawberry Shortcake—unless it's our Gingered Shortcake with Honey-Poached Peaches. Shortcakes are simply especially rich, sweetened baking-powder biscuits. For information on making biscuits, see Chapter 11.

PIES

STANDARD PASTRY

Since a food processor provides the fastest way to mix piecrust dough and makes pastry that is as good as that made by hand, our piecrust recipes are written with food-processor directions. If you prefer to mix the dough by hand, do not freeze the shortening. Chill it thoroughly, then cut it into the flour mixture using a pastry blender or two knives. See How to Make a Piecrust in the introduction to this chapter.

1. In a food processor, combine the flour and salt. Add the butter and shortening and whir until they are the size of small peas. With the motor running, add cold water, a little at a time, until the mixture holds together when lightly pressed.
2. Shape into a disc and wrap in plastic. Chill until the dough is workable, about 30 minutes.

Yield: enough for 1 single-crust pie or tart

1 cup all-purpose flour
1/2 teaspoon salt
4 tablespoons unsalted butter, cut into pieces and frozen
3 tablespoons vegetable shortening, well chilled
2 tablespoons (approximately) cold water

GREAT-GRANDMOTHER'S PASTRY

1. Combine the flour, salt, and sugar in a food processor and whir until well mixed. Add the butter and lard and whir until the butter and lard pieces are the size of small peas. With the motor running, add the vinegar and cold water, a little at a time, until the mixture forms a ball when lightly pressed together.
2. Press the dough into a disc shape. Wrap in plastic and chill until workable, at least 30 minutes.

Yield: enough for 1 single-crust pie or tart

1 cup all-purpose flour
1/2 teaspoon salt
3/4 teaspoon sugar
3 tablespoons unsalted butter, cut into pieces and frozen
4 tablespoons lard, well chilled, cut into pieces
3/4 teaspoon cider vinegar
2 tablespoons (approximately) cold water

GREEN TOMATO–MINCEMEAT PIE

2 recipes Great-Grandmother's Pastry
(see previous recipe)
2 cups chopped green tomatoes
1 cup raisins
½ cup light-brown sugar
2 tablespoons cider vinegar
½ cup boiled cider (see Note)
¼ cup orange juice
Grated zest of 1 orange
¼ teaspoon salt
½ teaspoon ground cinnamon
½ teaspoon ground cloves
¼ teaspoon grated nutmeg
¼ teaspoon ground allspice
2 tablespoons unsalted butter
2 tablespoons brandy or applejack
(optional)
1 egg yolk beaten with 1 tablespoon
heavy cream

1. Make the pastry dough, wrap, and refrigerate.
2. In a nonreactive saucepan, combine the next 8 ingredients and simmer until the tomatoes are tender and the juices are reduced by half, about 40 minutes. Stir in the spices, butter, and optional brandy or applejack.
3. Heat the oven to 375°F. Butter a 9-inch pie pan.
4. Roll out slightly over half the pastry dough and line the prepared pan. Cut off the dough even with the edge of the pan.
5. Fill the lined pie pan with the tomato mixture. Roll out the remaining dough 1 inch larger than the top of the pan. Tuck the edges of the top crust under the bottom crust all around the rim and flute. Brush with the egg glaze and vent with decorative slashes.
6. Bake in the preheated oven until golden, about 45 minutes. Serve slightly warm or at room temperature.

Yield: one 9-inch pie

Note: Boiled cider is also known as cider jelly and can be purchased from natural-food stores. If not available, you can make your own by boiling 2 cups fresh apple cider until reduced to ½ cup.

CRANBERRY LATTICE PIE

1½ recipes Standard Pastry or Great-
Grandmother's Pastry (see recipes,
this chapter)
1½ cups cranberries
½ cup seedless raisins
⅓ cup orange juice
½ teaspoon grated orange zest
¼ teaspoon grated lemon zest
½ cup dark-brown sugar
1½ tablespoons dark rum
1 tablespoon unsalted butter
1 egg yolk beaten with 1 tablespoon
milk

1. Make the pastry dough, wrap, and refrigerate.
2. Combine the cranberries, raisins, orange juice, and zests in a heavy 2- to 3-quart saucepan. Add the brown sugar and bring to a boil, stirring to dissolve the sugar. Lower heat and simmer, stirring often, until the cranberries have popped, 5 to 7 minutes. Remove from heat and stir in the rum and butter.
3. Heat the oven to 375°F. Butter a 9-inch pie pan.
4. Roll out about two-thirds of the pastry dough and line the prepared pan. Trim the edge leaving a ½-inch overhang. Fill with the cranberry mixture.
5. Roll out the remaining pastry and cut into ½-inch strips. Arrange the strips over the filling in a lattice.

Fold the overhang from the bottom crust over the edges of the strips. Flute the edge. Carefully brush the pastry with the egg glaze.

6. Bake in the preheated oven until the pastry is golden brown, about 45 minutes. Let cool and serve at room temperature.

Yield: one 9-inch pie

BUTTERMILK PIE

1. Make the pastry dough, wrap, and refrigerate for at least 30 minutes.
2. Butter a 9-inch pie pan. Roll out the chilled dough, line the pan, and flute the edge. Refrigerate until ready to use.
3. Heat the oven to 400°F.
4. In a mixing bowl, beat the eggs, adding the sugar gradually, until mixture forms a heavy ribbon as it falls from the beaters. Beat in the salt, flour, lemon zest, lemon juice, and vanilla. Beat in the buttermilk until incorporated and then stir in the melted butter.
5. Remove the pie pan from the refrigerator and fill with the buttermilk mixture. Bake in the preheated oven for 10 minutes. Reduce heat to 350°F and continue baking until the top is golden and the custard is just set, an additional 20 to 25 minutes. Serve warm.

Yield: one 9-inch pie

1 *recipe Standard Pastry (see recipe, this chapter)*
3 *eggs*
1 *cup sugar*
⅛ *teaspoon salt*
1 *tablespoon all-purpose flour*
Grated zest of 2 lemons
3 *tablespoons fresh lemon juice*
1 *teaspoon vanilla extract*
1 *cup buttermilk*
6 *tablespoons unsalted butter, melted*

FIG-PECAN TART

One of the most typical desserts in France is a tart shell filled
with pastry cream and topped with fruit. Here the idea is
adapted to the ingredients of our own South—pecans, figs,
and bourbon.

1 *recipe Standard Pastry (see recipe, this*
chapter)

Fig Topping

1½ *cups dried figs*
 2 *cups water*
 ½ *cup bourbon*
 3 *tablespoons sugar*
 2 *tablespoons lemon juice*
 1 *cup toasted pecan halves (see Note)*

Bourbon Pastry Cream

 ½ *cup sugar*
 6 *large egg yolks*
 ¼ *cup all-purpose flour*
   Pinch of salt
 2 *cups milk*
 3 *tablespoons (approximately) bourbon*

1. Make the pastry dough, wrap, and refrigerate for at least 30 minutes.
2. Butter a 12-inch tart pan. Roll out the chilled dough and line the pan. (See Prebaking in the introduction to this chapter.) Prick the bottom thoroughly with a fork. Cover with a double thickness of buttered aluminum foil, pressing it onto the base and up the sides. Freeze until firm, 15 to 30 minutes.
3. Heat the oven to 400°F. Put the lined tart pan in the preheated oven and bake for 10 minutes. Remove the foil, reduce the oven temperature to 375°F, and bake until golden brown, 12 to 15 minutes. Set aside to cool.
4. Meanwhile, make the topping. Simmer the figs, water, bourbon, sugar, and lemon juice in a saucepan for 10 minutes. Cool the figs in their syrup to room temperature.
5. Drain the figs thoroughly, reserving the liquid. Cut the figs in half and set aside. Reduce the liquid to ¼ cup over medium heat, about 15 to 20 minutes. Set aside.
6. To make the pastry cream, whisk the sugar with the egg yolks until they are lightened in color. Whisk in the flour and salt.
7. In a heavy saucepan, bring the milk to a boil. Whisking constantly, pour the hot milk into the egg mixture in a thin stream. Return the mixture to the saucepan and cook over medium heat, stirring constantly, until it comes to a boil. Boil for about 2 minutes, remove from heat, and cool. Stir in the bourbon, taste, and add 1 or 2 more teaspoons if desired.
8. Brush the inside of the pastry with the reduced fig poaching liquid. Spread with pastry cream and arrange the figs and pecans in a pattern on top of the

pastry cream. If kept longer than a few hours, refrigerate the tart but bring to room temperature before serving.

Yield: one 12-inch tart

Note: To toast pecans, put in a 325°F oven until crisp, 5 to 10 minutes.

CAKES

FUDGE CAKE WITH MILK-CHOCOLATE FROSTING

Fudge Cake

    3 cups sifted cake flour
    2 cups light-brown sugar
  2¼ teaspoons baking powder
   ¾ teaspoon baking soda
   ¾ teaspoon salt
  1½ cups milk
    3 eggs
  1½ teaspoons vanilla extract
    4 ounces unsweetened chocolate, broken
        into pieces
    6 ounces unsalted butter, softened

Milk Chocolate Frosting

    1 pound milk chocolate, broken into
        pieces
   ½ pound extra-bittersweet or semisweet
        chocolate, broken into pieces
   ¾ pound unsalted butter, softened

1. Heat the oven to 350°F. Butter two 9-inch cake pans and line them with buttered and floured parchment paper or waxed paper.
2. For the cake, mix the first 5 ingredients in a large bowl, breaking up any lumps of brown sugar.
3. In a small bowl, whisk about ⅓ cup milk with the eggs and vanilla and set aside. Melt the chocolate in a double boiler over hot water.
4. Add the remaining milk and the butter to the mixed dry ingredients and beat for 1½ minutes, scraping the sides of the bowl twice. Add the egg mixture in 3 parts, scraping the sides of the bowl and beating for 20 seconds after each addition. Add the melted chocolate and beat just until incorporated.
5. Pour the batter into the prepared pans and bake in the center of the preheated oven until the cake springs back when lightly pressed in the center, 25 to 30 minutes. Cool the cakes in their pans for 10 minutes and invert onto racks. Cool completely before frosting.

Decorate the top of the cake using a serrated knife and an up-and-down motion to make a zigzag design in the frosting.

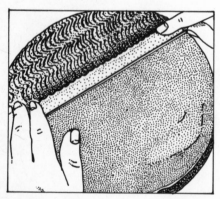

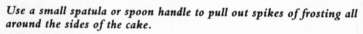

Use a small spatula or spoon handle to pull out spikes of frosting all around the sides of the cake.

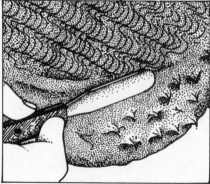

6. For the frosting, put the chocolate pieces in the upper container of a double boiler over hot water. Stir occasionally until completely melted. Remove the double boiler from heat and separate the top and bottom sections. Allow the chocolate to cool just until it is no longer warm to the touch, about 20 minutes.

7. Put the butter in a mixing bowl. Beat in the cooled chocolate until the mixture is evenly blended, about 3 minutes.

8. Frost the surface of one layer and put the second layer on top. Spread the remaining frosting on the top and sides of the cake. Decorate the top of the cake using a serrated knife and an up-and-down motion to make zigzags in the frosting. Use a small spatula or spoon handle to pull out spikes of frosting all around the sides.

Yield: one 9-inch cake

Note: Frosting can be stored at cool room temperature up to 3 days, or several months in the freezer.

MISSISSIPPI MUD CAKE

Cocoa
2 cups all-purpose flour
1 teaspoon baking soda
Pinch of salt
1½ cups strong, brewed coffee, or 4 teaspoons espresso powder mixed with 1½ cups boiling water
½ cup bourbon
5 ounces unsweetened chocolate, broken into pieces
½ pound unsalted butter
1¾ cups sugar
2 eggs, lightly beaten
1 teaspoon vanilla extract
Whipped cream

1. Heat the oven to 275°F. Butter a 9-inch tube pan and dust with cocoa.

2. In a large bowl, sift together the flour, baking soda, and salt.

3. In a double boiler over simmering water, heat the coffee and bourbon. Add the chocolate and butter and stir until the mixture is smooth. Remove from heat and stir in the sugar. Cool slightly.

4. Transfer the chocolate mixture to a mixing bowl and beat in the flour mixture, about ½ cup at a time. Add the eggs and vanilla and continue beating until smooth. Pour the batter evenly into the prepared tube pan and bake in the preheated oven until a cake tester or knife inserted in the cake comes out clean, about 1½ hours.

5. Cool the cake completely in its pan before unmolding onto a serving plate. Serve with whipped cream on top.

Yield: one 9-inch cake

POPPY-SEED CAKE WITH BROWN-SUGAR MERINGUE

Poppy-seed Cake

6 ounces unsalted butter
1 cup sugar
4 eggs
1¼ cups all-purpose flour
2 teaspoons baking powder
½ cup poppy seeds

Syrup

½ cup water
¼ cup sugar
2 tablespoons brandy

Brown-Sugar Meringue

3 egg whites
⅛ teaspoon cream of tartar
1 teaspoon vanilla extract
½ cup dark-brown sugar, rubbed through
   a strainer to remove any lumps
   Poppy seeds

1. Heat the oven to 325°F. Butter and flour a 6-cup brioche or other similar-size mold.
2. For the poppy-seed cake, cream the butter and sugar in a large mixing bowl. Add the eggs, 1 at a time, mixing well after each addition.
3. Sift the flour and baking powder together. Fold the sifted flour mixture into the egg-sugar mixture, making sure to remove any lumps. Add the poppy seeds and mix to distribute evenly. Pour the batter into the prepared mold.
4. Bake in the preheated oven until the cake springs back to the touch, about 1 hour. Set aside to cool in the mold for about 5 minutes and then turn out onto a rack to cool completely.
5. For the syrup, heat the water, sugar, and brandy in a heavy saucepan until the sugar dissolves. Boil the syrup for 1 minute. Remove from heat and pour the syrup over the cooled cake slowly so that it's absorbed thoroughly.
6. For the meringue, beat the egg whites in a mixing bowl until frothy and then add the cream of tartar. Continue beating until soft peaks form. Add the vanilla. Gradually add the brown sugar, beating until stiff peaks form and the meringue is smooth and shiny.
7. Put the meringue into a pastry bag fitted with a star tip and pipe the meringue over the top and down the sides of the cake in a crisscross pattern, or simply spread the meringue over the top and sides of the cake. Put under the broiler until evenly browned, about 60 seconds. Remove from the oven and sprinkle with poppy seeds.

Yield: 6 servings

APPLE STACK CAKES

1. In a saucepan, simmer the apples in water to cover until soft and most of the water is absorbed, 20 to 40 minutes. Add more water as necessary to keep from sticking, up to ½ cup. Add the sugar and cinnamon to taste and mash with a fork or back of a spoon until the mixture is the consistency of thick, chunky applesauce. Set aside.
2. Heat the oven to 350°F. Butter 2 large baking sheets.
3. For the cakes, sift the flour with the baking powder, salt, ginger, and baking soda. In a mixing bowl, cream the butter and the remaining ½ cup sugar until fluffy. Add the egg and beat well. In another bowl, mix together the buttermilk and molasses. Add the dry ingredients to the butter-sugar mixture alternately with the buttermilk-molasses mixture until the batter is well blended and smooth.
4. Evenly divide the batter into 2 mounds, one on each prepared baking sheet. Using a spatula or the back of a spoon, spread each mound to a 7- or 8-inch round about ¼-inch thick. Bake for 12 to 15 minutes in the preheated oven until the edges begin to brown and the cake is firm. Cool on sheets for about 7 minutes.
5. Spread two-thirds of the apples on the surface of one of the cake layers, set the second layer on top, and spread its surface with the remaining apples. Set aside for 4 to 8 hours, loosely covered, at room temperature before serving. Cut into wedges and serve with whipped cream, if desired.

Yield: one 7- to 8-inch cake

Apple Filling

  2 cups chopped or sliced dried apples
2¼ cups (approximately) water
  ¼ cup sugar
  ¼ to ½ teaspoon cinnamon

Cakes

  2 cups all-purpose flour
  1 teaspoon baking powder
  ½ teaspoon salt
  1 teaspoon ground ginger
  ½ teaspoon baking soda
  4 ounces unsalted butter, softened
  ½ cup sugar
  1 egg
  ½ cup buttermilk
  ½ cup molasses

  ¾ cup heavy cream, whipped (optional)

DARK FRUITCAKE

Pan preparation is one factor that is consistent for all fruitcakes. The pans should be deep. In shallow pans like layer-cake pans, the cakes will dry out. Loaf pans are good, as are bundt or tube pans. The pans' surfaces should be smooth, without indentations where pieces of fruit might stick. Well-buttered brown wrapping paper or parchment paper should be used to line the pans. Cut a piece of paper to fit each pan's bottom. Butter the pan well and fit with the paper. Then butter the paper. A standard loaf pan will hold about 1 pound of cake, enough for at least 8 to 10 servings. Allow at least 1 to 3 days for the cake to mellow before serving.

Fruitcake

- 1 pound raisins
- 1 pound currants
- 2 ounces citron, cut into small dice (about 1/3 cup)
- 2 ounces dried figs, cut into small dice (about 1/3 cup)
- 2 ounces pitted dates, cut into small dice (about 1/3 cup)
- 4 ounces almonds, blanched and slivered (about 1 cup)
- 4 ounces pecans, chopped (about 1 cup)
- 2 cups plus 2 tablespoons all-purpose flour
- 1/2 pound unsalted butter
- 1 cup sugar
- 5 eggs, separated
- 1/2 teaspoon ground cloves
- 1/2 teaspoon ground allspice
- 1/2 teaspoon mace
- 1 teaspoon salt
- 1/2 teaspoon baking soda
- 1/2 cup dark molasses
- 3/4 cup bourbon

Apricot Glaze

- 2 ounces (about 1/3 cup) dried apricots, soaked in 2/3 cup water overnight
- 1/3 cup light corn syrup

1. Heat the oven to 350°F. Line three 8½"- × - 4½" loaf pans with buttered paper (see instructions in head-note).
2. In a large bowl, toss the first 7 ingredients with ¼ cup flour.
3. Put the remaining flour into a shallow pan. Brown the flour in the preheated oven, stirring every minute or two, until it becomes golden and smells nutty, 7 or 8 minutes. Set aside to cool completely. Turn the oven down to 300°F.
4. In a large mixing bowl, cream the butter with the sugar until very light. Beat in the egg yolks 1 at a time, beating well after each addition.
5. Sift the browned flour with the cloves, allspice, mace, and salt and set aside.
6. Stir the baking soda into the molasses.
7. Combine the sugar mixture and flour mixture alternately with the molasses and mix well. Stir in ¼ cup bourbon and then add the fruits and nuts.
8. Beat the egg whites in another bowl until they form soft peaks and fold them into the batter. Fill the prepared pans about three-quarters full.
9. Put a shallow pan of water on the bottom shelf of the preheated oven. Bake the cakes until the tops are firm to the touch and the cakes have retracted slightly from the sides of the pans, 1½ to 2 hours.

Cool for 10 minutes in the pans. Remove the cakes from the pans and set on racks to cool completely.

10. Soak 3 large pieces of cheesecloth in the remaining ½ cup bourbon. Wrap the cakes in cheesecloth and then wrap again in aluminum foil. Let stand for 1 to 3 days.

11. For the apricot glaze, in a saucepan, cook the apricots gently in their soaking water until the water is absorbed and the fruit is very soft, 10 to 15 minutes. In a food processor or blender, puree the apricots. Strain through a sieve to remove any lumps. Return the puree to the saucepan, add the corn syrup, and simmer for 5 minutes. Brush the glaze generously over the surfaces of the cakes.

Yield: 3 loaf cakes

SHORTCAKES

BEST STRAWBERRY SHORTCAKE

Filling

 1 quart ripe strawberries, hulled and cut
      into quarters or *sliced if large*
⅓ cup sugar
 3 tablespoons unsalted butter, softened

Biscuits

¾ cup all-purpose flour
¼ cup cake flour
 2 teaspoons baking powder
¼ teaspoon salt
 1 tablespoon sugar
 5 tablespoons cold unsalted butter, cut
      into pieces
⅓ cup (approximately) milk

¾ cup heavy cream, whipped and
      sweetened

1. For the filling, toss the strawberries with the sugar in a bowl. Set aside.
2. Heat the oven to 375°F.
3. For the biscuits, sift the flours, baking powder, salt, and sugar into a bowl.
4. Incorporate the butter into the sifted dry ingredients, using a fork, a wire pastry blender, or your fingertips, until the mixture resembles coarse crumbs. Make a well in the center and add about 3½ tablespoons milk. Mix just until the dough holds together, adding more milk as necessary.
5. Turn the dough out onto a lightly floured work surface and knead 10 to 15 times. Gently roll or pat the dough to a ½- to ¾-inch thickness. Cut into 4 biscuits with a floured 2-inch-round biscuit cutter, being careful not to twist the cutter. Put the biscuits on an unbuttered cookie sheet.
6. In the preheated oven, bake the biscuits until golden brown, 12 to 15 minutes. Split the hot biscuits and slather each one with the softened butter.
7. To serve, put the bottom halves of the biscuits, cut side up, on individual dessert plates and distribute half of the sugared strawberries and their juices over them. Top with the remaining biscuit halves and remaining strawberries. Spoon on the whipped cream and serve immediately.

Yield: 4 servings

GINGERED SHORTCAKE WITH HONEY-POACHED PEACHES

1. For the peaches, bring the water, honey, and sugar to a boil in a large saucepan. Lower heat to simmer, add the orange zest, and cook for 5 minutes. Add the peaches and poach gently, spooning the hot syrup over the peaches until they are tender, about 15 minutes. Remove from heat and set aside to cool in the syrup.
2. Heat the oven to 375°F.
3. For the biscuits, in a small bowl, mix the ginger with 1½ teaspoons all-purpose flour. Stir in the sugar and set aside.
4. Sift the remaining flours, baking powder, and salt into a bowl. Incorporate the butter into the sifted dry ingredients, using a fork, a wire pastry blender, or your fingertips, until the mixture resembles coarse crumbs. Toss with the ginger-flour mixture. Make a well in the center and add about 3½ tablespoons milk. Mix just until the dough holds together, adding more milk as necessary.
5. Turn the dough out onto a lightly floured work surface and knead 10 to 15 times. Gently roll or pat the dough to a ½- to ¾-inch thickness. Cut out 4 biscuits with a floured 2-inch-round biscuit cutter, being careful not twist the cutter. Put the biscuits on an unbuttered cookie sheet and bake until golden brown, 12 to 15 minutes.
6. With a slotted spoon, remove the peaches and orange zest from the syrup. Return the syrup to medium-high heat and simmer until reduced by one-third, about 8 minutes. You should have about 1½ cups syrup.
7. To serve, split each biscuit in half. Put the bottom halves, cut side up, on individual dessert plates. Douse each evenly with half the syrup. Distribute half of the peach slices over the biscuits. Top with the remaining biscuit halves and syrup and spoon the remaining peaches over the biscuits.

Yield: 4 servings

Honey-Poached Peaches

1½ cups water
⅓ cup honey
¼ cup sugar
   Zest of ½ orange, removed in ½-inch-wide strips and cut crosswise into thin shreds
3 ripe peaches, peeled and sliced

Gingered Biscuits

1 teaspoon grated fresh ginger
¾ cup plus 1½ teaspoons all-purpose flour
1 tablespoon sugar
¼ cup cake flour
2 teaspoons baking powder
¼ teaspoon salt
5 tablespoons cold unsalted butter, cut into pieces
⅓ cup (approximately) milk

Chapter

13 | One-Dish Desserts

One-dish American desserts provide a glimpse into how the first generations of Americans adapted Old World recipes to fit New World ingredients. Porridge, for instance, about as English as cricket and scones, was made in America with cornmeal, which was available and cheap. First served as a side dish to accompany the meat course, it was easily turned into a dessert with the addition of maple syrup or molasses. Thus we invented Indian pudding.

Puddings were well suited to the American kitchen. The variations were endless; they were easy to make and could take advantage of available, local ingredients. The Shaker version of Indian pudding, for example, called for the addition of whatever berries happened to be in season along with the more traditional ingredients, cornmeal and maple syrup. Ozark Pudding, a dish favored by Bess Truman, was a simple flour-sugar-egg pudding, leavened with baking powder and flavored with an American standby—the apple. The prevalence of puddings as an American staple is attested to by the Hasty Pudding Club, which was started in 1795 by a group of disgruntled Harvard University undergraduates and was dedicated to the notion that "hasty pud-

218

ding," cooked up in their own fireplace pots, was preferable to the culinary offerings of Harvard kitchens.

Other desserts, now thought to be as American as apple pie, went through similar transformations. Cobblers, bettys, even soufflés were adapted to the New World. In fact, soufflés, along with puddings, form a major category in contemporary American one-dish desserts. The recipes in this chapter reflect both traditional American dishes and more recent innovations, such as a Pumpkin Crème Brûlée and a Cream Cheese Soufflé with Rhubarb Sauce.

PUDDINGS

There are three basic types of puddings: baked, stirred, and steamed. Baked puddings are often custards or include an egg and milk or cream custard in the ingredients or at least are bound by egg. The Ozark Pudding, Whole-Wheat Bread Pudding with Blueberry-Maple Sauce, and Pumpkin Crème Brûlée in this chapter are all good examples of baked puddings. Stirred puddings, like the Grits 'n' Honey Pudding, are also egg-bound but are cooked on top of the stove over low heat rather than in the oven and then continue to thicken as they cool. Steamed puddings, an old English favorite, are cooked in a covered mold and subjected to steam heat over a long period of time. This method produces moist, heavy puddings with rich, full flavor. The Steamed Brownie Pudding in this chapter is an updated version of this traditional method.

The ingredients for puddings are basic: eggs, milk, and sweetener as the usual foundation, plus flavorings, fruits, and spices. Cooking time and temperature are critical to puddings; an undercooked pudding will not achieve the proper consistency and an overcooked one is tough and leathery. We suggest using heavy pans for stirred puddings and metal containers, rather than heat-retaining types like enameled iron, for baked puddings. Remove puddings from the oven when they still seem a trifle underdone since they will continue to cook in the pan after they're taken out of the oven. Cooking times in smaller containers will be shorter. If using individual ramekins, be especially careful to avoid overcooking.

SOUFFLÉS

A soufflé has two principle parts: beaten egg whites and the thickened and flavored yolk base. The most usual base is a dense white sauce made of butter, flour, and milk and enriched with the egg yolks. You can add any flavoring to this base (vanilla, chocolate, Grand Marnier, et cetera) to make the soufflé one of the most versatile dishes available to the innovative cook.

The second type of base is made with yolks in combination with anything that is thick enough on its own to provide the foundation for the soufflé. Melted chocolate, for instance, can be made into a flourless soufflé, and pureed fruit is frequently used. In our unusual Cream Cheese Soufflé with Rhubarb Sauce, cream cheese provides the necessary substance for the base. Whatever the base, it can be prepared in advance, leaving only the beating and incorporation of the egg whites for the last minute.

The beaten egg whites are folded into the base, no matter which type you use, and the mixture is baked. The air trapped in the foamy egg whites expands when heated, making the mixture rise. Begin with egg whites at room temperature for greatest volume. An electric mixer will produce fine results although slightly more volume can be achieved with a balloon whisk. Tests have shown that a copper bowl will also increase volume—the albumin in the egg whites reacts chemically with the copper—but being somewhat weak of arm, we see no substantial benefit from the traditional balloon whisk and copper bowl stricture. An electric mixer fitted with a balloon whisk seems the ideal arrangement.

More crucial is the point to which the whites are beaten. Most soufflés that fall do so because the whites are beaten too long or are overfolded. Whites are ready when they maintain glossy peaks. You should be able to hold the bowl upside down without their falling out. Overwhipped whites will break up into small clumps when folded into the base rather than incorporating smoothly.

The second critical step is folding the whites into the

base. The hand is as good a tool as any for this process although a large rubber spatula works fine. Many chefs, rather unorthodoxly, swear by a whisk for the process. In any case, start by adding a small amount of the beaten whites to the base mixture and stirring thoroughly to lighten it. Then add the rest of the egg whites. Cut into the center of the mixture straight down to the bottom of the bowl. Run your hand or spatula along the bottom of the bowl and up toward you to the edge. Rotate the bowl and repeat. Folding the whites should be done quickly, in less than a minute. Do not worry if the mixture doesn't appear totally homogenous when you are done. You're better off with some pockets of white than overmixed, broken-down whites, which result in flat soufflés.

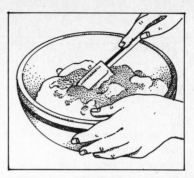

To fold the base and the beaten whites together, cut straight down into the center.

The soufflé dish must be the right size for your mixture. The uncooked soufflé should just fill the baking dish. Level it off with a long metal spatula so that it's even with the top. To promote an even rise, run a knife or your thumb around the edge of the dish, making a small groove in the mixture. A properly made soufflé has no need of a supporting collar. It will hold its high moment of glory on its own.

Run the spatula along the bottom of the bowl and up toward you to the edge.

Do not trust recipes, even ours, for soufflé cooking times. Due to the soufflé's fragile nature, small oven variances can significantly alter the scheduled timing. Check your soufflé about ten minutes before it should be done. *Do not overcook.* The center of a perfect soufflé is soft, slightly undercooked, and the consistency of thick soup, not firm. When spooned onto a plate, each serving should contain some of the browned crust, a portion of well-cooked perimeter, plus a good helping of the runny middle portion. A soufflé is a multitextured dessert.

Flip the mixture back into the center and rotate the bowl.

A soufflé will rise straight up without the aid of a collar.

OZARK PUDDING

2 *eggs*
½ to ¾ cup sugar *(depending upon tartness of apples)*
3 *tablespoons all-purpose flour*
2 *teaspoons baking powder*
  Pinch of salt
2 *tart apples (such as Greening or Granny Smith), peeled, cored, and chopped*
½ *cup chopped toasted walnuts*
1 *teaspoon vanilla extract*
1 *cup heavy cream, whipped to soft peaks*

1. Heat the oven to 350°F. Butter a 9-inch pie pan.
2. In a large mixing bowl, beat the eggs with the sugar until light in color and the mixture forms a heavy ribbon when trailed from the beater. Blend in the flour, baking powder, and salt. Fold in the apples, nuts, and vanilla.
3. Pour the mixture into the prepared pie pan and bake until the top is well browned and puffed, 30 to 35 minutes. Remove from the oven. The puffed top will fall during cooling. Serve warm or at room temperature with whipped cream.

Yield: 6 to 8 servings

WHOLE-WHEAT BREAD PUDDING WITH BLUEBERRY-MAPLE SAUCE

Pudding

4 *eggs*
½ *cup plus 2 teaspoons sugar*
4½ *cups heavy cream*
1½ *tablespoons vanilla extract*
2 *large, fresh loaves (about 1½ pounds each) whole-wheat bread, crusts removed, cut into 1-inch cubes (8 cups)*

Blueberry-Maple Sauce

1½ *cups pure maple syrup*
3 *pints blueberries*

1. For the pudding, whisk the eggs thoroughly in a large mixing bowl. Gradually whisk in ½ cup sugar, cream, and vanilla. Add the bread cubes and stir gently to coat well. Set aside for 30 minutes, stirring once or twice.
2. Heat the oven to 325°F. Butter a large baking pan.
3. Using a slotted spoon, spread the soaked bread in a single layer in the prepared pan. Pour the remaining egg mixture evenly over the bread.
4. Bake in the upper third of the preheated oven for 35 minutes. Sprinkle the remaining 2 teaspoons sugar over the pudding and continue cooking until the pudding is just set, about 15 minutes more. Be careful not to overcook; the pudding will thicken further as it cools.
5. For the sauce, bring the maple syrup to a boil in a large, heavy saucepan. Reduce heat to medium–high and cook, stirring occasionally so that the syrup won't boil over. Cook until reduced by about one-third, 20 to 25 minutes. Add the blueberries and continue to cook, covered, over low heat until the berries begin

to yield juices, about 5 minutes. Uncover, raise heat, and bring to a boil, stirring. Skim off any foam and reduce to simmer. Continue to cook until all the berries have burst and the sauce has thickened slightly, about 10 more minutes.

6. Serve the pudding warm or at room temperature with the sauce, either warm or cool, poured over each serving.

Yield: 10 to 12 servings

Note: Unused sauce will keep for several weeks, refrigerated, and is good over pancakes, waffles, or ice cream.

GRITS 'N' HONEY PUDDING

1. In a large, heavy saucepan, bring the milk and salt to a boil. Gradually add the grits, stirring constantly. Stir in the raisins, lower heat, and cook, covered, stirring occasionally, until very thick, about 15 minutes.
2. In a mixing bowl, whisk together the egg yolks and honey. Whisk 1 cup of the thickened grits mixture into the honey-egg mixture and then slowly whisk this mixture back into the hot grits.
3. Return to low heat and cook, stirring constantly, until the mixture just reaches a boil, about 5 minutes. The mixture will be very thick. Remove from heat and set aside.
4. In another mixing bowl, whip the egg whites until they form soft peaks. Sprinkle with sugar and continue to beat until the whites form stiff peaks. Lighten the grits mixture by stirring in ¼ cup egg whites. Then fold in the remaining whites. Cool to room temperature and cover with plastic wrap, pressing it onto the surface of the pudding to prevent the formation of a skin. Refrigerate at least 6 hours before serving.
5. Spoon pudding into individual bowls and drizzle with heavy cream.

4 cups milk
½ teaspoon salt
1 cup white hominy grits
1 cup raisins
5 egg yolks
¾ cup honey
3 egg whites
1 tablespoon sugar
Heavy cream

Yield: 8 to 10 servings

PUMPKIN CRÈME BRÛLÉE

Crème brûlée is popularly believed to have originated in King's College, Cambridge, although in style at least it seems more French than English. Whatever its origin, it has become a great favorite in the United States. This version is not a firm custard but is meant to be soft to contrast with the crackling brown-sugar topping.

5 egg yolks
1½ cups unsweetened fresh or canned pumpkin puree
½ cup granulated sugar
4½ teaspoons vanilla extract
1 teaspoon ground cinnamon
½ teaspoon ground cloves
¼ teaspoon grated nutmeg
3 cups heavy cream
½ cup light-brown sugar

1. Heat the oven to 325°F.
2. In a mixing bowl, whisk the egg yolks, 1 at a time, into the pumpkin puree. Slowly whisk in the sugar. Stir in the vanilla and spices and set aside.
3. In a saucepan, bring the cream to a boil. Slowly whisk the cream into the egg-pumpkin mixture and pour into an 8-inch-square baking pan. Put the square pan into a large baking pan and set in the upper third of the preheated oven. Pour enough boiling water into the larger pan to come halfway up the sides of the pudding.
4. Bake until golden but not firm, about 1 hour, being careful not to overcook; the pudding will thicken as it cools. Remove the pan from the water bath and cool to room temperature. Cover and refrigerate until very cold.
5. Heat broiler.
6. Force the brown sugar through a sieve in an even layer over the top of the chilled pudding. The sugar layer should be loose and fluffy, not packed down. Set the pudding under the preheated broiler, 5 to 6 inches from heat source if electric, as far as possible from flame if gas. Rotate the pan often for even broiling. Time varies, but in 30 seconds to 3 minutes, the sugar will begin to liquefy and caramelize. When the topping is a rich dark brown, remove. Serve warm or cool.

Yield: 6 to 8 servings

APPLE BROWN BETTY

Brown betty is a simple, old-fashioned dessert most commonly made with apples, although other fruits can be used, too. Bettys are composed of layers of fruit and bread crumbs, and it's the crunch of the crumbs that makes the warm, deep-dish dessert special. Using toasted bread crumbs makes the difference between good and mediocre betty. If you add a tablespoon or so of an alcohol that corresponds in flavor to the fruit (we use applejack here), it becomes a slightly more sophisticated dessert.

1. Heat the oven to 350°F. Butter a baking pan or shallow casserole.
2. In a bowl, toss the apples with the next 7 ingredients.
3. In another bowl, toss the bread crumbs with the butter.
4. Spread one-third of the bread crumb mixture in the bottom of the prepared baking dish or casserole. Add half of the apple mixture and sprinkle with half of the applejack or cider. Spread with another one-third bread crumbs, add the rest of the apples and applejack, and top with the remaining bread crumbs.
5. Cover with foil and bake in the preheated oven for 35 minutes. Uncover, raise the oven temperature to 400°F, and continue baking until the topping is well browned and crisp, about 10 minutes. Serve warm with cream poured over each serving.

Yield: 6 to 8 servings

Note: To toast the walnuts, place the nuts on a baking sheet and put in a 325°F oven for 5 to 7 minutes.

4 *large tart apples (such as McIntosh or Granny Smith), peeled, cored, and cut into ¼-inch-thick slices*
2 *teaspoons lemon juice*
⅓ *cup granulated sugar*
⅓ *cup dark-brown sugar*
½ *teaspoon ground cinnamon*
¼ *teaspoon grated nutmeg*
¼ *teaspoon grated lemon zest*
½ *cup chopped toasted walnuts (see Note) or raisins*
2½ *cups toasted coarse bread crumbs*
6 *tablespoons unsalted butter, cut into bits*
6 *tablespoons applejack or apple cider Heavy cream*

STEAMED BROWNIE PUDDING

Pudding

    3   ounces unsweetened chocolate
    4   tablespoons unsalted butter
    1   cup dark-brown sugar
    2   eggs
    ⅓   cup buttermilk
    2   teaspoons vanilla extract
    1   teaspoon instant espresso
    ½   teaspoon ground cinnamon
    ½   teaspoon salt
    1   cup chopped walnuts or pecans
    1¼ cups sifted flour
    2   teaspoons baking powder
    ½   teaspoon baking soda

Custard Sauce

    ⅓   cup sugar
    5   egg yolks
    1¾ cups half and half
    ½   vanilla bean, or 1 tablespoon vanilla
        extract

1. Butter a 6- to 7-cup pudding mold (see Note) and lid. Set a metal rack in the bottom of a large pot that is tall enough to hold the pudding mold sitting on a rack. Add enough water to the pot to come halfway up the sides of the pudding mold. Bring water to a boil, reduce heat, and keep hot over low heat while you make the pudding.

2. For the pudding, melt chocolate, butter, and brown sugar together in a large, heavy saucepan over low heat, stirring occasionally. Remove from heat and cool for 10 minutes.

3. Beat the eggs, 1 at a time, into the cooled chocolate mixture. Whisk in the buttermilk, vanilla, espresso, cinnamon, and salt. Stir in the nuts.

4. In a small bowl, combine the flour, baking powder, and soda. Add the dry ingredients to the chocolate mixture and stir to combine thoroughly.

5. Spoon the batter into the prepared mold and smooth the top with the back of the spoon. Clamp the lid in place. Return the water in the pot to a full boil, set the mold on the rack, reduce heat, and tightly cover the pot. Adjust heat so that the water maintains a steady, gentle simmer for 1½ hours. Keep a kettle of hot water on the stove and add to the water in the pot as the level drops.

6. For the sauce, whisk the sugar into the egg yolks in a mixing bowl. Continue whisking until the mixture is pale yellow and thickened and forms a ribbon when trailed from the whisk, 3 to 4 minutes.

7. Put the half and half into a saucepan. If using a vanilla bean, slit it, scrape the seeds into the half and half, and drop the pod in. Bring the half and half just to a boil and remove from heat.

8. Slowly whisk the hot half and half into the egg mixture. Pour the mixture into the saucepan and set over low heat. Do not allow to boil. Stir constantly with a wooden spoon until thick enough to coat the back of the spoon, 5 to 8 minutes. Remove from heat and strain into a small bowl. If using vanilla extract, stir

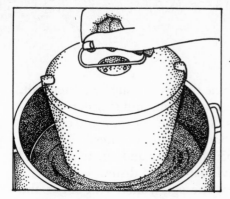

A pudding mold being set inside a larger pot to steam.

it into the warm custard. Cool to room temperature, cover, and refrigerate. Remove vanilla bean pods before serving.

9. Lift the pudding mold from the water and remove the lid. Cool the pudding for 15 minutes. To unmold, invert a plate over the mold. Gently reverse the plate and mold so that the pudding drops out onto the plate. Cool to room temperature, cover well, and chill. Slice when chilled but allow to return to room temperature before serving with cold custard sauce.

Yield: 8 servings

Note: The ideal pudding mold is a 6- to 7-cup cylindrical one with a hollow central core and a clamp-on lid.

BANANA SOUFFLÉ WITH BOURBON-BUTTERSCOTCH SAUCE

Bourbon-Butterscotch Sauce

½ cup light-brown sugar
2 tablespoons unsalted butter
Pinch of salt
½ cup heavy cream
2 tablespoons (approximately) bourbon

Banana Soufflé

4 egg yolks
⅔ cup sugar
3 tablespoons unsalted butter
3 tablespoons all-purpose flour
½ cup milk
6 egg whites, room temperature
⅛ teaspoon salt
3 ripe bananas
1 tablespoon lemon juice

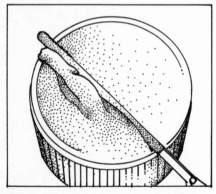

Sweep a long metal spatula across the dish to even the surface of the soufflé.

To promote an even rise, run a knife around the edge of the dish, making a small groove.

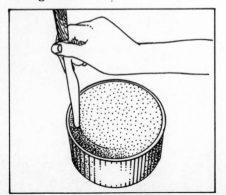

1. For the sauce, combine the brown sugar, butter, salt, and heavy cream in a saucepan, and simmer, uncovered, for 15 minutes. Stir in the bourbon and continue to cook, stirring, about 2 more minutes.

2. Heat the oven to 350°F. Butter and sugar a 2-quart soufflé dish or individual soufflé dishes.

3. For the soufflé, beat the egg yolks with sugar and set aside.

4. In a saucepan, melt the butter, add the flour, and cook, stirring, 1 to 2 minutes. Stir in the milk and continue to cook, stirring, until it is smooth and thick, 2 to 3 more minutes. Stir some of the hot liquid into the yolk mixture, then add the yolk mixture to the saucepan containing the hot liquid. Cook, stirring, until the sauce is thick and smooth, 2 to 3 minutes. Do not boil. Cool slightly.

5. In another bowl, beat the egg whites with salt until they form firm peaks.

6. In a food processor, puree the bananas with lemon juice. You should have about 1 cup. Stir the puree into the yolk mixture, working quickly so the bananas will not discolor. Fold the egg whites into the banana mixture and pour into the prepared soufflé dish or dishes. Level the top with a spatula and run a knife around the edge to make a small groove. Bake in the preheated oven until well risen and golden brown, 35 to 40 minutes. If using individual dishes, bake 10 to 15 minutes.

7. Just before the end of baking, reheat the sauce. Taste and add more bourbon if desired. Serve the soufflé immediately with the warm sauce.

Yield: 6 to 8 servings

CREAM CHEESE SOUFFLÉ WITH RHUBARB SAUCE

The cream cheese makes this a foolproof soufflé recipe. It always rises high and maintains its shape once out of the oven. The tangy rhubarb sauce is a perfect balance to its rich creaminess.

1. For the sauce, combine the rhubarb with sugar and orange juice in a small saucepan. Bring to a boil, reduce heat to medium-low, and simmer, uncovered, until the sauce is thickened and reduced to ⅔ cup, 15 to 20 minutes.
2. Heat the oven to 375°F. Butter and sugar a 1½-quart soufflé dish.
3. For the soufflé, split the vanilla bean and scrape out the seeds. Pound the vanilla seeds and cardamom in a mortem with a pestle. Combine with the sugar.
4. Whir the vanilla-cardamon mixture, cream cheese, egg yolks, and lemon zest in a food processor until very smooth. Transfer to a large bowl.
5. In another bowl, beat the egg whites with salt until they form soft peaks. Add the lemon juice and continue beating until the whites form stiff peaks.
6. Add one-third of the whites to the cream cheese mixture and mix well. Fold in the remaining whites and pour into the prepared soufflé dish. Level the top and run a knife around the edge to make a small groove. Bake in the preheated oven until the top is golden, about 30 minutes.
7. Just before the end of baking, reheat the rhubarb sauce. Serve the soufflé immediately with the hot rhubarb sauce.

Yield: 4 to 6 servings

Butter and then sugar the soufflé dish by shaking sugar over the bottom and then rolling the dish around to coat the sides. Pour out excess sugar.

Rhubarb Sauce

 1 rib rhubarb, peeled and diced
¼ cup sugar
 1 cup orange juice

Cream Cheese Soufflé

 ½ vanilla bean
 ¼ teaspoon cardamom seeds
 5 tablespoons sugar
12 ounces cream cheese, softened
 3 egg yolks, room temperature
 ½ teaspoon grated lemon zest
 4 egg whites, room temperature
   Pinch of salt
 1 teaspoon lemon juice

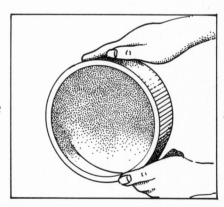

RASPBERRY-PEACH COBBLER

A cobbler is simply sweetened fruit covered with a layer of biscuit dough. Cut and mix the fruit just before you plan to bake the cobbler since it will hold its shape and retain its flavor better if not allowed to sit combined with sugar for too long. The sweet, rich biscuit dough, much like that used for shortcake, should be handled quickly and lightly. Let the weight of the rolling pin do most of the work for you. For more on biscuit dough, see Chapter 11.

The dough is placed over the fruits, but not so as to completely seal them in. The dough lid should provide steam to cook the fruits but also allow some of the liquid to evaporate. You might want to prepare cobblers the old-fashioned way with cut-out rounds of dough instead of a solid top. Be sure to leave adequate room between "cobbles" for escaping steam.

See the Variations at the end of this recipe for other fruit cobblers.

Dough

- 2 cups all-purpose flour
- 1 teaspoon salt
- 1 tablespoon baking powder
- 1 tablespoon sugar
- 4 tablespoons cold unsalted butter, cut into small pieces
- 1 cup heavy cream, plus more if necessary

Fruit

- 2 pints raspberries
- 2 pounds peaches, peeled and sliced (about 4 cups)
- ⅔ cup sugar
  Grated zest and juice of 1 lemon
- 3 tablespoons unsalted butter
  Confectioners' sugar

1. For the dough, stir together the flour, salt, baking powder, and sugar in a mixing bowl. Rapidly blend the butter into the flour mixture, using the tips of your fingers or a pastry blender. Gradually add the cream, stirring with a fork or working with your fingertips until the dough holds together in a ball. Blend in additional drops of cream if necessary to make a firm dough. Do not overwork. (The dough can be used immediately or wrapped in plastic and stored in the refrigerator.)
2. For the fruit, in a bowl, combine the raspberries and peaches with the sugar.
3. Heat the oven to 400°F.
4. On a lightly floured work surface, roll out the dough until it is about ¼ inch thick and slightly smaller than a shallow, 10- to 11-cup baking dish. Trim the edges and crimp the dough to make an attractive border and to even up any rough edges.
5. Put the fruit mixture in the baking dish. Scatter with the grated lemon zest and lemon juice. Dot with the butter.

6. Lay the rolled-out dough over the fruit. Cut several steam vents in the dough.
7. Bake until golden brown, 30 to 35 minutes. Cool on a rack for 10 to 15 minutes before serving. Sprinkle with confectioners' sugar before spooning onto plates.

Yield: 6 to 8 servings

Variations: For *Apple-Blackberry Cobbler*, replace raspberries and peaches with 3 tart green apples, peeled, cored, and sliced ¼ inch thick, and 2 pints blackberries. Increase sugar to ¾ cup.

For *Papaya Cobbler*, replace raspberries and peaches with 3 large papayas (about 1½ pounds each), peeled, seeded, and cut into ¼-inch slices. Use ½ cup dark-brown sugar instead of white sugar, and add ¼ teaspoon grated nutmeg and ¼ teaspoon ground cinnamon.

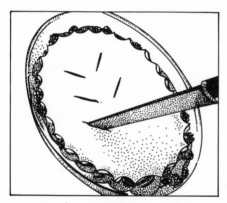

The edges of the dough should not touch the sides of the dish. Cut several steam vents in the dough.

MARGARITA MOUSSE WITH STRAWBERRIES

A *mousse*, which means "foam" in French, is a light, frothy mixture that can be made from almost anything—sweet or savory. Though puddinglike, in its simplest form it resembles nothing so much as an uncooked soufflé. A base of egg yolk and flavoring is lightened with beaten egg whites and then chilled. Whipped cream can be folded in instead of or in addition to the whites, and gelatin is sometimes added, providing more structure. This contemporary mousse tastes remarkably like a margarita.

¼ cup cold water
1 envelope unflavored gelatin
¼ teaspoon salt
½ cup lime juice
1½ teaspoons minced lime zest, blanched in boiling water for 30 seconds
3 tablespoons Triple Sec
⅓ cup tequila
4 eggs, separated
⅔ cup sugar
1 pint strawberries, sliced

1. Oil a 6-cup mold.
2. Put the water in a bowl and sprinkle the gelatin over it. Let it stand until spongy, 4 to 5 minutes. Put the bowl over simmering water until the gelatin dissolves, about 2 minutes.
3. Whisk the salt, lime juice, blanched lime zest, Triple Sec, and tequila into the gelatin. Put the bowl over ice water and stir until the mixture is the consistency of unbeaten egg whites, about 10 minutes.
4. In another bowl, beat the egg yolks with ⅓ cup sugar until the yolks thicken and form a ribbon when trailed from a whisk, 4 to 5 minutes. Stir thoroughly into the gelatin mixture.
4. In a third bowl, beat the egg whites until they form soft peaks. Slowly add the remaining ⅓ cup sugar. Beat until the whites form stiff peaks. Fold into the gelatin mixture.
5. Turn the mousse into the prepared mold. Chill until firm, at least 2 hours. Unmold and serve with the sliced strawberries.

Yield: 8 servings

14 Cookies and Candies

Despite America's current fitness fixation, we still find cookies and candy irresistible. The sybaritic nature of sweets—their main purpose, after all, is pure pleasure—has linked them to delights of another sort, too: The terminology of affection owes a lot to confection. Endearments such as "sweetheart," "honey," and "sugar" all indicate the connection in our minds between the two gratifications.

Candy making is a skill that has assumed an aura of alchemy, but given the right equipment (most important is a reliable thermometer) and the right weather (cool and dry), the sweet satisfaction of homemade candies can be yours. And making cookies is usually even easier.

COOKING AND HANDLING SUGAR SYRUP

Candy is most often simply a mixture of sugar and water to which flavoring is added. What determines the texture and appearance—gumdrop, fudge, or taffy—is the temperature to which this syrup is cooked and the amount of crystallization that takes place. In soft, opaque candies like fudge and taffy, the syrup is cooked to 238° and 250° Fahrenheit respectively, and then it's beaten (fudge) or pulled (taffy) to obtain the desired opacity. Hard candies, on the other hand, are cooked to 290° Fahrenheit or more and cooled undisturbed.

There are several ways to prevent the crystallization that causes cloudy or grainy candy. The simplest method is to cover the pan tightly for a few minutes after the sugar has dissolved so that steam will wash down any crystals that may appear on the side of the pan. Corn syrup, a fat such as butter or chocolate, or an acid such as lemon juice or vinegar will act as an interfering agent, and the addition of even a small amount of these substances will effectively prevent undesired crystallization. Sugar syrup foams up immensely when cooking, and so be sure your pan is a heavy-weight one that will hold at least four times the volume of the ingredients.

The candies in this chapter have been arranged according to the temperatures they reach during cooking. For the soft Clove Gumdrops, a pectin mixture and a sugar syrup are simply brought to a boil separately and then combined at around 212° Fahrenheit. Cooking a sugar syrup to 234° Fahrenheit will produce a creamy, melt-in-the-mouth texture as in our Buttermilk Pralines. For the finest fudge, the syrup should be cooked to 238° Fahrenheit, cooled to 110° to 120°, and then beaten. Temperatures between 250° and 260° will produce textures like those of chewy taffy and divinity.

SWEETENERS

The texture of cookies depends more on ingredients than temperature. Crisp or lacy cookies like the Macadamia Nut Wafers and Gingered Florentine Twins are made with a low proportion of flour to butter. Softer, chewier cookies have more flour and sometimes call for liquid sweeteners.

Sweeteners other than sugar can be used in both cookies and candies with consequent variations in flavor and texture. Honey, maple syrup, and molasses are most frequently used in baking. Corn syrup, viscous and sweet, has qualities that make it especially valuable to candy makers.

Honey was a European staple until more easily stored sugar became available at the very tail end of the Middle

Ages, and honey-based alcoholic beverages, mead and hydromel, were popular until the development of sweet grape wines. Since honey contains a high level of fructose, many varieties can be tolerated without ill effect by some diabetics, although other medicinal claims for pollen and royal jelly are at best unsubstantiated. Honey does contain small amounts of hydrogen peroxide, which explains the early use of the sweet substance as an antiseptic.

Cookies made with honey will stay moist longer and not spoil as quickly as their all-sugar counterparts. Any liquid sweetener—honey, maple syrup, corn syrup, or molasses—will result in a slightly chewier cookie.

Maple syrup, an all-American sweetener, was used on this continent almost exclusively until the arrival here of the honeybee around 1625. Even after the Revolution, many Americans eschewed cane sugar since its production was dependent upon the labor of slaves. With the discovery of cheap and readily available sugar from beets in the early nineteenth century, the demand for maple syrup declined drastically, and it remains a small industry.

Molasses is a by-product of the cane sugar refining process. Depending on how many times it is centrifuged to remove the sucrose, the leftover molasses is mild or strong in flavor. When processed three times, blackstrap molasses is the result—very dark in color, very concentrated in flavor, but not as high in nutrients as food faddists or your grandmother would have you believe. It contains only small amounts of minerals and B vitamins.

The same is true of brown sugar. In spite of its appearance, brown sugar is refined—it's simply a combination of pure sucrose crystals and molasses.

Powdered sugar or confectioners' sugar is very finely ground white sugar, most often packed with a small amount of cornstarch to help prevent clumping. It should be sifted before measuring.

Fructose, also known as levulose, is simply half of the sucrose (white sugar) molecule. The other half is known as glucose or dextrose. Fructose is highly refined, but tastes sweeter than sucrose and contains only about half the calories. Its nutritional benefits are nil. In liquid form, it is used primarily by commercial soft drink companies, and only a small percentage of the fructose produced is available to the home cook.

The recipes that follow range from homespun to sophisticated. The techniques involved are reliable and simple to master, and the results are sweet indulgence.

GINGERED FLORENTINE TWINS

Thin, lacy florentines are traditionally made with chopped candied fruit in the batter and a bottom coating of chocolate. Here, crystallized ginger replaces the fruit, and the cookies are sandwiched with chocolate and ginger preserves.

1. Heat the oven to 350°F. Butter and flour several baking sheets.
2. In a mixing bowl, cream the butter and add the confectioners' sugar and heavy cream alternately, beating well after each addition. Stir in the hazelnuts and combine thoroughly. Add the crystallized ginger, mix well, and then stir in the flour, combining thoroughly.
3. Drop the batter by teaspoons onto the prepared baking sheets, about 8 cookies to a sheet. Bake in the preheated oven, 1 sheet at a time, until the cookie edges are lightly browned and the centers are set, 6 to 7 minutes. Remove from the oven and cool a minute until they are manageable. Transfer the cookies to waxed paper to cool.
4. Put the chocolate in the top of a double boiler set over hot water. Stir until melted, remove from the hot water, and cool slightly.
5. Spread the chocolate in a very thin layer on half of the cookies. Spread about ¼ teaspoon ginger preserves on each remaining cookie. Press the chocolate-coated and ginger-coated cookies together in pairs and set on a rack to firm.

Yield: 2 to 2½ dozen cookies

2½ tablespoons unsalted butter
2 cups sifted confectioners' sugar
½ cup heavy cream
1 cup ground hazelnuts
2 tablespoons minced or shredded crystallized ginger
½ cup sifted all-purpose flour
2½ ounces bittersweet chocolate, broken into small pieces
3 tablespoons chopped ginger preserves

CHOCOLATE-MINT CREAM SQUARES

Chocolate Mint Squares have a brownielike cookie as their base, which is split, spread with creamy mint filling, and then dipped in a rich chocolate-mint glaze. To vary this recipe, replace the peppermint extract with orange, coffee, or nut-flavored liqueur.

Chocolate Cookies

2 ounces unsweetened chocolate
5 tablespoons unsalted butter
1 cup sugar
2 eggs, lightly beaten
½ teaspoon almond extract
¾ cup sifted all-purpose flour
¼ teaspoon baking powder
  Pinch of salt

Mint Cream Filling

4 tablespoons unsalted butter, softened
2 cups sifted confectioners' sugar
1 tablespoon heavy cream, plus more if
  necessary
¼ teaspoon peppermint extract

Chocolate-Mint Coating

6½ tablespoons light corn syrup
¼ cup water
4 tablespoons unsalted butter, cut into
  small pieces
¼ teaspoon peppermint extract
½ pound bittersweet chocolate, broken
  into small pieces

32 tiny candied mint leaves (optional)

1. Heat the oven to 350°F. Butter an 8-inch baking pan.
2. For the cookies, melt the chocolate and butter in the top of a double boiler over hot water, stirring continuously. Remove from the water, add the sugar, and mix well. Add the eggs and almond extract and mix well.
3. In a bowl, sift together the flour, baking powder, and salt. Add to the chocolate mixture and stir to combine. Pour the batter into the prepared pan and bake in the preheated oven until a toothpick inserted in the center comes out clean, about 30 minutes. Cool in the pan. Cut into quarters with a sharp knife. Remove 1 quarter at a time from the baking pan, using a wide spatula. Set aside.
4. For the filling, cream the butter in a mixing bowl. Add the confectioners' sugar gradually and mix until smooth. Add the cream and peppermint extract and combine thoroughly. Add more cream if necessary, 1 teaspoon at a time, combining thoroughly after each addition, until the mixture is spreading consistency.
5. Split each of the 4 cookie sections into 2 layers by slicing in half horizontally with a thin, sharp, serrated knife. Spread the bottom layers evenly with the filling. Put the top layers over them and press lightly. Set on a flat plate and chill until the filling is firm, at least 1 hour.
6. For the coating, combine the corn syrup, water, butter, and peppermint extract in a small saucepan. Cook over medium heat, stirring, just to boiling. Remove from heat, add the chocolate, and stir until melted.
7. With a sharp knife, evenly trim outside edges of the 4 cookie squares. Cut each cookie section into 8 pieces. Spear the squares in the bottom, 1 at a time, with a

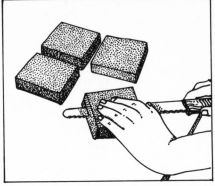

Split each of the four sections into two layers, slicing in half horizontally with a serrated knife.

sharp-tined fork. Dip the sides and top into the warm chocolate coating, allowing the excess coating to drip off. Set the squares on a rack set over a plate to catch the dripping chocolate until firm, several hours.

8. Garnish each piece with a candied mint leaf if you wish.

Yield: 32 cookies

SOFT MOLASSES OR HONEY COOKIES

1. In a bowl, sift together the flour, baking soda, salt, ginger, cinnamon, and allspice. Set aside.
2. In another bowl, cream together both sugars and the butter until light and fluffy. Beat in the molasses or honey, egg, and zest until smooth. Stir or beat at low speed, adding the flour mixture gradually until the dough is well combined. Chill the dough, covered, until firm enough to handle, 1 to 2 hours.
3. Heat the oven to 350°F. Lightly grease several baking sheets.
4. Form the dough into 1- to 1½-inch balls. Roll each ball in the granulated sugar and place on the prepared baking sheets leaving 2 inches between the balls.
5. Bake in the preheated oven for 12 to 15 minutes, until just set. Transfer to racks to cool. Store in an airtight container.

Yield: about 2 dozen cookies

2 *cups sifted all-purpose flour*
½ *teaspoon baking soda*
½ *teaspoon salt*
½ *teaspoon powdered ginger*
½ *teaspoon ground cinnamon*
½ *teaspoon ground allspice*
¼ *cup granulated sugar, plus about ¼ cup more for rolling*
¼ *cup light-brown sugar*
4 *ounces unsalted butter, softened*
½ *cup molasses* or *honey*
1 *egg*
1 *tablespoon grated orange zest*

RICH MACAROON SQUARES

Cookies

½ pound unsalted butter, *softened*
1 cup sugar
    Pinch of salt
    Grated zest of 2 oranges
1 extra-large egg plus 1 yolk, *lightly beaten*
2 tablespoons milk
2 teaspoons vanilla extract
2 cups cake flour
1½ cups all-purpose flour
2 ounces unsweetened chocolate

Macaroon Topping

2⅔ cups almonds with skins
⅔ cup hazelnuts with skins
3 cups sugar
2 teaspoons vanilla extract
½ teaspoon almond extract
10 egg whites (a generous ¾ cup)

1. For the cookies, cream the butter in a mixing bowl. Add the sugar, salt, and orange zest and beat until fluffy. Beat in the egg and extra yolk, milk, and vanilla. Add the flours and mix just until they are incorporated. (Be careful not to overmix or dough will be tough. The dough should be soft but not sticky.) Gather the dough together, dust with flour, wrap, and chill well.

2. Heat the oven to 400°F. Lightly butter a 10½"-×-15½"-×-1" baking pan.

3. On a lightly floured work surface, roll out the chilled dough so that it is slightly larger than the prepared baking pan. Transfer the dough to the pan. Trim the edges of the dough flush with the pan and prick the dough all over with a fork. Chill for about 10 minutes.

4. Bake in the preheated oven until golden, about 16 minutes. Melt the chocolate in a double boiler. Remove the pan from the oven and brush the pastry with a thin layer of melted chocolate. Cool on a rack until the chocolate is set. Lower the oven to 375°F.

5. For the macaroon topping, put the almonds, hazelnuts, and sugar in a food processor. Whir until powdered but not oily, working in batches if necessary. Add the vanilla and almond extracts and egg whites and process until the mixture forms a smooth paste.

6. Gently spread the topping over the cooled crust, being careful not to allow the chocolate to blend with the topping. Smooth the surface with a spatula and bake until crisp and golden brown, 30 to 35 minutes. Cool on a rack.

7. Use a sharp knife to cut into 1½- to 2-inch squares.

Yield: 5 to 6 dozen cookies

COCONUT KISSES

Superfine sugar dissolves more completely than granulated. Be sure to measure it carefully; too much will make the cookies sticky and chewy. These light cookies are delicious with fresh fruit or sorbets.

¾ cup water
1 cup superfine sugar
4 egg whites
⅛ teaspoon cream of tartar
1 teaspoon vanilla extract
¾ cup grated fresh coconut

1. Heat the oven to 200°F (see Note). Butter a baking sheet, cover it with parchment paper, and butter and flour the parchment paper.
2. In a heavy saucepan, heat the water and sugar until the sugar dissolves. Boil the mixture to 238°F on a candy thermometer. Remove from heat.
3. In a mixing bowl, beat the egg whites until frothy. Add the cream of tartar and continue beating until soft peaks form. With the mixer running, drizzle the hot sugar syrup into the egg whites. Continue beating until the meringue cools and stiff peaks form, 8 to 10 minutes. Stir in the vanilla and coconut.
4. Fill a pastry bag fitted with a ½-inch star tip with the meringue. Pipe small round kisses, about 1 inch in diameter, onto the prepared baking sheet 1 inch apart.
5. Bake in the preheated oven until the kisses are light and dry, 1½ to 1¾ hours. Carefully loosen the kisses on the baking sheet as soon as they are removed from the oven and allow to cool on the baking sheet. Store in an airtight container.

Yield: 7 to 8 dozen kisses

Note: The kisses must be baked in a cool oven so that they dry without browning. While still warm, the kisses will be soft and pliable, but they will become crisp and fragile when cool.

With a star tip, pipe small round kisses onto the prepared baking sheet.

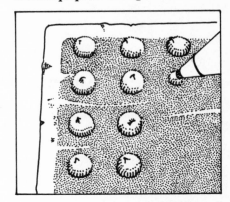

BUTTERMILK PRALINES

This buttermilk variation on southern pralines is as creamy as ever but has an extra tang.

1   cup sugar
½   tablespoon light corn syrup
½   cup buttermilk
½   teaspoon baking soda
1½ tablespoons unsalted butter
1   cup toasted pecan halves (see Note)
½   teaspoon vanilla extract

1. In a large, heavy saucepan, combine the sugar, corn syrup, buttermilk, and baking soda. Bring to a boil over medium heat, stirring constantly to dissolve the sugar. Cover and cook over low heat for about 2 minutes. Uncover the pan and cook over medium heat until the temperature on a candy thermometer reaches 220°F.
2. Add the butter and pecans and cook to 232° to 234°F. Remove from heat and let stand for 2 to 3 minutes. Add the vanilla and beat with a wooden spoon until the mixture begins to thicken and becomes creamy, 2 to 3 minutes.
3. Drop the pralines by tablespoons onto waxed paper. Allow to cool and become firm.

Yield: about ¾ pound

Note: To toast the pecans, spread them in a single layer on a baking sheet and put in a preheated 325°F oven until lightly browned, 5 to 10 minutes.

CRISP MACADAMIA WAFERS

6   ounces unsalted butter, softened
½   cup sugar
2   egg whites
½   teaspoon vanilla extract
½   cup ground toasted macadamia nuts,
        plus ½ cup chopped toasted
        macadamia nuts (see Note)
½   cup all-purpose flour

1. Heat the oven to 350°F. Use nonstick baking sheets or butter and flour the baking sheets.
2. In a mixing bowl, cream the butter until light. Add the sugar and beat until fluffy. Stir in the egg whites and vanilla. Gently stir in the ground nuts and flour.
3. Drop the batter by teaspoons onto the prepared pans, leaving 3 inches between each wafer. Flatten the wafers slightly with the back of a spoon dipped in cold water. Sprinkle each wafer generously with the chopped nuts.
4. Bake in the preheated oven until the wafer edges are golden, 8 to 10 minutes. Transfer to a rack to cool.

Yield: about 4 dozen wafers

Note: To toast the nuts, spread them in a single layer in a shallow pan and put in a preheated 325°F oven until golden brown, 5 to 10 minutes.

CLOVE GUMDROPS

1. Butter an 8-inch pan.
2. In a large, heavy saucepan, combine the liquid pectin or reconstituted powdered pectin with 2 tablespoons water. Stir in the baking soda. In another heavy saucepan, combine sugar and the corn syrup.
3. Cook both mixtures over high heat, stirring both until the foam in the pectin mixture has thinned and the sugar mixture is boiling rapidly, 3 to 5 minutes.
4. Slowly drizzle the pectin mixture into the sugar mixture, stirring constantly. Continue to boil, stirring, for 1 minute more.
5. Immediately remove from heat and stir in the clove oil. Pour the syrup into the prepared pan. Set aside to cool and firm, at least 2 hours.
6. Turn the candy out and, with a knife rinsed in cold water, cut into small diamonds. Roll each piece in sugar. Store loosely covered.

Yield: about 1 pound

Note: Clove oil is available from candy-making supply houses and old-fashioned pharmacies. For different flavors, add other flavoring oils. Food coloring can be added just before the oil.

6 *ounces liquid pectin, or one 1¾-ounce packet powdered pectin reconstituted with ¾ cup water*
2 *tablespoons water*
½ *teaspoon baking soda*
1 *cup sugar, plus some for rolling*
1 *cup light corn syrup*
1 *to 2 drops clove oil (see Note)*

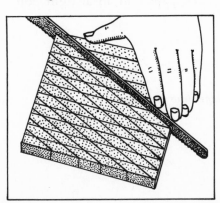

Cut the gumdrop mixture into small diamond shapes by cutting crosswise and then diagonally.

VANILLA OR CINNAMON SALTWATER TAFFY

1⅓ cups sugar
 1 tablespoon cornstarch
 1 cup light corn syrup
⅔ cup water
 1 split vanilla bean or broken cinnamon
     stick
1½ tablespoons unsalted butter
½ teaspoon salt
     Few drops food color (optional)

1. Butter a large marble slab or heavy baking sheet.
2. In a large, heavy saucepan, combine the sugar, cornstarch, corn syrup, water, and vanilla bean or cinnamon stick. Bring to a boil, stirring to dissolve the sugar. Cover the pan and cook over medium-low heat for 2 minutes. Uncover, add the butter and salt, and cook until the syrup registers 250°F on a candy thermometer.
3. Remove from heat and, without stirring, pour the mixture onto the prepared marble slab or baking sheet. Sprinkle with food color if desired and remove the vanilla bean or cinnamon stick. Cool for 2 to 4 minutes.
4. Generously butter your hands. To pull taffy, first gently pick up the edges, which will be cooler than the center, and fold over the center to keep the temperature as even as possible. Pull the candy into a 12- to 15-inch rope. Fold the rope in half and pull again. Continue folding and pulling, keeping your hands buttered, until the candy begins to harden and no longer sags when stretched. Make a final pull to an even rope of about ½ inch in diameter. The rope should be opaque and creamy. The entire pulling process will take 10 to 20 minutes, depending upon room temperature and your stamina. (Taffy hardens more quickly at cool temperatures.)
5. Butter or oil kitchen shears and quickly cut the rope into 1- to 1½-inch pieces. Store the candies, individually wrapped in waxed paper, in an airtight container.

Yield: about 1 pound

To pull taffy, first fold the edges into the center.

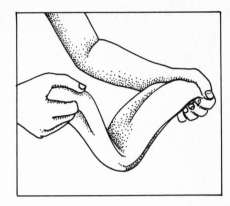

Pull the taffy into a 12- to 15-inch rope, fold the rope in half, and pull again.

DIVINITY

1. In a large, heavy saucepan, combine the sugar, water, and corn syrup. Bring to a boil over medium heat, stirring to dissolve the sugar. Cover the pan and cook over medium-low heat for about 2 minutes. Uncover and cook without disturbing the pan until the temperature on a candy thermometer reaches 256° to 260°F.

2. Beat the egg whites with an electric mixer to firm but not dry peaks.

3. With the mixer on medium speed, very slowly drizzle the hot syrup onto the whites and then slowly increase to a thin stream until all the syrup is incorporated. Beat in the vanilla and continue beating until the mixture cools and becomes creamy and stiff, 5 to 10 minutes more. Quickly beat in the nuts and fruits.

4. Drop the candies by rounded teaspoons onto waxed paper and leave until firm. Store in an airtight container to prevent divinity from absorbing moisture from the air.

Yield: about 1 pound

2 cups sugar
½ cup water
½ cup light corn syrup
2 egg whites
1 teaspoon vanilla extract
½ cup coarsely chopped pistachio nuts
½ cup coarsely chopped dried apricots or a combination of dried apricots and candied cherries

TOFFEE BITTERSWEET CRUNCH

1 cup packed light-brown sugar
1 tablespoon light corn syrup
4 ounces unsalted butter
1 teaspoon vanilla extract
½ cup chopped blanched almonds, plus 1
    cup chopped lightly toasted blanched
    almonds (see Note)
6 ounces extra bittersweet or 5 ounces
    bittersweet plus 1 ounce
    unsweetened chocolate, broken into
    small pieces

1. Butter a cookie sheet.
2. In a heavy saucepan, combine the sugar, corn syrup, and butter and cook over medium heat, stirring constantly, until the sugar dissolves and the mixture boils. Cover the pan for 1 minute. Uncover and cook over medium heat until the mixture reaches 290°F on a candy thermometer.
3. Remove from heat and stir in the vanilla and ½ cup chopped almonds. Pour onto the prepared cookie sheet and spread with a metal spatula until about ¼ inch thick.
4. Immediately scatter the chocolate pieces over the hot toffee. Press the chocolate pieces lightly with a spoon so the chocolate starts melting. When the chocolate is soft enough, 3 to 5 minutes, spread over the surface in an even layer and sprinkle with 1 cup toasted almonds. Cool completely and break into pieces. Toffee will stay crunchy for several days if stored in an airtight container in a dry, cool place.

Yield: about 1 pound

Note: To toast the nuts, spread them on a baking sheet in a single layer and put in a preheated 325°F oven until golden, 5 to 10 minutes.

MAPLE-WALNUT FUDGE

1½ cups sugar
 1 cup pure maple syrup
 1 cup half and half or light cream
 1 tablespoon light corn syrup
 1 tablespoon unsalted butter
 ½ teaspoon vanilla extract
1½ cups broken toasted black walnuts (see
    Note)

1. Butter an 8- or 9-inch pan.
2. In a large, heavy saucepan, combine the sugar, maple syrup, half and half or cream, and corn syrup. Bring to a boil over medium heat, stirring constantly to dissolve the sugar. Cover the pan and cook over medium-low heat for about 2 minutes. Uncover and cook over medium heat to 238°F on a candy thermometer.
3. Remove from heat and add the butter but do not stir. Cool, undisturbed, to about 110° to 120°F. Add the vanilla and beat the fudge with a wooden spoon until

it begins to thicken and lose its gloss. Beat in the walnuts.

4. Pour the mixture into the prepared pan, being careful not to scrape the bottom of the saucepan. Quickly spread to an even thickness. Cool completely and cut into 1-inch squares.

Yield: about 1½ pounds

Note: To toast the nuts, spread them in a single layer in a shallow pan and put in a preheated 325°F oven until lightly browned, 5 to 10 minutes.

15 Ice Creams, Sherbets, and Ices

Ice creams, sherbets, and ices have ranked among America's favorite desserts for more than two centuries, and we now consume more ice cream than any other country. From velvety smooth and decadently rich ice creams to light sherbets and ices with clear, sparkling flavors, frozen confections are the soul of versatility. They can be prepared in myriad flavors and dressed up or down to suit the occasion: served alone or partnered with other desserts; topped with sauce or garnished with fresh fruit; molded or insulated with other ingredients and then baked or fried. And today, with modern home freezers and contemporary ice-cream machines, frozen desserts are easy to prepare at home. Some excellent ready-made ice creams can be found, and these can certainly be used in our recipes, such as Fried Ice Cream and Baby Alaskas. Supermarket varieties, however, can be less than appetizing. Artificial flavors and colorings are allowed, and in the United States, over twelve hundred chemical stabilizers and emulsifiers are legal additives to ice cream—as is up to 50 percent air. When you make your own, freshness and flavor are assured.

FREEZING

It's good to chill the dessert before freezing. Prechilling allows the flavors to blend, and it cuts down on freezing time. Taste the cold mixture to see if any flavor adjustments are necessary; remember that freezing diminishes flavor, and so make the mixture slightly sweeter than it ultimately should be. Ice creams freeze more quickly than sherbets or ices because they contain (usually) less water and less sugar. Sugar lowers the freezing point of any mixture.

As ice creams, sherbets, and ices freeze, ice crystals are formed. The number and size of the ice crystals determine the texture of the final product. For ideal texture, the crystals should be tiny and well dispersed. The other element necessary for good texture is air, which affects the density of the mixture and prevents it from freezing solid.

In still-freezing, the mixture is stirred or beaten two or three times as it freezes. Each time it is beaten, the ice crystals are broken down and air is incorporated. In an ice-cream machine, a mechanically or electrically operated dasher or paddle evenly and constantly rotates through the mixture, exposing it to the cold, aerating it, and preventing the formation of ice crystals.

STILL-FREEZING

"Still-freezing" is something of a misnomer. When a clear liquid, unless it contains a very high proportion of alcohol, is frozen with no movement at all, the result is a large, flavored ice cube—or a giant unservable Popsicle. The "still-freeze" method generally involves beating or at least stirring during the process of solidification. Still-freezing produces sherbets and ices with a uniform, but slightly grainy texture. Ice cream, especially when made with all cream, can also be still-frozen. Prepare the sherbet or ice-cream mixture according to the recipe. Pour the mixture into metal ice-cube trays with the dividers removed (or a shallow cake pan or a metal bowl—the shallower the container, the faster the mixture will freeze) and set the trays directly on the floor of your freezer. When the mixture begins to harden around the edges but is still quite soft in the center (after about one hour, depending on the mixture), remove the trays from the freezer. Stir well, or better yet, beat the mixture until it is light and frothy, with a whisk or an electric mixer, or in a blender or a food processor fitted with a metal blade. Return the mixture to the freezer and then repeat the freezing and beating process one or two more times. Following the final beating, let the mixture freeze completely.

ICE-CREAM MACHINES

Ice cream used to be made in pot freezers in which the ingredients were first beaten by hand and then shaken vigorously in a container of ice and salt until solid. In the 1780s, we made a big step forward with the rotary paddle freezer. Jefferson used an eighteen-step method to make his ice cream in the up-to-date machine he purchased in 1784. Small, hand-cranked freezers were introduced in 1846, and we thought the job had been made as simple as possible.

Now, though hand-cranked models are still around, electrically operated machines make the work easy enough for the laziest cook. Some electric machines chill with a combination of ice and salt, while others contain

Ice and salt surround the cannister in a typical ice-cream machine.

When the ice cream is frozen, lift it out carefully so that no salty ice water gets into it.

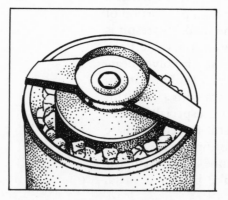

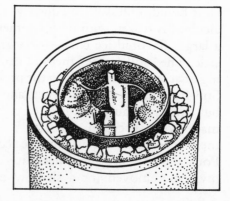

an internal refrigeration unit that relies on Freon. All models operate on the same principle: The mixture is poured into a cannister containing a dasher or a paddle. The cannister is chilled at an even temperature, and when the dasher or paddle rotates, it churns the mixture. As air is incorporated, the mixture increases in volume. For this reason, at the outset the cannister should be no more than two-thirds full for ice creams and three-quarters full for sherbets or ices.

Ice-cream machines vary greatly. When buying one, consider price, size, weight, ease of cleaning, operating and assembly requirements, and noise level. Most smaller machines are chilled with ice and salt and are perfectly adequate for the sometime ice-cream maker. Salt is always added to the ice to lower the temperature of the resulting brine. We don't recommend the small models that fit inside a refrigerator freezer for chilling. The larger, heavier, more expensive units are self-refrigerated. They produce the most reliable results and require the least effort.

ICE CREAMS
The most basic ice creams are a simple blend of cream, sugar, and a flavoring. A richer variety includes a custard base, made by thickening milk or cream with egg yolks. These ice creams are richer and heavier than those made without the yolks, and they have a smoother, silkier texture. The number of yolks is a variable. We've seen chefs push the limit, adding up to 18 per quart. Believe it or not, there can be too much of a good thing.

To prepare a custard–ice cream mixture, whisk the yolks with sugar until they lighten in color and thicken slightly. Add hot milk or cream, whisk well, and return the mixture to the saucepan. Cook the custard over low heat, stirring constantly, until it is slightly thickened, just enough to coat the back of a spoon. If the custard is not completely smooth, strain it. Otherwise pour the custard into a bowl and let it cool completely.

When the custard has cooled, any liquid or pureed flavorings can be added. Once there were three flavors—chocolate, vanilla, and strawberry. In the 1960s came a craze for new flavors that put even Howard Johnson's 28 to shame—everything from licorice to bubblegum flavoring went into ice cream. And we are still experimenting, albeit, one hopes, with a more refined palate. Any solid embellishments, such as chunks of fruit, chocolate bits, nuts, or pieces of candied fruit, should not be added to the mixture until it is partially frozen. If they were added earlier, they would sink to the bottom and never distribute evenly throughout the mixture as they should. If you plan to add dried or candied fruits, soak them in a little liqueur before adding them; the alcohol will prevent them from freezing solid. Once the custard has been flavored, pour it into the chilled cannister of an ice-cream machine and freeze according to the manufacturer's instructions.

When the ice cream is frozen, let it harden, or ripen, for 2 to 3 hours. This can be done in the cannister itself, if it is removable. Otherwise, transfer the ice cream to a metal bowl. Pack the ice cream down, cover it tightly, and set it in the freezer. To maintain its smooth consistency, ice cream should be stored between $-10°$ and $0°F$. All homemade ice creams should be eaten rather quickly; since they do not contain stabilizers or preservatives, both texture and flavor deteriorate after a week or so.

FRIED ICE CREAM

1. Line a metal tray with waxed paper.
2. Working quickly, form the ice cream into 4 equal balls, using an ice-cream scoop or 2 large spoons. Put the ice-cream balls on the prepared tray and return to the freezer until frozen very hard, at least 1 hour.
3. In a bowl, mix the cake with the chopped nuts. Remove the ice cream balls from the freezer 1 at a time, roll in the crumb-nut mixture, and return to the freezer. Remove the balls, 1 at a time, from the freezer, dip in the beaten egg, and roll again in the crumb mixture. Refreeze until the ice cream is very hard, at least 3 hours, before continuing.
4. Heat about 3 inches of oil in a deep fryer or a large, heavy saucepan to 375°F.
5. Remove 2 or more ice-cream balls from the freezer, depending on the size of fryer, and submerge in hot oil, using a basket or large slotted spoon. Fry the balls until gold brown, 30 to 40 seconds. Remove from the oil, drain, and repeat with the remaining ice-cream balls. Serve immediately in a pool of chocolate sauce.

Yield: 4 servings

1 pint Basic Vanilla Ice Cream (see recipe, this chapter)
½ cup crumbs from firm-textured cake (such as pound cake)
½ cup chopped pecans
1 egg, lightly beaten
Peanut oil
Basic Chocolate Sauce (recipe follows)

1. In a saucepan, heat the sugar with ¼ cup half and half until the sugar dissolves. Bring just to a boil and then remove from heat.
2. Add the chocolate and stir until melted and smooth. Add the remaining ¼ cup half and half and blend.

Yield: 1 cup

BASIC CHOCOLATE SAUCE

¼ cup sugar
½ cup half and half
4 ounces semisweet chocolate, broken into pieces

PECAN-PIE ICE CREAM AND PIE-PASTRY COOKIES

All the elements of traditional pie and ice cream are in this recipe, but arranged in a new way.

½ cup sugar
3½ tablespoons unsalted butter
¼ cup dark corn syrup
2 medium eggs, lightly beaten
1¼ cups chopped pecans, plus ¼ cup pecan halves
1 recipe Basic Vanilla Ice Cream (see recipe, this chapter)
Pie-Pastry Cookies (recipe follows)

1. Heat the oven to 350°F. Butter a 10-inch pie pan.
2. Combine the sugar, 2 tablespoons butter, and corn syrup in a small saucepan. Bring to a boil, stirring constantly, until the mixture is melted and smooth. Slowly pour the hot syrup in a thin stream into a bowl with the beaten eggs, whisking constantly. Add the chopped pecans and stir well.
3. Pour into the prepared pie pan and bake in the preheated oven until browned and a knife inserted in the center comes out clean, about 40 minutes. Cool and cut into small pieces.
4. Spread a 1-inch layer of ice cream in a baking dish. Distribute half the baked pecan mixture over the ice cream. Spread another 1-inch layer of ice cream onto the filling, layer with the remaining pecan filling mixture, and finish with another layer of ice cream. If the ice cream begins to melt while you are working, put it back in the freezer until firm again. Cover with plastic wrap. Freeze until firm.
5. Heat remaining 1½ tablespoons butter in a frying pan. Add the pecan halves and stir over medium-high heat to toast lightly.
6. Scoop the ice cream into chilled, stemmed glasses, top each serving with sautéed pecans, and serve with pie-pastry cookies.

Yield: 6 servings

PIE-PASTRY COOKIES

1¼ cups all-purpose flour
Pinch of salt
1½ tablespoons sugar, plus some for sprinkling
6 tablespoons cold unsalted butter, cut into small pieces
1 egg yolk beaten with 2 tablespoons cold water

1. Combine the flour, salt, and 1½ tablespoons sugar in a mixing bowl. Work the butter into the flour, using your fingertips or a pastry blender, until the butter pieces are about the size of peas. Make a well in the center of the butter-flour mixture. Pour in the egg yolk–water mixture and combine. Gather the dough into a ball.
2. Flour the heel of your hand and smear a handful of

dough at a time away from you on the work surface to complete blending. Gather the dough together with a pastry scraper, form into a ball, and wrap in plastic wrap. Refrigerate for at least 30 minutes.

3. Heat the oven to 375°F.

4. On a lightly floured work surface, roll out the pastry dough into a 10-inch square approximately ¼ inch thick. Trim the edges and cut the dough into four 2½-inch-wide strips. Cut the strips into pie-shaped triangles about 1½ inches wide. Put the triangles on an ungreased baking sheet. Flute the top edge of each triangle with your fingertips to resemble a piecrust. Sprinkle with sugar.

5. Bake in the preheated oven until golden around the edges, 8 to 10 minutes. Remove to a rack to cool. Store in an airtight container.

Yield: 32 cookies

Form smooth, round balls of ice cream by holding the scoop straight up and down perpendicular to the surface and scraping along the surface to roll up a ball.

BABY ALASKAS

Strawberry Ice Cream

1½ pints fresh strawberries, chopped
⅓ cup sugar
1½ tablespoons Grand Marnier
 2 egg yolks
½ cup heavy cream

Cake

⅓ cup all-purpose flour
    Pinch of salt
 2 eggs
⅓ cup sugar
¼ teaspoon vanilla extract

Praline

⅓ cup sugar
1½ tablespoons water
⅓ cup blanched almonds

Meringue

 4 egg whites
    Pinch of salt
⅛ teaspoon cream of tartar
 1 cup superfine sugar

1. For the ice cream, combine the strawberries, sugar, and Grand Marnier in a bowl. Cover and leave at room temperature for 4 to 8 hours.

2. Drain the strawberries and reserve the liquid. Combine the liquid, egg yolks, and cream in the top of a double boiler and cook over simmering water, stirring constantly, until the mixture thickens enough to coat the back of a spoon. Be careful not to let it get too hot or eggs will scramble. Cool. Put the mixture in an ice-cream maker and freeze according to the manufacturer's instructions. When it is partially frozen, add the strawberries and continue to freeze until firm.

3. Heat the oven to 350°F. Butter an 8-inch cake pan and dust with flour.

4. For the cake, sift the flour and salt together in a bowl. In another bowl, beat the eggs slightly and stir in the sugar. Beat vigorously until the mixture is pale yellow and trails in a ribbon when the whisk is lifted, 3 to 4 minutes. Add the vanilla. Add the flour to the batter in 3 batches, folding to incorporate after each addition. Pour into the prepared cake pan and bake in the preheated oven until the cake shrinks slightly from the side of the pan, 16 to 18 minutes. Set aside to cool in the pan for about 5 minutes and then turn out onto a rack to cool completely.

5. Butter a baking sheet.

6. For the praline, combine the sugar and water in a heavy saucepan and heat until the sugar dissolves. Boil until the syrup turns light caramel brown, 2 to 3 minutes. Remove from heat and stir in the almonds. Pour onto the prepared baking sheet to cool and harden. Break up the carmelized nuts and pulverize them in a food processor.

7. Cut the cake in half horizontally. With a 3½-inch cookie cutter, cut out 4 circles from the cake layers. Chill in the refrigerator for 30 minutes or longer.

8. Line a tray with waxed paper.

9. Scoop out 4 balls of ice cream with a 4-ounce ice-

cream scoop and put on the prepared tray. Freeze the ice-cream balls until they're very hard, about 1 hour. Remove from the freezer, roll the hardened balls in the praline, and put 1 ball on top of each cake round. Return to the freezer for another 30 minutes.

10. For the meringue, beat the egg whites and salt until foamy. Add the cream of tartar and beat until the whites form soft peaks. Still beating, add the sugar, 1 tablespoon at a time. Continue to beat until the whites are smooth, glossy, and form stiff peaks. Put the meringue into a large pastry bag fitted with a ½-inch star tip.

11. Butter a baking sheet.

12. Put the cake rounds with ice cream on the prepared baking sheet and pipe the meringue by circling the bottom of the cake and working up to the top, making sure to cover the ice cream and cake entirely. Return to freezer until ready to serve.

13. Heat the oven to 500°F.

14. Put the baking sheet directly from the freezer into the preheated oven. Bake until the meringue is browned, 4 to 5 minutes. Serve immediately.

Yield: 4 servings

CINNAMON ICE CREAM WITH CALVADOS

1. In a saucepan, bring the milk to a boil.
2. In a mixing bowl, whisk the egg yolks with sugar until thick and light in color. Add the cinnamon.
3. Slowly whisk half the hot milk into the egg yolk–sugar mixture and then return to the saucepan. Cook over low heat, stirring constantly, until the mixture thickens and coats the back of the spoon, about 10 minutes. Remove from heat and stir in the vanilla and cream.
4. Cool the mixture, stirring occasionally. Freeze in an ice-cream maker according to the manufacturer's instructions.
5. Serve with 2 teaspoons Calvados or apple brandy poured over each serving.

2 cups milk
6 egg yolks
¾ cup sugar
2 teaspoons ground cinnamon
1 teaspoon vanilla extract
1 cup chilled heavy cream
¼ cup Calvados or apple brandy

Yield: 1½ quarts (6 servings)

BASIC VANILLA ICE CREAM

2 cups milk
2 cups heavy cream
1 vanilla bean, split, or 1½ teaspoons
    vanilla extract
8 egg yolks
¾ cup sugar

A custard is thick enough when a finger drawn across the sauce-coated spoon leaves a clear trail.

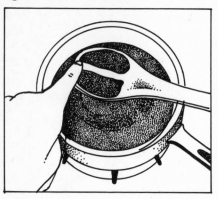

1. In a saucepan, combine the milk, cream, and vanilla bean if using. Bring just to a boil over medium heat.
2. In a mixing bowl, beat the egg yolks with the sugar until they are thick and light in color. Whisk in one half the hot milk mixture and then pour this mixture back into the saucepan with the remaining hot milk. Warm over low heat, stirring constantly, until the mixture begins to thicken slightly and coats the back of a spoon, about 10 minutes. Be careful not to boil or the mixture will curdle.
3. Remove from heat, stir in vanilla extract if using, and strain the mixture through a fine-mesh sieve into a bowl. Scrape the seeds from the vanilla bean, if using, into the custard. Lay plastic wrap directly on the surface to prevent a skin from forming. Cool completely.
4. Transfer the mixture to an ice-cream maker and freeze according to the manufacturer's instructions.

Yield: 1 to 1½ quarts

SHERBETS AND ICES

Among frozen deserts, sherbets and ices are the arena of most current experimentation by chefs and sophisticated home cooks. Cantaloupe and grapefruit show up in our sherbets here, and new combinations such as plum and Zinfandel become ices. The difference between sherbets and ices is that sherbets contain a bit of milk, egg white, or gelatin for smoother texture. Ices can include wine and often have more sugar than ice cream or sherbet to inhibit the formation of ice crystals. Sherbets and ices have brighter, deeper, clearer flavors than richer ice cream.

The ultimate texture of a sherbet or an ice will be determined in part by the ingredients in the mixture and in part by the freezing method. Sherbets and ices will always have a slightly coarse, grainy texture if they are frozen by the still-freeze method rather than in an ice-cream machine. However, even if these mixtures are frozen in a machine, they will never be as smooth as ice creams are.

Sherbets and ices do not keep as well as ice creams, and they should ideally be eaten within 8 hours. However, they can be melted down and rechurned to restore their fresh texture.

CANTALOUPE SHERBET

It's important to have an entirely ripe melon for this recipe. Other types, such as honeydew or casaba, can also be used.

1. In a saucepan, bring the sugar and water to a boil over medium heat, stirring constantly. Transfer to a chilled bowl and cool in the freezer for 10 to 15 minutes.
2. Scoop out the melon flesh, cut in chunks, and puree in a food processor. Measure out 2 cups of puree.
3. In a metal bowl, combine the cooled syrup with the 2 cups of melon puree and rum. Put the mixture into an ice-cream maker and freeze according to the manufacturer's instructions until the sherbet is just beginning to set.
4. In a mixing bowl, beat the egg whites until stiff. Fold into the partially frozen mixture and complete the freezing process in the ice-cream maker.

1 cup sugar
1 cup water
1 large cantaloupe, quartered and seeded
2 tablespoons rum (optional)
2 egg whites, room temperature

Yield: 1 quart

CRANBERRY-GRAPEFRUIT SHERBET MOLDS

Vermouth-Grapefruit Sherbet

½ cup grapefruit sections (about 1 grapefruit)
¼ cup superfine sugar
1½ teaspoons dry vermouth
1 egg white

Cranberry-Pear Sherbet

½ cup Whole Cranberry Sauce (recipe follows)
½ cup very ripe pear chunks
½ egg white (about 1 tablespoon)
½ tablespoon superfine sugar

4 half grapefruit shells, edges cut in zigzags, chilled (optional)
Mint leaves (optional)

1. For the vermouth-grapefruit sherbet, puree the grapefruit, all but 1 tablespoon sugar, and the vermouth in a food processor or blender. Strain.
2. In a mixing bowl, beat the egg white until soft peaks form and add the remaining tablespoon sugar. Continue beating for 30 seconds. Add the grapefruit puree and whisk to incorporate. Pour the mixture into a shallow pan or ice-cube trays, cover, and freeze until partially set, about 1 hour.
3. For the cranberry-pear sherbet, puree the cranberry sauce and pears in a food processor or blender. Strain.
4. In a mixing bowl, beat the egg white until soft peaks form. Add the sugar. Continue beating for 30 seconds and add the cranberry-pear puree. Whip to incorporate. Pour the mixture into a shallow pan or ice-cube trays, cover, and freeze until partially set, about 1 hour.
5. Put the partially set vermouth-grapefruit sherbet into a small mixing bowl and beat for 30 seconds. Cover and return to the freezer until partially set, about another hour. Repeat with the cranberry-pear sherbet.
6. Line four 6-ounce custard cups with plastic wrap, leaving an overhang. Chill the lined molds for about 30 minutes in the freezer.
7. Remove the grapefruit sherbet from the freezer and whip for 30 seconds. Fill each chilled custard cup halfway with grapefruit ice, smooth the surface, and return to the freezer to harden, about 1 hour.
8. Remove the cranberry sherbet from the freezer and whip for about 30 seconds. Remove half-filled custard cups from the freezer and fill with the cranberry ice, making the surface as smooth as possible. Freeze until completely frozen, 2 to 3 hours.

9. To unmold, remove ices from the cups by pulling out with the plastic wrap overhang (see Note) and invert into chilled grapefruit shells, if using. Peel off the wrap. Garnish with mint leaves, if desired.

Yield: 4 servings

Note: If the frozen desserts are difficult to remove from their cups, hold a towel dampened in warm water on the bottom of each for a few seconds and then remove as directed.

1. Combine the cranberries, sugar, and water in a small, nonreactive saucepan. Bring to a boil, stirring to dissolve the sugar.

2. Lower heat and simmer, uncovered, for about 5 minutes, until the cranberries have popped and are tender. Cool.

Yield: about 1½ cups

WHOLE CRANBERRY SAUCE

    2 cups (about ½ pound) fresh
         cranberries
    1 cup sugar
  ½ cup water

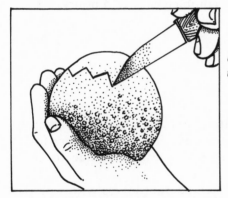

Cut grapefruit in a zigzag pattern, plunging the knife all the way to the center.

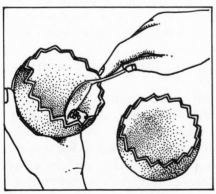

When the flesh is removed, the finished shell is an attractive container for the molded sherbet.

IDAHO RIESLING AND RHUBARB ICE

1½ pounds fresh rhubarb, cut into chunks
1½ cups late-harvest Idaho Riesling or
      other sweet dessert wine
¾ cup sugar
2 tablespoons lemon juice

1. Heat the oven to 375°F.
2. Put the rhubarb in a nonreactive baking dish. Bake in the preheated oven, covered, until soft, about 25 minutes. Transfer the rhubarb and its liquid to a food processor and puree until smooth.
3. Combine the rhubarb puree with the Riesling, sugar, and lemon juice. Cool. Put in an ice-cream freezer and freeze according to the manufacturer's instructions. Or pour the mixture into a large, shallow dish. Cover and freeze until the mixture just begins to harden around the edges but is still only partially frozen in the center, about 1 hour. Remove from the freezer and beat in a mixing bowl until frothy. Transfer back to the dish, cover, and refreeze until the mixture begins to harden again, about 30 minutes. Remove from the freezer, mix again, and return to the freezer to freeze completely, 2 to 3 hours.

Yield: 1½ quarts

PINEAPPLE-MINT ICE

3 cups water
2 cups sugar
2 cups firmly packed whole mint leaves,
      plus 1 cup minced mint leaves
1 ripe pineapple, peeled, cored, and cut
      into cubes (3½ to 4 cups)
  Juice of ½ lemon

1. In a saucepan, heat the water and sugar over medium heat, stirring until the sugar dissolves. Simmer for 3 minutes and remove from heat. Set aside to cool slightly.
2. In a bowl, crush the whole mint leaves with a pestle or other heavy, blunt instrument, bruising all the leaves to release as much flavor as possible. Pour half the sugar syrup over the mint, cover, and infuse for 30 minutes.
3. In a food processor, puree the pineapple with the remaining sugar syrup.
4. Strain the infused mint syrup through a fine sieve. Combine with the pineapple puree. Add the lemon juice and minced mint leaves and stir to blend.
5. Freeze in an ice-cream maker according to the manufacturer's instructions, then serve. Or, pour the mixture into a large, shallow dish. Cover and freeze just

until the mixture begins to harden around the edges but is still only partially frozen in the center, about 1 hour. Remove from the freezer and beat in a mixing bowl until frothy. Return to the dish, cover, and refreeze until the mixture begins to harden again, about 30 minutes. Remove from the freezer, mix again, and return to the freezer to freeze completely before serving, 2 to 3 hours.

Yield: 2 quarts

BANANA-CARAMEL SHERBET

1. In a food processor, puree the bananas with lemon juice.
2. In a saucepan, dissolve ¾ cup sugar in 1 cup water over medium heat, stirring. Raise heat to high and boil the syrup without stirring until it turns a rich amber color, 5 to 10 minutes. Remove from heat and cool for 1 minute. Add remaining ½ cup water, holding the pan at arm's length to avoid spatters. Stir in the cream.
3. Put the banana puree in a large bowl of an electric mixer. With the mixer on medium speed, slowly pour the caramel syrup into the puree and beat well to incorporate. Set aside.
4. In another bowl, beat the egg white with salt to soft peaks. Sprinkle on the remaining 1 tablespoon sugar and beat until stiff and glossy, about 30 seconds. Beat the banana-caramel mixture into the egg white at high speed.
5. Freeze in an ice-cream machine according to the manufacturer's instructions.
6. Serve garnished with banana chips and fresh mint if you like.

Yield: 6 servings

Note: For banana chips, make a caramel syrup as in step 2, using 1 cup sugar and ¼ cup water. Allow the syrup to cool slightly and then dip the dried banana chips into the syrup one by one. Allow to harden on oiled foil.

4 *large ripe bananas*
2 *tablespoons lemon juice*
¾ *cup plus 1 tablespoon sugar*
1½ *cups water*
3 *tablespoons heavy cream*
1 *egg white*
  Pinch of salt
12 *banana chips dipped in caramel (optional) (see Note)*
  Fresh mint sprigs (optional)

PLUM AND ZINFANDEL ICE

2 pounds red plums, pitted and chopped
1½ cups Zinfandel
½ cup water
1 cup sugar
1 2-inch piece cinnamon stick
2 bay leaves

1. In a large, nonreactive saucepan over medium heat, combine all the ingredients. Bring to a boil. Reduce heat and simmer, partially covered, skimming any foam that may form, until the plums are very tender, 20 to 25 minutes. Cool slightly and discard the cinnamon stick and bay leaves.
2. Force the mixture through a sieve or food mill into a metal container. Cover and freeze until firm, about 6 hours.
3. When ready to serve, transfer the container to the refrigerator to soften slightly, 5 to 10 minutes.

Yield: 1½ quarts

Chapter
16

Condiments and Vinegars

Condiments are served as additions or accompaniments to a dish, flavor that is added at the table rather than during the cooking. Some are preserved foods themselves, such as pickled vegetables, relishes, and catsups, while others, like mustards and hot sauces of all sorts, originally were used to mask the unpleasant flavor of spoiled food.

Today we have less need to preserve food by pickling it or making a relish out of it than was true previously, and we no longer need to hide the tang of high meat, but our taste for condiments lingers. Form has outlasted function, and today condiments serve us primarily as a point of contrast to the main dish, adding acidity, as with vinegar and pickles; sweetness, as with catsups, relishes, and some chutneys; or heat, as with mustard, salsa, or hot sauces.

Originally, most condiments were homemade, but the history of the manufacture of condiments is also an old one. Catsups, for instance, were widely made in the United States in the eighteenth and nineteenth centuries—and not just out of tomatoes. *The Home Cook Book*, 1882 edition, has recipes for four catsups—two tomato versions, a gooseberry catsup, and a cucumber catsup. But just about the time that book was published,

H. J. Heinz had begun the commercial preparation of catsup, and by the 1920s his brand and other similar ones had pretty well displaced homemade versions and established "tomato" as synonymous with "catsup."

The history of the manufacture of mustard goes back even farther—in England, for example, into the early nineteenth century. There, Jeremiah Colman of Norwich marketed his Colman's mustard, which still is a major English brand. And in France the secret recipes of the mustard-making families and merchants of Dijon are even older.

Most pickles, vinegar, relishes, mustards, and other condiments are made and distributed by large food-processing concerns today, but just as with many other kinds of foods, there has been a recent revival in the United States of cottage-industry condiments, especially mustards, vinegars, and relishes, and home cooks have found that many condiments are easy to prepare and can bring standards of flavor rarely matched by the commercial varieties. Until recently, the modern American taste in condiments ran to the simple, the sweet, and the commercial, but today the selection is as diverse as our cuisine itself.

CATSUP

Catsup (the *ketchup* spelling stems from H. J. Heinz's brand and was originally a registered company trademark) is essentially a saucelike concoction in which the principal ingredient is reduced by long cooking to form an intense flavoring. Among common early catsups were Oyster Catsup made with wine, brandy, sherry, shallots, and spices; Pontac or Pontack Catsup with elderberries; Windmere Catsup with mushrooms and horseradish; and Wolfram Catsup with beer, anchovies, and mushrooms. Homemade American tomato catsups were originally quite salty and piquant, but the commercial success of the Heinz company and other catsup makers adjusted the national preference toward the sweeter, blander style popular today.

Catsup making in the home is primarily a matter of patience, but the result, when tomato catsup, for instance, is made with good, ripe tomatoes, is a much different sauce from the familiar commercial kind and gives a new insight into why this became the country's most popular condiment in the first place.

MUSTARD

Until recently, French's was to mustard as Heinz was to catsup. But while catsup has long been primarily a commercial American condiment (there are only a few manufacturers of specialty catsups), mustard is one of the world's favorite condiments. American-style yellow mustard has always had at least some competition on U.S. shelves from French, German, English, and even Chinese mustards.

Mustard as a condiment is a paste made from the seeds of a variety of plants of the genus Brassica, especially the black mustard seed, the white mustard seed, and the brown mustard seed. The black mustard seeds are the hottest, and the white mustard seeds, used in American yellow (salad) mustard, are the mildest.

English prepared mustards are generally the strongest. French mustards range from mild to very hot. German mustard is of basically two types—the Düsseldorf style, which is usually hot, and the Bavarian or Munich style, which is milder and sometimes a bit sweet.

Mustard making in the United States is a growth industry now with lots of small producers putting out specialty mustards. Most of these are hotter and more complexly flavored than traditional commercial American mustards.

When making mustard at home, the important thing to remember is that heat inhibits the process and the pungency of the mustard develops best when it is mixed with a cold liquid. Begin with cold water, beer, or wine in order to have the sharpest flavor. For a milder result, heat the liquid before combining it with the mustard seeds. Different ingredients can be added to taste—salt, wine, herbs or spices, vinegar, or as in our recipe, garlic, soy sauce, and horseradish. Let the mixture rest for several hours or even a day or two while its flavor develops and mellows and then adjust the flavoring. If the mustard is too hot at this point, a little oil can be added to temper it without sweetening it.

RELISHES

Like many condiments, relishes were originally a means of preserving one year's fruit or vegetable harvest during the lean winter months. Piccalilli became a kind of American standard for home cooks by the nineteenth century, and then that wizard of the condiment, H. J. Heinz, started marketing his bottled version along with his catsup. By the mid-twentieth century, few home cooks were making any kind of relish.

With the renewal of interest in traditional American cooking and our contemporary zest to make for ourselves that which our parents bought from the food manufacturers, many American cooks are rediscovering the virtues of relishes—simple fruit or vegetable mixtures with vinegar or lemon, herbs, spices, onions, nuts, wine, sugar, or what have you. Many specialty relishes produced by small caterers or local cooks are on the market, and these provide the easiest way to sample the kinds of relishes our ancestors took for granted.

If you're making your own relishes, it's still best to use locally grown fruit or vegetables at the peak of the season. On the other hand, relishes made with supermarket produce during the off season are a way of enhancing fruits and vegetables that aren't really good enough to eat as they are.

PICKLES

It's probably a surprise for many modern Americans to learn that pickles and cucumbers aren't synonymous. Traditional American cooks knew that well, of course. They pickled tomatoes, onions, cauliflower, okra, cabbage, and other vegetables as well as cucumbers. *Pickling* means to preserve a vegetable or fruit in vinegar or brine. Brine is a strong saltwater solution; the standard formula is one pound of salt to a gallon of water. Long-brined pickles are cured simply by leaving them for two to four weeks in brine. When done they can be kept up to six months, in their brine, in a refrigerator or a cool place.

Short-brined pickles are kept in brine, or packed in salt, from one to twenty-four hours and then fermented in vinegar. Distilled vinegar is the best choice since it is usually cheaper and won't discolor the vegetables. Pickling herbs and spices—dill and mustard seeds, for instance—are added to the vinegar before starting the pickling process. The vinegar is then poured over the vegetables already packed in canning jars.

The most important thing to remember when following a pickling recipe is to use top-quality vegetables or fruits. They should be ripe but still firm, of moderate size, free from blemishes and spoiled spots, and very, very fresh. Vegetables pickled in vinegar must be canned, and you should follow standard procedures. A recipe for Cucumber, Onion, and Cauliflower Pickles follows.

CHUTNEY

Chutney is an Indian condiment, and in that country it is made much like an unsweetened relish or a Mexican fresh salsa. Chutneys in India vary by region and style of cooking. Nearly any ingredient can be used in a chutney as long as it's stimulating or refreshing. It's still common in India to use chutneys made fresh daily in the home rather than the bottled chutneys sold here.

In fact, most chutneys sold in this country are either of British manufacture or made in India specifically for export to the British or U.S. market. The British picked up the idea of chutney while ruling India but translated it into something more like a sweet pickle or chunky jam. For instance, a typical Indian mint chutney is often merely a mixture of mint leaves, chiles, onion, and lemon juice with perhaps some ground coconut or fresh coriander. An English chutney, on the other hand, is most likely a blend of apples or mangoes, raisins, onion, mustard, garlic, sugar, and salt, cooked until thickened.

Fresh chutneys can easily be made at home—just combine the ingredients and serve within an hour or two. Cooked chutneys are more like preserves and can be bottled and stored for later use.

HOT SAUCES

Hot sauces have one thing in common: They all come from parts of the world where the temperatures are very warm and food spoils easily. Hot sauces from Mexico, the Orient, or Louisiana, among other places, can mask the taste of spoiled meat, fish, or poultry, but this is no longer their main purpose. There is a sort of addictive quality to peppery foods that defies any easy explanation. Some of us just like it hot.

In Mexico, *salsa* simply means "sauce." There are varieties of Mexican hot sauces or salsas. *Salsa picante* literally means "spicy" or "hot sauce"; *salsa cruda* means "raw sauce"; *salsa verde* is "green sauce"; and *salsa ranchero* is "country-style sauce." *Salsa picante* and *cruda* are both usually made from chopped fresh tomatoes, chile peppers, lime juice, salt, and spices. *Salsa verde* substitutes Mexican green-husk tomatoes or tomatillos for tomatoes and is usually mixed with coriander, chile peppers, onion, and garlic. *Salsa ranchero* combines tomatoes, chile peppers, onion, and garlic—all cooked in oil. Salsas have become especially popular with American cooks in the Southwest, and increasingly elsewhere as that style has caught on across the country. A recipe for Tomatillo Salsa is included in this chapter.

The Orient is the source of a variety of hot sauces. Thailand probably holds pride of place among the Oriental cuisines for dedication to pure fieriness in the kitchen. We know a Thai cook who once stunned a whole room of American cooking students into silence with a Thai hot sauce and then merrily proclaimed that "In Thailand this sauce is just for babies." Thai fish sauce or *nam prik* is the prototypical Oriental hot sauce—it's a mixture of ground chiles, vinegar, sugar, and salt.

Louisiana is the home of the best-known native American hot sauces, and the McIlhenny family, producers of two hundred to three hundred bottles of Tabasco sauce a day, is the king of commercial hellfire. Tabasco is made from Avery Island peppers that are fermented and aged up to three years before going into the traditional thin-necked bottles.

VINEGAR

Vinegar is a sour liquid made by fermenting wine, cider, beer, grain, or fruit with acetic acid bacteria. During fermentation, the yeast turns sugar into alcohol, and then the alcohol is converted into acetic acid. The final liquid, the vinegar, will contain from 4 to 9 percent acetic acid. The best vinegars are made by a natural process called the Orleans method, during which they are subjected to minimum heat in order to retain maximum flavor. Commercial vinegars are usually made more rapidly, through processes that substitute heat for aging time.

The three principal types of vinegar available in the United States are cider, distilled, and wine. Cider vinegar is made from fermented apple cider and usually has an acid content of from 5 to 6 percent. It is especially good for homemade pickles and relishes.

Distilled vinegar is made from pure grain alcohol diluted with water. It's usually quite acidic and has a long shelf life. It's the vinegar most used in commercial mustards, pickles, catsups, and other condiments.

Wine vinegar is made from either red or white wine and usually has an acid content of 5 to 6 percent. With luck you can make wine vinegar simply by letting wine stand open in a warm, dark spot for several months. A surer and quicker method, however, is by adding a vinegar "mother" to the wine. Left alone, the "mother" will turn the wine into vinegar in four or five weeks. Vinegar "mothers" can be bought in specialty shops. Even if you don't make your own vinegar, you can easily make flavored vinegars with herbs or fruits. Start with a good-quality, Orleans-method wine vinegar and then add the desired fruit or herb so that the vinegar takes on the flavor and zest of the seasonings.

CATSUP

10 pounds ripe tomatoes, chopped
1 cup cider vinegar
2 tablespoons salt
¼ teaspoon grated nutmeg
2 teaspoons ground cinnamon
2 teaspoons ground allspice
½ teaspoon ground cloves
1 teaspoon cayenne
2 teaspoons baking soda
10 tablespoons sugar

1. In a large, nonreactive saucepan, cook the tomatoes over medium heat, stirring constantly, until soft, about 30 minutes.
2. Strain the tomatoes through a large sieve, forcing as much of the pulp through as possible. Discard the skins and seeds. Return the strained tomatoes to the pot and add all the remaining ingredients.
3. Simmer over medium heat, stirring occasionally until reduced to 6 cups, about 2 hours. The mixture should be thick and smooth.

Yield: 6 cups

LEMON-DILL VINEGAR

6 to 8 sprigs leafy dill
Zest of 1 lemon
4 cups Japanese rice wine vinegar

1. Put the dill and lemon zest in a large jar.
2. In a nonreactive saucepan, bring the vinegar almost to a boil and then pour it into the jar. Cool to room temperature and cover.
3. Steep for 48 hours and remove the lemon zest but leave the basil. Store in a cool place. The vinegar will keep for at least a year.

Yield: about 1 quart

BLUEBERRY-ORANGE VINEGAR

The same proportions of vinegar to sugar and berries can be applied to whatever berries you choose, and herbs can be added to the mixture, too.

1 cup blueberries, rinsed and drained
Zest of 1 orange, peeled off in strips
4 cups wine vinegar
⅓ cup sugar

1. Put the blueberries and orange zest in a large jar.
2. In a nonreactive saucepan, bring the vinegar and sugar almost to a boil. Stir to dissolve the sugar.
3. Pour the vinegar over the berries and zest, cool to room temperature, and cover.
4. Steep for 48 hours and then strain out the berries and zest. Store the vinegar in a cool place. Use within 1 year.

Yield: about 1 quart

CHILI SAUCE

Primarily a commercial preparation, chili sauce is a catsup variation. It's usually not very hot (our version is spicy but not fiery), and the texture is a bit chunkier than that of catsup.

1. In a nonreactive saucepan, simmer the tomatoes and juice over medium-low heat with the onion, red bell pepper, and garlic, stirring often, about 15 minutes.
2. Add the brown sugar, salt, and cayenne. Tie the cinnamon stick, cloves, mustard seeds, allspice, and black pepper in a cheesecloth bag and add to the saucepan. Stir in the vinegar and simmer, uncovered, for 45 minutes, adding a little water if the sauce gets too thick. Adjust the seasonings and discard the spice bags.
3. Remove from heat and let cool. Store, covered, in the refrigerator for at least 24 hours before using.

Yield: about ½ cup

2 ripe tomatoes, peeled, seeded, and
   chopped, juice reserved, or ¾
   pound canned Italian plum tomatoes
   with juice
½ small onion, minced
½ small red bell pepper, minced
¼ clove garlic, minced
½ to 1 tablespoon brown sugar
¼ teaspoon salt
   Pinch of cayenne
 1 ½-inch cinnamon stick
¼ teaspoon whole cloves
¼ teaspoon whole mustard seeds
¼ teaspoon whole allspice, or good pinch
   of ground allspice
 5 black peppercorns
¼ cup cider vinegar

To loosen tomato skins for easy peeling, cut a small x in the bottom of each tomato. Drop into boiling water for just a few seconds until the skin peels back at the cross.

Cut each tomato in half horizontally and scoop out the seeds.

TOMATILLO SALSA

½ yellow bell pepper
5 small tomatillos, cored and cut into
    small dice
2 small jalapeño peppers, cored, seeded,
    and minced (see Note)
2 small ripe tomatoes, cored, seeded, and
    cut into small dice
2 tablespoons thinly sliced black olives
1 small clove garlic, minced
1 pearl onion, cut into small dice
2 teaspoons minced fresh parsley
¼ teaspoon sugar
1 tablespoon vegetable oil
1 teaspoon white wine vinegar
1 teaspoon salt
⅛ teaspoon coarsely ground black pepper

1. Broil the yellow bell pepper until it blisters. Set aside until cool enough to handle and then peel, seed, and cut into small dice
2. Mix all the ingredients together in a nonreactive bowl.
3. Cover and let the flavors meld in the refrigerator for at least 20 minutes before serving.

Yield: 4 servings

Note: This salsa is mildly hot. For more fire, double the amount of jalapeño peppers.

BASIL-GARLIC VINEGAR

The following method can be used for any herb combination that you can come up with.

6 to 8 sprigs fresh basil
4 to 6 large cloves garlic, peeled
4 cups white wine vinegar

1. Put the basil and garlic in a large jar.
2. In a nonreactive saucepan, bring the vinegar almost to a boil and then pour it over the basil and garlic. Cool to room temperature and cover.
3. Steep for 48 hours and remove the garlic but leave the basil in the vinegar. Store in a cool place. The vinegar will be good for a year.

Yield: about 1 quart

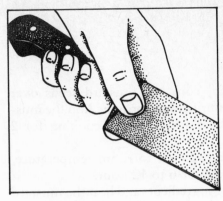

For nearly all cutting and chopping, maximum control of the knife is achieved by gripping the top of the blade firmly between thumb and forefinger.

To chop shallots, onions, or garlic, after peeling cut in half from root to stem and place each half, cut side down, on the work surface. Start from the stem end and cut horizontally almost through the root end.

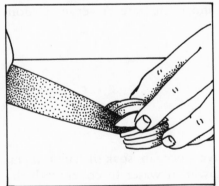

Next, make vertical cuts in the same way.

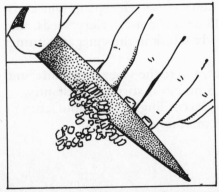

Finally, chop across your previous cuts.

BROWN BEER MUSTARD

½ cup yellow mustard seeds
2 tablespoons mustard powder
½ cup beer
1 tablespoon peanut oil
5 tablespoons cider vinegar
1 clove garlic, chopped
1 tablespoon water
½ teaspoon sugar
2 teaspoons salt
2 teaspoons soy sauce
2 peppercorns, crushed
1 teaspoon chopped horseradish

1. In a small saucepan, cook the mustard seeds over medium-high heat until golden brown. Add the mustard powder and beer and continue cooking for 2 minutes.
2. Remove from heat and cool to room temperature. Cover and refrigerate for 6 to 12 hours.
3. Stir in the remaining ingredients and heat the mustard in a small saucepan over a low flame for 10 minutes.
4. Puree in a food processor. The mustard will keep, refrigerated, for up to a month.

Yield: about ¾ cup

ORANGE AND LEMON RELISH

3 oranges, unpeeled, cut into ⅛-inch-thick slices
2 lemons, unpeeled, cut into ⅛-inch-thick slices
½ cup sweet sherry
½ cup water
4½ cups sugar
¼ teaspoon dried tarragon
⅛ teaspoon dried sage
½ teaspoon dried thyme
¼ teaspoon dried marjoram

1. In a large, nonreactive saucepan, combine the fruit, sherry, and water and bring to a boil.
2. Reduce heat and simmer until the peel is tender, about 20 minutes. Stir in the remaining ingredients and simmer, uncovered, until the mixture thickens, about 30 minutes. Cool and refrigerate or serve at room temperature.

Yield: 6 to 7 cups

CUCUMBER, ONION, AND CAULIFLOWER PICKLES

9 large cucumbers, peeled and cut into ½-inch-thick slices
9 large onions, sliced
1 small head cauliflower, broken into florets
¼ cup salt
2 cups sugar
¼ cup flour
2 teaspoons turmeric
1 teaspoon celery seeds
1 teaspoon mustard seeds
2 cups cider vinegar

1. In a large, nonreactive saucepan, soak the cucumbers, onions, and cauliflower in water to cover with the ¼ cup salt for 8 to 24 hours.
2. In another large, nonreactive saucepan, whisk together the sugar, flour, turmeric, celery seeds, and mustard seeds. Slowly whisk in the vinegar. Simmer for 10 minutes.
3. Drain the vegetables, add to the vinegar mixture, and simmer gently for 5 minutes, stirring constantly.
4. Process in sterile jars, according to the manufacturer's instructions, for 15 minutes.

Yield: about 3½ quarts

BEET MARBLES

1. In a saucepan, cover the beets with cold water and bring to a boil. Cook until just tender, about 15 minutes. Let the beets stand in the water until they are cool enough to handle. Rub off the skins and cut off the root ends and tops.
2. In a large saucepan, combine the remaining ingredients and bring to a boil. Reduce heat and cook until slightly thickened, about 15 minutes.
3. Add the beets and simmer for 2 to 3 minutes. Cool and refrigerate. The beet marbles will keep for several weeks.

Yield: 3 cups

3 cups tiny, uniformly sized beets
½ cup sugar
¾ cup distilled white vinegar
¼ cup water
¼ teaspoon salt
⅛ teaspoon ground cloves
⅛ teaspoon black pepper

FIG CHUTNEY

1. In a large saucepan, bring the sugar and vinegar to a boil. Add the figs, raisins, ginger, salt, cayenne, pecans, garlic, lemon, and chili powder. Tie the cloves, allspice, cinnamon, and mace in a cheesecloth bag and add to the saucepan. Return to a boil.
2. Turn heat to low and gently cook the chutney, stirring occasionally, until very thick, 1¼ to 2 hours. Discard the spice bag.
3. Cool and refrigerate the chutney. Serve right away or allow the flavor to mellow overnight. The chutney can be refrigerated for 3 to 4 weeks in an airtight container.

Yield: 4 cups

Note: To soften dried figs, cover with boiling water and let stand for 20 minutes.

1 cup brown sugar
1 cup cider vinegar
2½ cups diced softened figs (see Note)
½ cup raisins
¼ cup crystallized ginger
1 scant teaspoon salt
Pinch of cayenne
¼ cup chopped pecans
1 clove garlic, minced
½ lemon, peeled, seeded, and minced
1 tablespoon chili powder
6 cloves
6 allspice berries, or *pinch of ground allspice*
1 cinnamon stick
6 blades mace, or *pinch of grated nutmeg*

RECIPE CREDITS

APPLE STACK CAKES *Polly Beste*

BABY ALASKAS *Susy Davidson*

BAKED FISH CHOWDER *Rebecca Reilly*

BANANA-CARAMEL SHERBET *Abigail Johnson*

BANANA SOUFFLÉ WITH BOURBON-BUTTERSCOTCH SAUCE *Sarah Belk Rian*

BASIC SPOON BREAD *Anne Byrn Phillips*

BASIL-GARLIC VINEGAR *Michael McLaughlin*

BAY SCALLOPS WITH LIME AND MINT *Sara Moulton*

BEET MARBLES *Laura Lewis Harwood*

BEST STRAWBERRY SHORTCAKE *Emily Crumpacker*

BLUEBERRY-ORANGE VINEGAR *Michael McLaughlin*

BLUE CHEESE TRIANGLES WITH TOASTED HAZELNUTS *Susy Davidson*

BRAISED MONKFISH WITH CURRIED FRUIT *Charles Pierce*

BRAISED SPRING KALE WITH OREGANO *Susan Herrmann Loomis*

BUTTERMILK BISCUITS *Anne Byrn Phillips*

BUTTERMILK PIE *Roberta Frechette*

CAJUN CABBAGE WITH SMOKED SAUSAGE *Paul Prudhomme of K-Paul's Louisiana Kitchen*

CALF'S LIVER WITH SEVEN ONIONS *Dale Shedd Whitesell and Susan Goloboy*

CANNELLONI WITH SUN-DRIED TOMATO SAUCE *Nancy Barr*

CANTALOUPE SHERBET *Nancy Arum*

CAPELLINI WITH SMOKED SALMON AND BLACK CAVIAR *Sara Moulton*

CHICKEN AND ARTICHOKES WITH FRESH MARJORAM *Marian Morash of The Straight Wharf*

CHICKEN AND SEAFOOD GUMBO *Carmen Jones*

CHICKEN AND SQUAB STEW *Lydie Marshall*

CHICKEN SALAD WITH BLUEBERRY-ORANGE VINAIGRETTE *Michael McLaughlin*

CHOCOLATE-MINT CREAM SQUARES *Anita Borghese*

CHOCTAW SHRIMP STEW *Barrie Kavasch*

CINNAMON ICE CREAM WITH CALVADOS *Michael Foley of Printer's Row*

COCONUT KISSES *Emily Crumpacker*

CORN CHOWDER *Rebecca Reilly*

COUNTRY VENISON SAUSAGES WITH SAUTÉED POTATOES AND VINEGAR *Lawrence Forgione of An American Place*

CRANBERRY-GRAPEFRUIT SHERBET MOLDS *Susy Davidson*

CREAM CHEESE SOUFFLÉ WITH RHUBARB SAUCE *Sara Moulton*

CRISP MACADAMIA WAFERS *Richard Sax*

CURRIED APPLE AND ONION SOUP *Marcel Desaulniers of The Trellis*

DOUBLE-BARBECUED RIBS *Phillip S. Schulz*

DUCK BREASTS WITH CIDER SAUCE *Russell Siu*

FEDELINI WITH DUCK, GRAPES, AND CRACKED PEPPERCORNS *Sara Moulton*

FETTUCCINE WITH SHELLFISH CUSTARD SAUCE *Adrienne Welch*

FIG CHUTNEY *Steven Raichlen*

FIG-PECAN TART *Sarah Belk Rian*

FRESH PEA SOUP WITH ORANGE *Sarah Belk Rian*

FRIED CATFISH WITH MUSTARD SAUCE *Charles Pierce*

FRIED ICE CREAM *Harriet Reilly*

FRIED MUSHROOM PASTA *Nancy Barr*

FRIED PUMPKIN OR SWEET POTATO CHIPS WITH CAYENNE AND CORIANDER *Norman Van Aken of Sinclair's*

FUDGE CAKE WITH MILK-CHOCOLATE FROSTING *Rose Levy Beranbaum*

GINGERED FLORENTINE TWINS *Anita Borghese*

GINGERED SHORTCAKE WITH HONEY-POACHED PEACHES *Emily Crumpacker*

GLAZED CARROTS WITH MACE AND BASIL *Julie Sahni*

GREEN CHILI WITH PORK *Michael McLaughlin of The Manhattan Chili Company*

GREEN-PEPPER CAPPELLETTI WITH RED-PEPPER SAUCE *Nancy Barr*

GREEN TOMATO–MINCEMEAT PIE *Roberta Frechette*

GRILLED BEEF KEBABS CARIBBEAN-STYLE *Phillip S. Schulz*

GRILLED SHRIMP WITH PASTA *Jonathan Waxman of Jam's*

GRITS 'N' HONEY PUDDING *Michael McLaughlin*

GUINEA HEN SAUTÉ WITH NEW ENGLAND FALL VEGETABLES *Lawrence Forgione of An American Place*

HAM AND THREE-CHEESE PASTA ROLL *Sarah Belk Rian*

HEARTY DUCK AND WILD RICE SOUP *Lawrence Forgione of An American Place*

IDAHO RIESLING AND RHUBARB ICE *Len Allison of Hubert's*

JERUSALEM ARTICHOKES   *Barrie Kavasch*

LAMB AND HAM SAUSAGE WITH PECANS   *Judy Rodgers*

LAMB AND WHITE-BEAN SALAD   *Nancy Barr*

LAMB CHILI WITH JALAPEÑO HOMINY   *Michael McLaughlin of The Manhattan Chili Company*

LAMB WITH TOMATO CHUTNEY AND MINT SAUCE   *Sara Moulton*

LEMON-DILL VINEGAR   *Michael McLaughlin*

MAPLE-AND-COB-SMOKED HAM   *Phillip S. Schulz*

MARGARITA MOUSSE WITH STRAWBERRIES   *Carol E. Smaglinski*

MESCLUN SALAD   *Alice Waters of Chez Panisse*

MUSSELS IN RED PEPPER MAYONNAISE   *Sara Moulton*

NEW ENGLAND CLAM CHOWDER   *Rebecca Reilly*

ORANGE AND LEMON RELISH   *Emily Crumpacker*

OYSTER AND SPINACH SOUP   *Lydia Shire of Seasons*

OZARK PUDDING   *Roberta Frechette*

PAN-ROASTED QUAIL WITH THYME AND GREEN GRAPES   *Norman Van Aken of Sinclair's*

PASTA WITH PEAS AND STRING BEANS   *Sarah Belk Rian*

PEPPER BEEF   *Sara Moulton*

PINEAPPLE-MINT ICE   *Charles Pierce*

PINTO BEAN AND PARSLEY SALAD   *Marian Morash of The Straight Wharf*

PIQUANT PRODIGAL LAMB   *Phillip S. Schulz*

PLUM AND ZINFANDEL ICE   *Michael McLaughlin*

POACHED SALMON WITH CUCUMBER SAUCE   *Sara Moulton*

POPPY-SEED CAKE WITH BROWN-SUGAR MERINGUE   *Emily Crumpacker*

PORK STEW IN CIDER   *Lydie Marshall*

PUMPKIN CRÈME BRÛLÉE   *Michael McLaughlin*

RADISH REMOULADE   *Sara Moulton*

RASPBERRY-PEACH COBBLER   *Michael James*

RICH MACAROON SQUARES   *Richard Sax*

ROASTED PUMPKIN-GARLIC SOUP   *Judy Rodgers*

ROAST GOOSE STUFFED WITH WILD RICE AND CRANBERRIES   *Barrie Kavasch*

ROQUEFORT APPETIZER CHEESECAKE   *Mimi Gormezano*

SALMON AND AMERICAN CAVIAR CHECKERBOARD   *Susy Davidson*

SALMON AND PASTA SALAD WITH LEMON-DILL VINAIGRETTE   *Michael McLaughlin*

SAN FRANCISCO–STYLE SOURDOUGH BREAD   *Sara Pitzer*

SAUTÉED SOFT-SHELL CRABS WITH GINGER-LIME BUTTER   *Len Allison of Hubert's*

SAUTÉ OF JULIENNED TOMATOES WITH CREAM AND HERBS   *Elizabeth Wheeler*

SCALLOPED OYSTERS   *Nellie Altvater*

SHRIMP AND FENNEL TRIANGLES   *Nancy Barr*

SMOKED AND SIZZLED CORNISH GAME HENS   *Phillip S. Schulz*

SMOKED OYSTER CANAPÉS WITH CHERRY TOMATOES   *Susy Davidson*

SPAGHETTI WITH PARSLEY SAUCE   *Carol Cutler*

SPICY HAM AND PHYLLO TRIANGLES   *Sarah Belk Rian*

SPOON BREAD WITH CORN   *Anne Byrn Phillips*

STEAK AND CAVIAR TARTARE WITH VODKA   *Sara Moulton*

STEAMED BROWNIE PUDDING   *Michael McLaughlin*

STEAMED PARSLEY SERVED WARM OR COLD   *Carol Cutler*

STUFFED SNOW PEAS   *Sarah Belk Rian*

SUMMER SAUSAGE WITH LAVENDER   *Judy Rodgers*

SWEET AND SOUR RED CABBAGE SOUP   *Sara Moulton*

SWEET POTATO–PECAN BISCUITS   *Anne Byrn Phillips*

SWORDFISH TONNATO WITH LEMON-THYME MAYONNAISE   *Marian Morash of The Straight Wharf*

TOFFEE BITTERSWEET CRUNCH   *Rose Levy Beranbaum*

TURKEY CONFIT   *Sara Moulton*

TWO-CHICKEN BALSAMICO   *Nancy Barr*

VEAL CHOPS WITH CAVIAR BUTTER   *Sara Moulton*

VEAL WITH SHIITAKE MUSHROOM SAUCE   *Renie Steves and Louise Lamensdorf*

VENISON STEW   *Lydie Marshall*

WARM MOREL SALAD ON STEAMED SPRING LETTUCE   *Susan Herrmann Loomis*

WARM POTATO SALAD WITH SUGAR SNAP PEAS AND BACON DRESSING   *Sarah Belk Rian*

WHEAT-KERNEL ROUND LOAF   *Carmen Jones*

WHOLE-WHEAT BREAD PUDDING WITH BLUEBERRY-MAPLE SAUCE   *Michael McLaughlin*

WILD MUSHROOMS ON FRIED GRITS   *Len Allison of Hubert's*

WINTER GRATIN   *Lawrence Forgione of An American Place*

YOUNG PHEASANTS MANDAMIN   *Lawrence Forgione of An American Place*

INDEX

Page numbers in italic denote illustrations.

acorn squash, baked (as for sweet dumpling squash), 173
almond(s)
  in macaroon squares, 240
  in praline, for "baby Alaska," 256–257
  toasting, 246
  in toffee bittersweet crunch, 246
American caviar
  and mascarpone filling for snow peas, 18
  and (smoked) salmon canapés, 23, *23*
anchovy/ies
  in lemon-thyme mayonnaise, with swordfish, 114
  -tomato sauce, for artichokes, 32–33
andouille smoked sausage, with cabbage, Cajun style, 33
appetizers, 24–33
  development of, 24–26
apple(s)
  -blackberry cobbler, 231
  brown betty, 225
  with cabbage and sausage, Cajun style, 33
  with guinea hen, sautéed, 99–100
  and onion soup, curried, 45
  in Ozark pudding, 222
  in pork stew, with cider, 72–73
  stack cakes, 213
apple brandy
  with cinnamon ice cream, 257
  with duck in cider sauce, 95
  in green tomato-mincemeat pie, 206
apple brown betty, 225
apricot(s)
  curried, with monkfish, 112
  in divinity (candy), 245
  glaze: for fruitcake, 214–15; for ham, 123
artichoke(s)
  with chicken and fresh marjoram, 90–91
  fried, with tomato-anchovy sauce, 32–33
  trimming, *32*
asparagus, 169
  with lemon beurre rouge, 169
  preparation of, for cooking, *169*
  and red pepper, with orange zest, 137
avocado(s) with scallops marinated in lime and mint, 29

baby Alaska, 256–57
bacon dressing, with potato salad (warm), 140
baked fish chowder, 50
baked sweet dumpling squash, 173
baking powder, 179
banana(s)
  -caramel sherbet, 263
  chips, 263
  soufflé, with bourbon-butterscotch sauce, 228
barbecued ribs, 122
barbecuing, 117–20
  equipment for, 119, *119*
  fire for, 120
  fuel for, 120
barbecue sauces, 118
  for Cornish game hens, 129
  for ribs, 122
basil, 174
  with carrots, glazed, 174
  -garlic vinegar, 274
  -tomato mayonnaise, homemade (for clams), 30–31
bay scallops
  broiled with beef, 65
  with lime and mint, 28–29
  regional varieties of, 105
  in shellfish custard sauce, with pasta, 156
bean(s), green: with peas and pasta, 154
bean(s), pinto: and parsley salad, 140
bean(s), white (dry): and lamb salad, 138
Béchamel, 154
beef, 64–69
  cuts of, 61, *61*
beef, brisket (herbed), 66
beef, chuck: in chili, 53
beef, prime rib: broiled with scallops
beef, sirloin
  with bell peppers, 64
  and caviar tartare, with vodka, 27
  for kebabs, grilled Caribbean-style, 126
beef, steak
  and caviar tartare, with vodka, 27
  porterhouse, grilled over herbs and garlic, 127
beer mustard, 276
beet marbles (pickled), 277
berries, *see* blackberry; blueberry/ies; cranberry; raspberry; strawberry/ies
best strawberry shortcake, 216
beurre rouge, lemon (with asparagus), 169

biscuits, 187
  buttermilk, 188
  guidelines for making, 187
  reheating method, 187
  shortcake, 216; gingered, 217
  sweet potato-pecan, 188
  see also cobbler: dough for
blackberry-apple cobbler, 231
black walnut(s)
  and maple fudge, 246–47
  toasting, 247
blueberry/ies
  in chicken salad, 143
  -maple sauce, for bread pudding, 222–23
  -orange vinaigrette, 143
  -orange vinegar, 272
blue cheese
  American tradition of, 22
  canapés, with hazelnuts, 22
bobwhite (quail)
  pan-roasted, with thyme and green grapes, 91
  stock, 91
Boston cream doughnuts, 196–97
bourbon
  -butterscotch sauce, for banana soufflé, 228
  in fruitcake, 214–15
  pastry cream, for fig-pecan tart, 208–9
Brady, "Diamond" Jim, 17
braised monkfish, with curried fruit, 112
braised spring kale with oregano, 171
braising meat, 62–63
brandy, apple
  with cinnamon ice cream, 257
  with duck in cider sauce, 95
  in green tomato-mincemeat pie, 206
bread pudding (whole-wheat), with blueberry-maple sauce, 222–23
breads, 175–77
  baking powder and baking soda type, 179
  biscuits, 187–88
  doughnuts, 194–98
  egg-white type, 179–80
  muffins, 189–90
  "short rise method" for, 182
  spoon bread, 191–93
breads, yeast-type, 177–78
  doughnuts, 194–97
  oatmeal, 181
  sourdough, San Francisco-style, 184–85; starters for, 186
  wheat-kernel round loaf, 182–83, *183*

Brillat-Savarin, Anthelme, 84
brisket of beef, herbed, 66
broiled beef and scallop ribbon, 65
broiled lemon sole, 109
brown beer mustard, 276
brown betty, apple, 225
brownie pudding, steamed, 226–27
Brussels sprouts, timbales of, 172
Burgundy cherry sauce, for turkey,
    131
butter, flavored
    caviar, for veal chops, 69
    ginger-lime, for soft-shell crab, 110
    horseradish-parsley, for trout, 129
    lemon beurre rouge, 169
buttermilk
    biscuits, 188
    pie, 207
    pralines, 242
butternut squash, with guinea hen,
    sautéed, 99–100
butterscotch-bourbon sauce, for
    banana soufflé, 228

cabbage
    Cajun style, with smoked sausage,
        33
    shredding, *139*
    in slaw, creamy, 139
cabbage, red
    in slaw, creamy, 139
    soup, sweet and sour, 45
Cajun cabbage with smoked sausage,
    33
cakes, 210–15
    apple stack, 213
    in "baby Alaska," 256–57
    flour for, 200
    freezing, 204
    fruitcake, dark, 214–15
    fudge, with milk chocolate
        frosting, 210–11
    how to make and bake, 201–2
    Mississippi mud (with coffee and
        chocolate flavoring), 211
    poppy-seed, with brown-sugar
        meringue, 212
    shortening for, 200–1
calf's liver, with onions, 77
Calvados, with cinnamon ice cream,
    257
candies
    divinity, 245
    gumdrops, clove, 243
    maple-walnut fudge, 246–47
    pralines, buttermilk, 243
    saltwater taffy, vanilla or cinnamon,
        244
    sugar syrup for, 233–34
    toffee bittersweet crunch, 246
cannelloni (filled with spinach), with
    sun-dried tomato sauce, 154–55
cantaloupe sherbet, 259
capellini, 158
    with smoked salmon and black
        caviar, 158

caper(s)
    in lemon-thyme mayonnaise, with
        swordfish, 114
    with steak and caviar tartare, 27
cappelletti (green-pepper flavored),
    with red pepper sauce, 162
caramel-banana sherbet, 263
carrots, glazed (with mace and basil),
    174
catfish, 106
    fried, with mustard sauce, 109
catsup, 265–66
    basic recipe, 272
    guidelines for making, 266–67
cauliflower pickles (with cucumber
    and onion), 276
caviar, American
    and mascarpone filling for snow
        peas, 18
    and smoked salmon canapés, 23, *23*
caviar, black
    butter, with veal chops, 69
    with capellini and smoked salmon,
        158
    with steak tartare and vodka, 27
cayenne, with pumpkin or sweet
    potato chips, 16
canapés, 13, 22
    blue cheese triangles with
        hazelnuts, 22
    salmon and caviar, 23
    smoked oysters with cherry
        tomatoes, 22
celery
    dicing, *141*
    in pinto bean and parsley salad, 140
checkerboard of salmon and
    American caviar, 23
cheese, *see* blue cheese; cream cheese;
    Gorgonzola; mozzarella cheese;
    ricotta cheese; Roquefort
    cheesecake
cheesecake, Roquefort (as appetizer),
    29
cherry/ies, candied: in divinity
    (candy), 245
cherry-Burgundy sauce, for turkey,
    131
cherry tomato(es)
    and chutney stuffing, for lamb, 71
    and smoked oyster canapés, 22
chestnut(s)
    fresh, simmering of, 100
    with guinea hen and vegetables,
        99–100
chicken, 84–85
    with artichokes and fresh
        marjoram, 90–91
    categories of, 85
    fried, with cornmeal cakes and
        cream sauce, 88–89
    salad: balsamico (warm), 144; with
        blueberry-orange vinaigrette, 143
    and seafood gumbo, 51
    and squab: stew, 92–93; stock, 93
chicken liver(s), in chicken salad

(warm), 144
chicken stock, 35–36
    recipe, 41; with squab, 92–93
chile pepper(s)
    in green chili with pork, 55
    in pinto bean and parsley salad, 140
chili, 38–40, 53
    green, with pork, 55
    guidelines for making, 39–40
    lamb, with jalapeño hominy, 54
    Texas style, 53
chili powder
    in chili, 53–55
    commercial *vs.* homemade, 39–40
chili sauce, 273
    for dressing for seafood Louis, 142
Chimichurri sauce, 127
chips, fried
    potato, development of, 16
    pumpkin or sweet potato, 16
chive-lemon butter, for shad roe, 113
chocolate
    in brownie pudding, steamed, 226–
        227
    cakes: fudge, 210–11; Mississippi
        mud (with coffee), 211
    in cookies; gingered florentines,
        237; macaroon squares, 240;
        -mint cream squares, 238–39
    frosting, 210–11
    glaze, for cream-filled doughnuts,
        196–97
    sauce, basic, 253
    in toffee bittersweet crunch
        (candy), 246
Choctaw shrimp stew, 111
chopping vegetables, technique for,
    275
    celery, *141*
chorizo tortas, 121
chowders, 37–38, 48
    clam, New England style, 48
    corn, 49
    fish, 50
chutney, 269
    fig, 277
    -tomato stuffing, for leg of lamb,
        70–71
cider
    with guinea hen and vegetables,
        99–100
    pork stewed in, 72–73
    sauce, for duck, 94–95
cider, boiled (*or* cider jelly), 206
    in green tomato-mincemeat pie,
        206
cinnamon
    ice cream, with Calvados, 257
    saltwater taffy, 244
clam(s)
    chowder, New England style, 48
    fried, with tomato-basil
        mayonnaise, 30–31
    regional varieties of, 105
    removing from shell, *30–31*
clove gumdrops, 243

cobbler
  apple-blackberry, 231
  dough for, 230–31, *231*
  papaya, 231
  raspberry-peach, 230–31
coconut kisses (candies), 241
cocktail foods, 11–23
  as first course, 25
  guidelines for making, 13–15
  how much to prepare, 14–15
  tradition of, 11–13
  variety of, 14
coffee: in Mississippi mud cake, 211
cole slaw, 139
condiments, 265–70
  catsup, 265–66, 272
  chutney, 269, 277
  mustard, 266, 267–68, 276
  pickles, 266–67, 276, 277
  relishes, 268, 276
confit, turkey, 94
cookies
  chocolate-mint cream squares, 238–239, *239*
  coconut kisses, 241
  gingered florentines, 237
  macadamia wafers, 242–43
  macaroon squares, 240
  pie-pastry, 254–55
  soft, molasses or honey, 239
  sweeteners for, 234–36
coriander, with pumpkin or sweet potato chips, 16
corn
  chowder, 49
  cutting and scraping from cob, *49*
  dressing, for pheasant, 98–99
  in shrimp stew, Choctaw style, 111
corn bread, 190
  in dressing for pheasant, 98–99
Cornish game hen(s)
  with corn dressing (as for pheasant), 98–99
  smoked and sizzled, 129
  stuffed with leeks, 89
cornmeal
  cakes, with fried chicken, 88
  in spoon bread, 193
  stone-ground *vs.* water-ground, 190
country venison sausages, with sautéed potatoes and vinegar, 81
crab
  grilled on seaweed, with ginger sauce, 122–23
  in gumbo, chicken and seafood, 51
  regional varieties of, 105–6, 108
  in seafood Louis, 142
crab, soft-shell, 106, 110
  sautéed, with ginger-lime butter, 110
cranberry
  lattice pie, 206–7
  -pear sherbet, 260
  sauce, 261
  and wild rice stuffing, for roast goose, 96

cranberry-grapefruit sherbet molds, 260–61
crayfish, regional varieties of, 106, 107, 108
cream cheese
  fillings: for pasta roll, with ham and other cheeses, 160–61; for snow peas, with caviar or Gorgonzola (as for mascarpone), 18
  in Roquefort appetizer cheesecake, 29
  in salmon and American caviar checkerboard, 23
  soufflé, with rhubarb sauce, 229
cream sauce, 88–89
creamy three-cabbage slaw, 139
crème brûlée, 224
  pumpkin-flavored, 224
crème fraîche
  in fillings for snow peas, 18
  homemade, 18
  in radish remoulade, 27
crisp macadamia wafers, 242
croutons, pepper, 44
cucumber(s)
  pickles (with onion and cauliflower), 276
  sauce: cold, for lamb (grilled), 125; for poached (smoked) salmon, 115
cumin
  in chili, 53–54
  how to toast, 54
curry dishes
  apple and onion soup, 45
  fruit with monkfish, 112
custard sauce, 226
cutting vegetables, technique for, *275*
  celery, *141*

dark fruitcake, 214–15
desserts, 199–264
  see also cakes; cobbler; cookies; mousse; piecrust; pies; puddings; shortcakes; soufflés
dill
  -lemon vinaigrette, 157
  -lemon vinegar, 272
  with salmon: and caviar canapés, 23; filling for snow peas, 18; and pasta salad, 157
divinity (candy), 245
double-barbecued ribs, 122
doughnuts, 194
  Boston cream (with chocolate glaze), 196–97
  guidelines for making, 194, *195*
  molasses-spice cake, 198
  spudnuts, 195
dressings
  bacon, for potato salad (warm), 140
  for parsley, steamed, 170
  for seafood Louis, 142
  for slaw, 139
  vinaigrette, 136; blueberry-orange

flavored, for chicken salad, 143; herbed, for chicken salad (warm), 144
duck, 86
  breasts of, with cider sauce, 94–95
  with fedelini, grapes, and cracked peppercorns, 158–59
  stock, 158–59
  and wild rice soup, 42–43

egg pasta, homemade, 152, *152*, 153

Farmer, Fannie: *Boston Cooking School Cook Book*, 34, 72, 132
fedelini, 153
  with duck, grapes, and cracked peppercorns, 158–59
  with shrimp, grilled, 153
fennel
  and shrimp pasta triangles, 151
  with summer sausage, 82–83
fettuccine with shellfish custard sauce, 156
fig(s)
  chutney, 277
  -pecan tart, 208–9
  softening, 277
filé powder, 51, 52, 111
finger foods, 14
  see also cocktail foods
first courses, 24–33
  development of, 24–26
fish, 101–8
  broiled, 109
  categories of, 102–3; substituting, rule of thumb for, 103
  chowder, baked, 50
  fillets of, in flat fish and round fish, *103*
  fresh and frozen, 104
  nutritional aspects of, 102
  regional varieties of, 104–8
  see also anchovy/ies; catfish; monkfish; salmon; salmon, smoked; shellfish; sole; swordfish; tuna
fish stock, 113
florentines, gingered, 237
flour
  for bread, 176–77
  for cakes, 200
  for piecrust, 200
fresh pea soup with orange, 43
fresh tomato sauce, 192
fried baby artichokes, with tomato-anchovy sauce, 32–33
fried catfish, with mustard sauce, 109
fried chicken with cornmeal cakes and cream sauce, 88–89
fried ice cream, 253
fried Ipswich clams, with tomato-basil mayonnaise, 30–31
fried mushroom pasta, 20
fried pumpkin or sweet potato chips, with cayenne and coriander, 16
fritters, oyster, 17

frosting for cake
　how to apply, *210*
　milk chocolate, 210–11
fructose (*or* levulose), 235–36
fruit
　curried, with monkfish, 112
　see also apple(s); apricots(s);
　　banana(s); blackberry;
　　blueberry/ies; cantaloupe; cherry;
　　cranberry; fig(s); grape(s);
　　grapefruit; orange(s); papaya;
　　peach(es); pear(s); pineapple;
　　plum; prune(s); raspberry;
　　rhubarb; strawberry/ies
fruitcake
　dark, with apricot glaze, 214–15
　guidelines for making, 214
fudge, maple-walnut, 246–47
fudge cake, with milk chocolate
　frosting, 210–11

game birds, 86–87
　see also game hens, Cornish; guinea
　　hen(s); pheasant; quail
game hens, Cornish
　with corn dressing (as for
　　pheasant), 98–99
　smoked and sizzled, 129
　stuffed with leeks, 89
garlic
　-basil vinegar, 274
　chopping technique for, *275*
　with ham in phyllo triangles, 20–
　　21
　with kale, braised, 171
　peeling, *171*
　with porterhouse steak, grilled, 127
　with potatoes (whipped) and herbs,
　　174
　-pumpkin soup, 44
ginger
　in cookies, 239
　with Cornish game hens, smoked
　　and sizzled, 129
　florentines, 237
　with ham in phyllo triangles, 20–
　　21
　-lime butter, with soft-shell crab,
　　110
　sauce, with crab (grilled), 123
　shortcake, with honey-poached
　　peaches, 217
gingerbread-pumpkin muffins, 190
glazed carrots with mace and basil,
　174
glazes
　apricot: for fruitcake, 214–15; for
　　ham, 123
　for doughnuts, 195; chocolate, 196–
　　197
gluten, 176, 177
goose, 86–87
　carving, *97*
　roasted, stuffed with wild rice and
　　cranberries, 96–97
　trussing, *96*

Gorgonzola and mascarpone filling,
　for snow peas, 18
grape(s), green
　with fedelini, duck, and cracked
　　peppercorns, 158–59
　with quail, 93
grapefruit
　shells, for sherbet, 261, *261*
　-vermouth sherbet, 260
gratin of potatoes, 170–71
great-grandmother's pastry, 205
green chili with pork, 55
green pepper cappelletti with red
　pepper sauce, 162
green tomato-mincemeat pie, 206
grilled beef kebabs, Caribbean-style,
　126
grilled shrimp with pasta, 153
grilled tuna steak, with mozzarella-
　sage stuffing, 116
grilling, 117–20
grills, 119, *119*
grits
　fried, with mushrooms (wild), 28
　'n' honey pudding, 223
guinea hen(s), sautéed, with New
　England fall vegetables, 99–100
gumbo
　chicken and seafood, 51
　rabbit and oyster, 52
gumdrops, clove, 243

ham
　in gumbo, chicken and seafood, 51
　and lamb sausages, with pecans, 80
　maple-and-cob-smoked, 123
　in phyllo triangles, 20–21, *21*
　and three-cheese pasta roll, 160–61
　see also prosciutto
hazelnut(s)
　and blue cheese canapés, 22
　in gingered florentines, 237
　in macaroon squares (cookies), 240
hearty duck and wild rice soup, 42–
　43
Heinz, H. J., 266, 268
herbed brisket, 66
herbs, 167
　chopping leaves of, *168*
　with porterhouse steak, grilled, 127
　with potatoes, whipped, 174
　and rice muffins, 189
　with sauté of julienned tomatoes
　　and cream, 168
　see also specific herbs
Home Cook Book, The, 143, 265
hominy, jalapeño-flavored, with lamb
　chili, 54
hominy grits and honey pudding, 223
honey
　cookies, soft, 239
　'n' grits pudding, 223
　-poached peaches, with gingered
　　shortbread, 217
　as sweetener for cookies, 234–35
hors d'oeuvre, 13

　see also appetizers; cocktail foods
horseradish
　in brown beer mustard, 276
　-parsley butter, for trout, 128
　with steak and caviar tartare, 27
hot sauces, 270
　chili sauce, 273
　tomatillo salsa, 274

ice cream, 248–52
　basic vanilla, 258
　cinnamon, with Calvados, 257
　custard mixture for, 252
　freezing, 249
　fried, 253
　machines for making, 250, *250*, 251
　pecan-pie, with pie-pastry cookies,
　　254–55
　"still-freezing," 249–50
　strawberry, in "baby Alaska," 256–
　　257
　see also ices; sherbets
ices, 248–51, 259
　differentiated from sherbet and ice
　　cream, 259
　Idaho Riesling and rhubarb, 262
　pineapple-mint, 262–63
　plum and Zinfandel, 264
icing for cake
　how to apply, *210*
　milk chocolate, 210–11
Idaho Riesling and rhubarb ice, 262
Ipswich clams (razor clams), fried,
　with tomato-basil mayonnaise,
　30–31

jalapeño pepper(s)
　in Chimichurri sauce, 127
　in hominy, with lamb chili, 54
　in salsa, tomatillo, 274
Jerusalem artichoke(s), 173
　with dill, chives, and garlic, 173
　in shrimp stew, 111

kebabs (beef), grilled Caribbean-
　style, 126
ketchup, 265–66
　basic recipe, 272
　guidelines for making, 266–67
kielbasa with cabbage, Cajun style, 33
Kiradjieff, Anthanas, 55

lamb, 70
　categories of, 70
　chili, with jalapeño hominy, 54
　cuts of, 61, *61*
　grilled, with cucumber and/or mint
　　sauce, 124
　and ham sausages, with pecans, 80
　leg of, boned: rolling, with
　　stuffing, *71*
　stew (as for chicken or squab), 92–
　　93
　with tomato chutney and mint
　　sauce, 70–71
　and white bean salad, 138

lavender, with summer sausage, 82–83
leek(s)
 with calf's liver, 77
 in curried apple and onion soup, 45
 stuffing, for Cornish game hens, 89
lemon
 beurre rouge, with asparagus, 169
 -dill vinaigrette, for salmon and pasta salad, 157
 -dill vinegar, 272
 and orange relish, 276
 -thyme mayonnaise, for swordfish, 114
lemon sole, broiled, 109
lime
 -ginger butter, for soft-shell crab, 110
 marinade for scallops, 28–29
 (zest), for margarita soufflé, 232
liver, 76
 nutritional value of, 76
liver, calf's
 cooked *en papillote*, 77, 77
 with onions, 77
liver, chicken: in chicken salad (warm), 144
liver, pheasant's: with roast pheasant, 98
lobster
 regional varieties of, 105, 106
 in seafood Louis, 142

macadamia nut(s)
 toasting, 243
 wafers of, 242–43
macaroon squares (cookies), 240
maee, with glazed carrots and basil, 174
mandamin style pheasants (with corn dressing), 98–99
maple-and-cob-smoked ham, 123
maple syrup
 -blueberry sauce, for bread pudding, 222–23
 in fudge, with black walnuts, 246–247
 with goose, roasted, 97
 with squash, baked, 173
 as sweetener for cookies, 235
maple-walnut fudge, 246–47
margarita mousse, with strawberries, 232
marinades and marinating, 28, 59
 for beef, 64
 for Cornish game hens, 129
 for lamb: grilled, 124; and white bean salad, 138
 for quail, 91
 for scallops, 28–29
marjoram (fresh), with chicken and artichokes, 90–91
mascarpone, in fillings for snow peas, 18
mayonnaise, homemade

lemon-thyme, for swordfish, 114
 with red peppers, for mussels, 19
 tomato-basil, for clams, 30–31
meat, 56–63
 American tradition of, 56–57
 cooking techniques for, 59–63; poaching or simmering, 63; roasting, 61–62; sautéing and pan-frying, 62; stewing and braising, 62–63
 cuts of, 58, 61, *61*
 fat in, 58
 selecting, 57–59
 tenderizing, 59
 tenderness of, 58
 see also beef; ham; lamb; pork; rabbit; veal; venison
Melancom, Bobby, 17
meringue
 in "baby Alaska," 256–57
 brown-sugar, for poppy-seed cake, 212
mesclun salad (mixed greens), 136
milk-chocolate frosting, 210–11
mincemeat-green tomato pie, 206
mint
 -chocolate cream squares (cookies), 238–39
 with lamb and white bean salad, 138
 -pineapple ice, 262–63
 sauce, for lamb, 70, 125
 with scallops in lime marinade, 28–29
Mississippi mud cake, 211
molasses
 cookies (soft), 239
 -spice cake doughnuts, 198
 as sweetener for cookies, 235
monkfish
 bones, for stock, 113
 braised, with curried fruit, 112
 trimming membrane from, *112*
morel salad (warm), on steamed spring lettuce, 136–37
mortadella and spinach, in cannelloni, 155
mousse, 232
 margarita, with strawberries, 232
mozzarella cheese
 with mushrooms in pasta cases, fried, 20
 -sage stuffing, for tuna steaks, 116
muffins, 189
 guidelines for making, 189
 herbed rice, 189
 pumpkin-gingerbread, 190
mushroom(s)
 with chicken and artichokes, 90–91
 in pasta cases, fried, 20
mushroom(s), wild
 in corn dressing for pheasant, 98
 in duck and wild rice soup, 42–43
 on grits (fried), 28
 morel salad (warm) on steamed spring lettuce, 136–37

shiitake sauce, for veal, 68
mussel(s)
 American tradition of, 18–19
 in red pepper mayonnaise, 19
 removing from shell, *19*
mustard, 266, 267
 beer-flavored, 276
 guidelines for making, 267–68
 in remoulade of radishes, 27
 sauce: for catfish, 109; for turkey, 130; for venison sausages, 81

New England clam chowder, 48
noodles, *see* cannelloni; capellini; cappelletti; fedelini; fettuccine; pasta; spaghetti
nuts, *see* almond(s); black walnut(s); chestnut(s); hazelnut(s); macadamia nut(s); pecan(s); pine nut(s); pistachio nut(s); walnut(s)

oatmeal bread, 181
O'Connor, Hyla: *Early American Cooking*, 72
okra, in chicken and seafood gumbo, 51
onion(s)
 and apple soup, curried, 45
 with calf's liver, 77
 chopping technique for, *275*
 pickles (with cucumber and cauliflower), 276
orange(s)
 for beef kebabs, Caribbean-style, 126
 -blueberry vinaigrette, 143
 -blueberry vinegar, 272
 and lemon relish, 276
 and pea soup, 43
 zest: with asparagus and red pepper, 137; in chicken salad, 143
oregano, with kale (braised), 171
ovens, 199
oyster(s)
 American tradition of, 17
 fritters, 17
 and rabbit gumbo, 52
 regional varieties of, 105, 106, 108
 removing from shell, *46–47*
 scalloped, 110–11
 smoked, with cherry tomatoes, canapés of, 22
 and spinach soup, 46–47
Ozark pudding, 222

pan-roasted quail, with thyme and green grapes, 91
papaya cobbler, 231
parsley, 170
 -horseradish butter, for trout, 128
 and pinto bean salad, 140
 sauce, for spaghetti, 27
 steamed, served warm or cold, with dressings, 170
partridge, 87
pasta, filled, 151

cannelloni (filled with spinach), with tomato sauce, 154–55
green pepper cappelletti, with red pepper sauce, 162
ham and three-cheese pasta roll, 160–61, *161*
how to fill and close, 151, *162*
mushrooms in, fried, 20
shrimp and fennel triangles, 151
pasta, fresh (homemade), 145–50
cooking, 150
cutting, 149, *149*
dough-making for, 146–47; egg pasta, 152, *152*, 153; in food processor, 147
freezing dough, 149
machine for, 147, *148–49*, 149
rolling dough, 147, *148*, 149, *149*
spinach-flavored, 153
pasta dishes
with duck, grapes, and cracked peppercorns, 158–59
with peas and string beans, 154
salad, with salmon and lemon-dill vinaigrette, 157
with shellfish custard sauce, 156
with shrimp, 153
with smoked salmon and black caviar, 158
with tomato sauce, 154–55
see also pasta, filled
pastry, *see* cobbler: dough for; phyllo pastry; piecrust
pastry bag, piping cookie dough from, *241*
pea(s)
and orange soup, 43
with pasta: and smoked salmon and black caviar, 158; and string beans, 154
see also snow pea(s); sugar snap pea(s)
peach(es)
honey-poached, with gingered shortcake, 217
-raspberry cobbler, 230–31
pear(s)
caramelized, 75
-cranberry sherbet, 260
pecan(s)
in brownie pudding, steamed, 226–227
in buttermilk pralines, 242
-fig tart, 208–9
in fried ice cream balls, 253
in lamb and ham sausages, 80
-pie ice cream and pie-pastry cookies, 254–55
-sweet potato biscuits, 188
toasting, 242
pepper(s), hot
with beef kebabs, Caribbean-style, 126
with chorizo tortas, 121
with Cornish game hens, smoked and sizzled, 129

with ribs, double-barbecued, 122
see also chile pepper(s); jalapeño pepper(s)
pepper(s), sweet
with asparagus and orange zest, 137
with beef, 64
with cappelletti, 162
with ham, in phyllo triangles, 20–21
in mayonnaise (homemade), for mussels, 19
peppercorn(s), cracked: with fedelini, duck, and grapes, 158–59
pepper croutons, 44
pheasant, 87
mandamin style, with corn dressing, 98–99
sautéed, with New England fall vegetables (as for guinea hen), 99–100
phyllo pastry: spicy ham in, 20–21, *21*
pickles, 266–67
beet, 277
cucumber, onion, and cauliflower, 276
piecrust
flour for, 200
freezing, 204
"great-grandmother's" recipe, 205
how to make, *202, 203*
prebaking, 203
standard recipe, 205
pie-pastry cookies, 254–55
pies, 205–9
buttermilk, 207
cranberry lattice, 206–7
fig pecan tart, 208–9
green tomato-mincemeat, 206
see also piecrust
pineapple-mint ice, 262–63
pine nut(s), with chicken salad (warm), 144
pinto bean and parsley salad, 140
piquant prodigal lamb, 124
pistachio nut(s), in divinity (candy), 245
plum and Zinfandel ice, 264
poached salmon, with cucumber sauce, 115
poaching meat, 63
poppy-seed cake, with brown-sugar meringue, 212
pork
cuts of, 61, *61*
with green chili, 55
ribs, barbecued, 122
stew, in cider, 72–73
see also bacon; prosciutto; salt pork; sausage
porterhouse steak grilled over herbs and garlic, 127
potato(es)
chips: development of, 16
in chowders, 48, 49, 50
garlic-herb whipped, 174

salad (warm), with sugar snap peas and bacon dressing, 140
sautéed, with venison sausages, 81
and sweet potatoes, gratin of, 170–171
poultry, 84–86
frozen, 87
see also chicken; Cornish game hen(s); duck; game birds; goose; squab; turkey
praline(s)
in "baby Alaska," 256–57
buttermilk, 242
prosciutto with mushrooms, in pasta cases (fried), 20
prune(s), curried (with monkfish), 112
puddings, 218, 219
brownie (chocolate-nut), steamed, 226–27
grits 'n' honey, 223
guidelines for making, 219
molds for, 227, *227*
Ozark (with apples and walnuts), 222
whole-wheat bread, with blueberry-maple sauce, 222–23
pumpkin
chips (fried), with cayenne and coriander, 16
crème brûlée, 224
-garlic soup, 44
-gingerbread muffins, 190

quail, 87
pan-roasted, with thyme and green grapes, 91
stock, 91
quick breads, 179
biscuits, 187; buttermilk, 188; sweet potato-pecan, 188
doughnuts, molasses-spice cake flavor, 198
muffins, 189; herbed rice, 189; pumpkin-gingerbread, 190

rabbit and oyster gumbo, 52
radish remoulade, 27
raspberry-peach cobbler, 230–31
razor clams, fried, with tomato-basil mayonnaise, 30–31
red cabbage
in slaw, creamy, 139
soup, sweet and sour, 45
red pepper(s), hot, *see* pepper(s), hot
red pepper(s), sweet
with asparagus and orange zest, 137
with ham, in phyllo triangles, 20–21
in mayonnaise (homemade), for mussels, 19
sauce, for green peper cappelletti, 162
relishes, 268
orange and lemon, 276
remoulade, radish, 27

rhubarb
  and Idaho Riesling ice, 262
  sauce, for cream cheese soufflé, 229
ribs, double-barbecued, 122
rice, wild
  and cranberry stuffing, for roast
    goose, 96
  and duck soup, 42–43
rice and herb muffins, 189
rich macaroon squares, 240
ricotta cheese
  with mushrooms, in pasta cases
    (fried), 20
  in pasta roll, with ham and other
    cheeses, 160–61
  with spinach, in cannelloni, 154–55
roasted pumpkin-garlic soup, 44
roast goose stuffed with wild rice and
  cranberries, 96–97
roasting meat, 61–62
rock Cornish game hens
  with corn dressing (as for
    pheasant), 98–99
  smoked and sizzled, 129
  stuffed with leeks, 89
Roquefort cheesecake, as appetizer, 29

sage-mozzarella stuffing, for tuna
  steaks, 116
salad dressings
  bacon, for potato salad (warm), 140
  for seafood Louis, 142
  for slaw, 139
  vinaigrette, 136; blueberry-orange
    flavored, for chicken salad, 143;
    herbed, for chicken salad (warm),
    144
salads, 132–35
  asparagus and red pepper, with
    orange zest, 137
  chicken with blueberry-orange
    vinaigrette, 143
  composed, 134–35
  as first course, 25
  guidelines for, 134–35
  hot, see salads, warm
  lamb and white bean, 138
  mesclun (mixed greens), 136
  pinto bean and parsley, 140
  salmon and pasta, with lemon-dill
    vinaigrette, 157
  simple, 133–34
  three-cabbage slaw, creamy, 139
salads, warm, 133
  chicken, balsamico style, 144
  morel, on steamed spring lettuce,
    136–37
  potato, with sugar snap peas and
    bacon dressing, 140
salmon, 115
  and pasta salad, with lemon-dill
    vinaigrette, 157
  poached, with smoked salmon and
    cucumber sauce, 115
  regional varieties of, 107
salmon, smoked, 115

  with capellini and black caviar, 158
  and caviar canapés, 23, *23*
  and dill filling for snow peas, 18
  poached, with salmon steaks and
    cucumber sauce, 115
salmon and American caviar
  checkerboard, 23, *23*
saltpeter, 83
salt pork, in chowders, 48, 49, 50
salsa, 270
  tomatillo, 274
saltwater taffy, vanilla or cinnamon,
  244
San Francisco-style sourdough bread,
  184–85
  starters for, 186
sauces
  barbecue, 118; for Cornish game
    hens, 129; for ribs, 122
  Béchamel, 154
  Burgundy cherry, for turkey, 131
  Chimichurri, for steak, 127
  cider, for duck, 94–95
  cream, for fried chicken, 88–89
  cucumber: cold, for lamb (grilled),
    125; for smoked salmon
    (poached), 115
  ginger, for crabs (grilled), 123
  mint, for lamb, 70, 125
  mustard: for catfish, 109; mousse,
    for turkey, 131; for venison
    sausages, 81
  parsley, for spaghetti, 27
  for pasta dishes, 154–55, 156, 159,
    162
  red pepper, for green pepper
    cappelletti, 162
  shellfish custard, for pasta, 156
  shiitake mushroom, for veal, 68
  tomato, *see* tomato sauce
  see also butter, flavored; dressings;
    marinades and marinating;
    mayonnaise; sauces, dessert;
    sauces, hot; tomato sauce
sauces, dessert
  blueberry-maple, for bread
    pudding, 222–23
  bourbon-butterscotch, for banana
    soufflé, 228
  chocolate, basic (for ice cream), 253
  cranberry, 261
  custard, for steamed brownie
    pudding, 226
  rhubarb, for cream cheese soufflé,
    229
sauces, hot, 270
  chili, 273
  salsa, tomatillo, 274
sausage, 78
  chorizo tortas, 121
  homemade, 78, *79*
  Italian (sweet), in green pepper
    cappelletti, with red pepper
    sauce, 162
  of lamb and ham, with pecans, 80
  storage of, 78

  summer, with lavender, 82–83
  venison, with sautéed potatoes and
    vinegar, 81
sausage, smoked: with cabbage,
  Cajun style, 33
sautéed soft-shell crabs, with ginger-
  lime butter, 110
sautéing meat, 62
sauté of julienned tomatoes, with
  cream and herbs, 168
scallion(s)
  with beef: kebabs, Caribbean-style,
    126; and scallops, broiled, 65
  in wild rice and cranberry stuffing,
    96
scallop(s)
  broiled with beef, 65
  with lime and mint (marinated),
    28–29
  regional varieties of, 105
  in shellfish custard sauce, with
    pasta, 156
scalloped oysters, 110–11
seafood
  and chicken gumbo, 51
  Louis, 142
  see also clam(s); crab; crayfish; fish;
    lobster; mussel(s); oyster(s);
    scallop(s); shad roe; shrimp
seaweed, for grilling crabs, 123
sesame seeds
  in dressing for parsley (steamed),
    170
  toasting, 170
shad roe, in lemon-chive butter, 113
shallot(s)
  with calf's liver, 77
  chopping technique for, *275*
  with monkfish and fruit, curried,
    112
shellfish
  custard sauce, with pasta, 156
  regional varieties of, 105–8
  see also clam(s); crab; crayfish;
    lobster; mussel(s); oyster(s);
    scallop(s); shrimp
sherbets, 248–51, 259
  banana-caramel, 263
  cantaloupe, 259
  cranberry-pear, 260–61
  differentiated from ices and ice
    cream, 259
  freezing, 249
  machines for making, 250, *250*, 251
  molds of, removing from cups, 261
  "still-freezing," 249–50
  vermouth grapefruit, 260
shiitake mushroom sauce, for veal, 68
shortcakes, 204
  gingered, with honey-poached
    peaches, 217
  strawberry, 216
shrimp
  and fennel pasta triangles, 151
  grilled, with fedelini, 153
  in gumbo, chicken and seafood, 51

regional varieties of, 106, 108
in seafood Louis, 142
in shellfish custard sauce, for pasta, 156
stew, Choctaw style, 111
simmering meat, 63
sirloin
  and caviar tartare, with vodka, 27
  kebabs, grilled Caribbean-style, 126
  as pepper beef, 64
slaw, creamy three-cabbage type, 139
smoked and sizzled Cornish game hens, 129
smoked oyster canapés, with cherry tomatoes, 22
smoked salmon, 115
  with capellini and black caviar, 158
  and caviar canapés, 23, *23*
  and dill filling for snow peas, 18
  poached, with salmon steaks and cucumber sauce, 115
smoked sausage, with cabbage, Cajun-style, 33
smoked trout, with horseradish-parsley butter, 128–29
smoking (cooking method), 118
  for Cornish game hens, 129
  for ham, 123
  for trout, 128, *128*
  for turkey, 130
  water smoker for, 119, *119*
snacks, 12
  see also appetizers; cocktail foods
snow pea(s)
  with pasta and string beans, 154
  stuffed (with choice of three fillings), 18
  see also sugar snap pea(s)
soft molasses or honey cookies, 239
soft-shell crab(s), 106, 110
  sautéed, with ginger-lime butter, 110
sole, lemon (broiled), 109
soufflés, dessert, 219, 220–21
  banana, with bourbon-butter-scotch sauce, 228
  cream cheese, with rhubarb sauce, 229
  dish for cooking, 221, *221*
  guidelines for making, 220–21, *221, 228–29*
soups, 34–38, 42
  chowder, 37–38; clam, 48, corn, 49; fish, 50
  curried apple and onion, 45
  duck and wild rice, 42–43
  guidelines for making, 36–37
  oyster and spinach, 46–47
  pea and orange, 43
  pumpkin-garlic, 44
  stocks for, 34–36
  sweet and sour red cabbage, 45
sourdough bread, San Francisco-style, 184–85
  starters for, 186
spaghetti

with parsley sauce, 27
with peas and string beans, 154
spicy ham and phyllo triangles, 20–21, *21*
spinach
  in cannelloni, with tomato sauce, 154–55
  and oyster soup, 46–47
  pasta, 153; roll, stuffed with ham and three cheeses, 160–61; salad, with salmon, 157
spoon bread, 191
  basic recipe, 192
  with corn, 193
spudnuts, 195
squab
  boning breasts of, *92*
  and chicken stew, 92–93
  and chicken stock, 93
  with corn dressing (as for pheasant), 98–99
squash, acorn: baked (as for sweet dumpling squash), 173
squash, butternut: with guinea hen, sautéed, 99–100
squash, sweet dumpling (baked), 173
standard pastry, for piecrust, 205
steak
  and caviar tartare, with vodka, 27
  porterhouse, grilled over herbs and garlic, 127
steamed brownie pudding, 226–27
steamed parsley, served warm or cold, 170
stewing meat, 62–63
stews, 72
  chicken and squab (or veal or lamb), 92–93
  pork, in cider, 72–73
  shrimp, Choctaw style, 111
  venison, 74–75
stocks, 34–36
  chicken, 35–36; recipe, 41; and squab, 93
  duck, 158–59
  fish, 113
  quail, 91
  rules for preparing, 36
strawberry/ies
  ice cream, in "baby Alaska," 256–257
  with margarita mousse, 232
  shortcake, 216
string beans, *see* bean(s), green
stuffed snow peas, 18
stuffings
  leek (braised), for Cornish game hens, 89
  mozzarella-sage, for tuna steak, 116
  for pasta, *see* pasta, filled
  for snow peas, 18
  tomato-chutney, for lamb, 71
  wild rice and cranberry, for roast goose, 96
sturgeon caviar and salmon checkerboard, 23, *23*

sugar
  brown or powdered, for sweetening cookies, 235
  superfine, 241
sugar snap pea(s)
  with potato salad (warm) and bacon dressing, 140
sugar syrup, for candy, 233–34
summer sausage, 82
  with lavender, 82–83
sweet and sour red cabbage soup, 45
sweet dumpling squash, baked, 173
sweet potato(es)
  chips, fried, with cayenne and coriander, 16
  -pecan biscuits, 188
  and white potatoes, gratin of, 170–171
swordfish, 107
  tonnato, with lemon-thyme mayonnaise, 114

taffy (saltwater), vanilla or cinnamon, 244
tart, fig-pecan, 208–9
tequila, in margarita mousse, with strawberries, 232
Texas chili, 53
three-cabbage slaw, creamy, 139
three-cheese pasta roll with ham, 160–61
thyme
  -lemon mayonnaise, for swordfish, 114
  with porterhouse steak, grilled, 127
  in pumpkin-garlic soup, 44
  with quail and green grapes, 91
  with summer sausage, 82–83
timbale, of Brussels sprouts, 172
toffee bittersweet crunch, 246
tomatillo salsa, 274
tomato(es), 168
  -basil mayonnaise, homemade (for clams), 30–31
  halving and scooping out seeds of, *273*
  julienned, sauté of, with cream and herbs, 168
  in lamb chili, 54
  peeling, preparation for, *273*
  sauce, *see* tomato sauce
  with shrimp and pasta, 153
  in sweet and sour cabbage soup, 45
tomato(es), cherry
  and chutney stuffing, for lamb, 71
  and smoked oyster canapés, 22
tomato(es), green: and mincemeat pie, 206
tomato(es), sun-dried, 155
  sauce of, for cannelloni, 155
tomato-chutney stuffing, for lamb, 71
tomato sauce
  with anchovies, for artichokes, 32–33
  for chicken and squab stew, 93
  with ham and three-cheese pasta

tomato sauce *(cont.)*
    roll, 160–61
    with red peppers, for green pepper
        cappelletti, 162
    salsa, tomatillo, 274
    for spoon bread, 192
    sun-dried, for spinach-filled
        cannelloni, 155
    see also catsup; chili sauce
trout, 106
    smoked, with horseradish-parsley
        butter, 128, *128*
tuna
    in lemon-thyme mayonnaise, with
        swordfish, 114
    steaks (grilled), with mozzarella-
        sage stuffing, 116
turban squash, baked (as for sweet
    dumpling squash), 173
turkey, 85–86
    confit of, 94
    wood-smoked, with two sauces,
        130–31
turnip(s), in pork stew, with cider,
    72–73
two-chicken balsamico, 144

vanilla
    ice cream, basic recipe, 258
    saltwater taffy, 244
veal, 67
    categories of, 67
    chops: with caviar butter, 69;
        slicing pocket in, *69*
    cuts of, 61, *61*
    ground: in green pepper cappelletti,

with red pepper sauce, 162
    with shiitake mushroom sauce, 68
    stew (as for chicken and squab),
        92–93
vegetables, 163–67
    cutting and chopping, technique
        for, *275*
    recipes, 168–74
    seasonal, 165–67
    see also specific vegetables
venison
    sausages (homemade), with sautéed
        potatoes and vinegar, 81
    stew, 74–75
vermouth-grapefruit sherbet, 260
vinaigrette dressing, 136
    blueberry-orange flavored, for
        chicken salad, 143
    with herbs, for chicken salad
        (warm), 144
    lemon-dill, for salmon and pasta
        salad, 157
vinegar, 271
    basil-garlic, 274
    blueberry-orange, 272
    lemon-dill, 272
    types of, 271
vodka, with steak and caviar tartare,
    27

walnut(s)
    in apple brown betty, 225
    in brownie pudding, steamed, 226–
        227
    in Ozark pudding, 222
    toasting, 225

see also black walnut(s)
warm morel salad on steamed spring
    lettuce, 136–37
warm potato salad, with sugar snap
    peas and bacon dressing, 140
water smoker, 119, *119*
wheat kernel(s), 183
    round bread from, 182–83, *183*
whipped potatoes, with garlic-herb
    flavoring, 174
white bean(s), dry: and lamb salad,
    138
whole-wheat bread pudding, with
    blueberry-maple sauce, 222–23
wild mushroom(s)
    in corn dressing for pheasant, 98
    in duck and wild rice soup, 42–43
    on grits (fried), 28
    morel salad (warm), on steamed
        spring lettuce, 136–37
    shiitake sauce, for veal, 68
wild rice
    and cranberry stuffing, for roast
        goose, 96
    and duck soup, 42–43
winter gratin (of white and sweet
    potatoes), 170–71
woodcock, 87
wood-smoked turkey, with two
    sauces, 130–31

yogurt, in marinade for grilled lamb,
    124
young pheasants mandamin, 98–99

Zinfandel and plum ice, 264

PHOTO CREDITS

RICHARD FELBER

Steamed Parsley Served Warm or Cold

VINCENT LEE

Fudge Cake with Milk-Chocolate Frosting
Lamb and White-Bean Salad
Oyster and Spinach Soup
Pinto Bean and Parsley Salad
Swordfish Tonnato with Lemon-Thyme Mayonnaise
Two-Chicken Balsamico
Veal with Shiitake Mushroom Sauce

NANCY McFARLAND

Bay Scallops with Lime and Mint
Best Strawberry Shortcake

Cannelloni with Sun-Dried Tomato Sauce
Fried Catfish with Mustard Sauce
Fried Mushroom Pasta
Green-Pepper Cappelletti with Red-Pepper Sauce
Pecan-Pie Ice Cream and Pie-Pastry Cookies
Pepper Beef
Radish Remoulade
Raspberry-Peach Cobbler
Steamed Brownie Pudding

MICHAEL WATSON

Crabs Grilled on a Bed of Seaweed with Fresh Ginger Sauce
Ham and Three-Cheese Pasta Roll
Lamb with Tomato Chutney and Mint Sauce
Spicy Ham and Phyllo Triangles